Dyslexia
A Practitioner's Handbook

Dyslexia
A Practitioner's Handbook

Gavin Reid
Centre for Specific Learning Difficulties
Moray House Institute of Education
Heriot-Watt University

JOHN WILEY & SONS
Chichester · New York · Weinheim · Brisbane · Singapore · Toronto

Other Wiley Editorial Offices

John Wiley & Sons, Inc., 605 Third Avenue,
New York, NY 10158-0012, USA

WILEY-VCH Verlag GmbH, Pappelallee 3,
D-69469 Weinheim, Germany

Jacaranda Wiley Ltd, 33 Park Road, Milton,
Queensland 4064, Australia

John Wiley & Sons (Asia) Pte Ltd, 2 Clementi Loop #02-01,
Jin Xing Distripark, Singapore 129809

John Wiley & Sons (Canada) Ltd, 22 Worcester Road,
Rexdale, Ontario M9W 1L1, Canada

Library of Congress Cataloging-in-Publication Data

Reid, Gavin, 1950–
    Dyslexia : a practitioner's handbook / Gavin Reid.
        p.   cm.
    Includes bibliographical references and index.
    ISBN 0-471-97391-2
    1. Dyslexic children—Education—Handbooks, manuals, etc.
    2. Dyslexic children—Ability testing—Handbooks, manuals, etc.
    3. Curriculum planning—Handbooks, manuals, etc. I. Title.
LC4708.R45   1997
371.91'44—dc21
                                                97-17407
                                                CIP

British Library Cataloguing in Publication Data

A catalogue record for this book is available from the British Library
ISBN 0-471-97391-2 (paper)

Typeset in 10/12pt Times by Dorwyn Ltd, Rowlands Castle, Hampshire
Printed and bound in Great Britain by Bookcraft (Bath) Ltd, Midsomer Norton, Somerset
This book is printed on acid-free paper responsibly manufactured from sustainable forestry, in which at least two trees are planted for each one used for paper production.

Contents

About the Author   ix
Preface   xi

Chapter 1   **ISSUES AND CONSIDERATIONS**   **1**
             Defining Dyslexia   1
             Discrepancies   3
             Factors Associated with Dyslexia   4
             Practical Issues   5

Chapter 2   **THE ACQUISITION OF LITERACY**   **9**
             Children's Perception of Reading   10
             Reading Skills   11
             Reading Development   13
             Reading Models and Methods   15
             Nature of Reading   19
             The Reading Debate   24
             Reading Strategies   26

Chapter 3   **ASSESSMENT APPROACHES**   **31**
             Aims and Rationale   31
             Approaches and Strategies   34
             Standardised and Diagnostic   35
             Phonological Assessment   45
             Screening   49
             Metacognitive Assessment   53
             Observational Assessment   61

Chapter 4	**ASSESSMENT PROCESS**	**67**
	Models of Identification	68
	An Assessment Framework	71
	Identifying Emerging Literacy Skills	78
Chapter 5	**TEACHING APPROACHES**	**81**
	The Context	81
	Assessment and the Curriculum	81
	The Learner	82
	Programmes and Strategies	82
	Individualised Programmes	84
	Programmes in Practice	85
	Support Approaches and Strategies	105
	Assisted Learning	120
Chapter 6	**CURRICULUM ACCESS**	**127**
	Reading Projects	127
	The Curriculum	130
	Secondary School Dimensions	131
	Metacognitive Aspects	132
	Learning Styles	134
	Study Skills	141
Chapter 7	**DYSLEXIA IN FURTHER AND HIGHER EDUCATION**	**151**
	Is Disability Related to Context?	151
	Experiencing Further and Higher Education	151
	Institutional Supports	153
	Succeeding in Further and Higher Education	153
	Essay Writing	154
	Tutor's Role	157
	Institutional Guidance	158
Chapter 8	**REVIEW OF RESOURCES**	**159**
	General Texts	159
	Reading	170
	Teaching Programmes	177
	Learning Skills/Self-Esteem	188

Assessment   196
Writing/Motor Skills   202
Spelling   205
Parents/Adults   208
References   213
Author Index   235
Subject Index   241

About the Author

Dr Gavin Reid is a lecturer at Moray House Institute of Education in Edinburgh and Course Leader for the Post-Graduate Awards in Specific Learning Difficulties (Dyslexia). He was instrumental in the development of the first Master's Award in Dyslexia in Scotland and in the conversion of the course into an open and distance learning format. The course has been run in many countries and he has made numerous keynote conference presentations throughout the UK, Europe, United States, Hong Kong and New Zealand.

He is the editor of the two volume text *Dimensions of Dyslexia*, author of *Specific Learning Difficulties (Dyslexia): A Handbook for Study and Practice* and co-author of *Specific Learning Difficulties (Dyslexia) A Resource Book for Parents and Teachers*. He has also written a number of book chapters for journal articles.

He is a member of the British Dyslexia Association Accreditation Board for Teacher Training and has been a consultant in many national and international working groups on assessment, teaching and dyslexia in higher education.

He has also many years' experience as a class teacher and as an educational psychologist. He is Associate Fellow of the British Psychological Society and has a PhD in Psychology from the University of Glasgow. He is committed to helping teachers develop an awareness of the learning needs and potential of dyslexic children.

Preface

This book is a substantially revised and updated edition of *Specific Learning Difficulties (Dyslexia), a Handbook for Study and Practice*. The revisions have been necessary due to the growth in interest in dyslexia and in particular teacher training courses. The field of dyslexia has benefited from considerable research activity and widespread interest in assessment and teaching approaches in recent years. This has resulted in new and varied forms of assessment and support strategies, most of which are described in this updated text.

The interest in teacher training courses in dyslexia provided the initial impetus for this book. Since the first edition was published in 1994 it has been recommended as one of the main text books for teacher training courses and is the set course book for the Moray House Masters Post Graduate Awards in Dyslexia which are run widely in the UK and Europe, and overseas.

In addition to being a set text for courses in dyslexia, the book will be useful for teachers wishing to enhance their awareness of resources and developments in the area of dyslexia.

By helping teachers gain more insights and knowledge of dyslexia it is hoped that dyslexic children and adults will feel more confident in dealing with their difficulty and that they may then fulfil their potential for learning.

This book is essentially the product of many years' involvement in the field of dyslexia and throughout that time I have been indebted to teachers, course tutors and colleagues who have provided a focus of discussion together with examples of good practice. I would also like to acknowledge the authors and publishers who have allowed their work to be used in this text.

Finally it is gratifying to have observed and to have been deeply involved in the considerable developments which have taken place in dyslexia in recent years. It is hoped, therefore, that this momentum will be maintained and extended, that teachers everywhere will benefit from training and that parents, children and dyslexic adults will benefit from the positive effects of such training.

GAVIN REID

Chapter 1

Issues and Considerations

The concept of dyslexia, its identification and assessment, and investigations, both into its possible causes and into different methods and approaches for dealing with it, have all been the subject of considerable attention from researchers, practitioners and parents and even the media. Interest in dyslexia is high and this impact is felt at all levels from early education through to further and higher education. It is now widely recognised and accepted that much can be achieved to help dyslexic children and adults fulfil their potential.

Professor Peter Pumfrey, when delivering the fifteenth Vernon-Wall Lecture of the British Psychological Society began by suggesting that the 'concept of dyslexia has a widespread and increasing currency' (Pumfrey, 1996); this is certainly the case. The awareness and conceptual understanding of dyslexia has developed considerably in recent years, almost certainly due to the interest and activities from researchers worldwide as well as those engaged in classroom and clinical practices. Although these activities have helped to achieve a wider and clearer understanding of the concept of dyslexia, in terms of aetiology, models of assessment and teaching, it should be noted that the field of dyslexia is still characterised by controversy, both in research and practice. It is perhaps beyond the scope of this book to deal in a detailed manner with these controversies, but it is hoped that, by providing guidance to practitioners, the book will help to clarify some of these issues and equip teachers to deal with dyslexia from a standpoint of knowledge and confidence. Both knowledge and confidence are important factors and these can be developed through a clear view of the issues and through appropriate and effective training. It is one of the aims of this book therefore to help teachers undergoing training courses in dyslexia achieve these objectives and to provide classroom teachers with some awareness of strategies and resources which can help dyslexic students.

DEFINING DYSLEXIA

It is important for the teacher and for those engaged in study in this field to have a clear definition of dyslexia. A definition, however, is only really useful and effective if it has widespread agreement within the fields of research and practice. Indeed, lack of such agreement has been a feature of dyslexia for some time and although there is now a better understanding of the difficulties associated with dyslexia, there is still some disagreement regarding actual definitions. There are, however, a number of well-accepted definitions currently in use.

The British Dyslexia Association, for example, use the following definition:

> Dyslexia is a complex neurological condition which is constitutional in origin. The symptoms may affect many areas of learning and function, and may be described as a specific difficulty in reading, spelling and written language. One or more of these areas may be affected. Numeracy, notational skills (music), motor function and organisational skills may also be involved. However, it is particularly related to mastering written language, although oral language may be affected to some degree. (British Dyslexia Association, 1997)

A definition, while it can be a useful general guideline, can and should be adapted and contextualised for the particular area and purpose for which it is to be used. For example, for the purpose of teacher training the Moray House Centre for the Study of Dyslexia developed the following definition.

> Specific Learning Difficulties/Dyslexia can be identified as distinctive patterns of difficulties relating to the processing of information within a continuum from very mild to extremely severe which result in restrictions in literacy development and discrepancies in performances within the curriculum. (Reid, 1996)

In relation to educational practice the above definition was extended in order to meet the needs of an education authority which wished to issue detailed guidelines on dyslexia to all schools: The extended definition is:

> Specific Learning Difficulties/Dyslexia is a pattern of difficulties of which the most obvious are significant, persistent problems in learning to read, write and spell. The following may also be affected: numeracy, motor skills, spoken language, information processing, memory and organisational skills. Pupils with Specific Learning Difficulties/Dyslexia may be identified by their ability to demonstrate orally their conceptual understanding. There will be significant discrepancies in performance between the area of difficulty (e.g. literacy) and other skills. Specific Learning Difficulties/Dyslexia occurs across ability levels and socio-economic groupings. (Partnership: Parents, Professionals and Pupils Fife Education Authority, 1996)

Similarly in the United States, for the joint purpose of research and influencing classroom practice, the Tennessee Center for the Study and Treatment of Dyslexia developed the following definition of dyslexia.

> A language-based learning disorder that is biological in origin and primarily interferes with the acquisition of print literacy (reading, writing and spelling). Dyslexia is characterised by poor word reading and poor spelling abilities as well as deficits in awareness of sounds in words and manipulation of sounds to spell words. (Tennessee Center for the Study and Treatment of Dyslexia, 1996)

It is feasible to suggest that while a definition can help to provide some guidance to teachers and researchers, the range of definitions in use may result in some confusion. Reid Lyon (1995) suggests that the negative consequences of inadequate definitions are serious as this can result in lack of information on the precise nature of the reading difficulties and consequently lead to inadequate training for teachers.

In relation to research, Reid Lyon asserts that the lack of an appropriate definition has resulted in a reliance on exclusionary criteria and lack of a clear selection criteria for the sample being studied. He suggests that a definition must be governed by a theoretical view supported by substantial research and clinical evidence. This should be based on 'constructs' which can be measured directly and consistently and should provide clear indications of how to identify whether a person is dyslexic.

Reid Lyon believes that the working definition which was initiated by the Orton Dyslexia Society Research Committee, in conjunction with the National Center for Learning Disabilities and the National Institute of Child Health and Human Development, takes account of these factors. It is seen as an example of a research-based definition.

> Dyslexia is one of several distinct learning disabilities. It is a specific language-based disorder of constitutional origin characterised by difficulties in single word decoding, usually reflecting insufficient phonological processing. These difficulties in single word decoding are often unexpected in relation to age and other cognitive and academic abilities; they are not the result of generalised developmental disability or sensory impairment. Dyslexia is manifest by variable difficulty with different forms of language, often including, in addition to problems with reading, a conspicuous problem with acquiring proficiency in writing and spelling. (The Orton Dyslexia Society Research Committee, April 1994)

Two of the key aspects in the above definition which will feature prominently in this book are 'insufficient phonological processing' and 'characterised by difficulties in single word decoding'. These will be discussed in the following chapter on literacy and in the chapters covering assessment and teaching.

DISCREPANCIES

One of the key issues in relation to the concept of dyslexia is the IQ–attainment discrepancy. Traditionally the IQ–attainment discrepancy has been used to identify dyslexics from other poor readers. Doubts, however, which have been cast on the role of intelligence tests have resulted in some controversy on their use in a diagnosis of dyslexia. In fact Stanovitch (1996a) suggests that the IQ–reading discrepancy does not have a role to play in the diagnosis of dyslexia and suggests if the label is retained it may be more appropriate to adopt an inclusive definition applying the label to all poor readers, regardless of the IQ–reading discrepancy.

Reid Lyon (1995) also suggests that the IQ–reading discrepancy is inappropriate because of the body of research which shows that, on measures assessing decoding, word recognition and phonological skills, high–IQ readers do not differ from reading disabled children with lower IQs. Reid Lyon, however, does point out that the characteristic 'unexpectedness' in literacy achievement in high IQ dyslexics may not necessarily be predicted by IQ but through some other cognitive measure. This may for example include listening comprehension (Aaron, 1994).

Miles (1996), however, suggests that intelligence tests do have a role to play, particularly in the identification of strengths and weaknesses since these marked differences are a feature of a dyslexic profile. He does, however, accept that the concept of global IQ may be misleading since many of the items in IQ tests are not suitable for dyslexics.

In terms of performance Reid and Weedon (1997) suggest that data from their study on diagnostic criteria for early literacy difficulties show that the discrepancy between reading and listening comprehension was evident in a significant number of dyslexics and was, in fact, one of the best predictors in identifying dyslexia.

It is therefore suggested that it may be possible to supplement the traditional IQ–reading discrepancy with other types of discrepancies involving aspects of phonological skills, single word reading and listening comprehension with other measures, such as chronological age. Nicolson (1996) however suggests that there is some confusion between the cause of reading difficulties and the cause of dyslexia. He suggests that dyslexia is more than one end of the poor reading continuum and that, in addition to a phonological deficit, dyslexic children can display a pattern of difficulties which can include visual processing and rapid auditory processing as well as neuro-anatomical and genetic factors. Other areas of research also associated with dyslexia include automaticity (Nicolson and Fawcett, 1990), motor skills (Blyth, 1992: Nicolson and Fawcett, 1996) and visual factors (Wilkins, 1995; Eden *et al.*, 1996).

In Chapter 3 of this book the role of the discrepancy between decoding and comprehension, will be discussed more fully within the context of a range of assessment strategies since it is recognised that no single test exists which can adequately diagnose dyslexia.

FACTORS ASSOCIATED WITH DYSLEXIA

Pumfrey (1996) suggests that dyslexia is increasingly being described as a 'variable syndrome'. This implies that there is a strong view that there are qualitatively different types of dyslexia, although even this is not without its critics, particularly from those who suggest a single underlying cause. Certainly if one examines the research on dyslexia and listens to teachers and practitioners in related fields a considerable collection of factors associated with causes, identification and teaching can be accumulated. This in itself points to a variable syndrome. The list in the box highlights some of these factors.

Although dyslexia is widely recognised as being associated with phonological difficulties, the list illustrates that other factors may be implicated to a greater or lesser extent within the dyslexic profile. Wolf (1996) for example

---

SOME FACTORS ASSOCIATED WITH DYSLEXIA
Causes, Identification and Teaching

Phonological processing (Stanovich, 1996; Snowling, 1995; Reason and
  Frederickson, 1996)
Atypical brain symmetry (Galaburda, 1993)
Cortical anomalies (Hynd, Marshall and Gonzalez, 1991)
Balance theory (Bakker, 1990; Bakker *et al.*, 1994)
Visual difficulties (Wilkins, 1995; Eden *et al.*, 1996)
Residual primitive reflexes (Blyth, 1992)
Creativity and visualisation (West, 1991)
Naming speed deficit (Wolf, 1991, 1996)
Automaticity (Nicolson and Fawcett 1990)
Cerebellar impairment (Fawcett, Nicolson and Dean, 1996)
Genetic factors (Pennington, 1990, 1996)
Metacognitive delay (Tunmer and Chapman, 1996)
IQ–reading discrepancy controversies (Stanovich, 1996)
Role of listening comprehension and non-word reading (Aaron, 1989)
Role of analogous reading (Goswami, 1994)
Phonological approaches in teaching (Wilson, 1993; Frederickson and
  Wilson, 1996)
Role of learning styles (Given, 1996)
Curriculum integrative models (Dyson and Skidmore, 1996; Padget, Knight
  and Sawyer, 1996)
Computer-based assessment and teaching (Singleton, 1996)

---

suggests that dyslexics can be identified by what she describes as a double deficit, which includes phonological deficits and naming speed problems. In fact she argues that naming speed is the single best predictor of reading difficulties.

There are also research studies which support the role of visual factors in dyslexia. Eden *et al.* (1996), for example, provide research evidence of a biological marker for dyslexia independent of reading. Eden suggests that dyslexics can have a selective deficit in the magnocellular subsystem of the brain which would indicate physiological abnormalities in the processing of visual movement. Frith and Frith (1996), in interpreting the findings of the research by Eden and colleagues, suggest it is possible that phonological and visual disorders can co-exist in dyslexics.

PRACTICAL ISSUES

In view of the boxed list, which is by no means exhaustive, it is important that classroom teachers receive some training in dyslexia offering both theoretical insights and practical assistance. The role of the class teacher is, however, governed to a great extent by the policy of the education authority, the attitude of the school management and the awareness and training of the class teacher. These factors would largely determine the available expertise and resources for dealing with dyslexia in the classroom. Pumfrey (1996) acknowledges that establishing a resource allocation decision-making model that is 'explicit, open, fair and theoretically defensible, requires considerable professional knowledge' (Pumfrey, 1996, p. 20). In practice, however, criteria used to allocate resources for dyslexia often have a reactive as well as a proactive element. The reactive element usually emerges from parental pressure (Heaton, 1996) and the proactive aspect from an objective attempt by education authorities to establish some form of working criteria for identifying and dealing with dyslexia within their budgetary considerations. This, however, usually results in discrepancy criteria being employed – for example, reading scores two standard deviations below prediction from IQ, or perhaps reading accuracy at or below second percentile for age (Pumfrey, 1996). Although this form of measurement may have some advantage for the authority it also has some limitations. This form of measurement represents a formal structure which appears to be controlled and directed by resources and budgetary concerns. By focusing on discrepancy criteria, only those children who are the most severely affected by their dyslexic difficulties will receive special consideration within the education authority.

Alternatively, education authorities could establish a programme of early identification and intervention which could prevent later failure. This may also make discrepancy criteria for intervention unnecessary. At the same time enhanced awareness among class teachers and the school management on the needs of dyslexic children in assessment, teaching and curriculum delivery could help to cater for all dyslexic children and not just the most severe. This view is in fact incorporated in a key paper on the working practices of educational psychologists in Scotland (Kirkcaldy, 1997). Kirkcaldy suggests that empowerment of teachers through consultancy and training can provide an effective means of identifying and dealing with dyslexic difficulties in the classroom.

An interesting integrative model for the study and treatment of dyslexia can be seen in Tennessee. The model addresses identification, intervention, teacher education and research. The aim of the model is to establish best practices and to implement these in school settings. This model is similar to many of the policies which have been developed in education authorities (e.g. Fife Education Council, 1996) combined with specialist training from recognised university courses on dyslexia (e.g. Moray House (Reid, in press). This model highlights the impact of specialist training on educational policy and provision.

Duffield, Riddell and Brown (1995) report on research conducted in Scotland which suggests that in most cases schools have systematic procedures for identifying specific learning difficulties. In many of these cases, however, the responsibility for identification rests with the specialist learning support teacher. Duffield *et al.* also suggest that there needs to be a shared understanding of the problems of specific learning difficulties/dyslexia among educationalists, health practitioners and parents. This shared understanding can be achieved through improvements in communication. They suggest six areas of conflict or tension which need to be addressed, although they admit that these are 'not open to easy resolution' (p. 206). These are:

- friction between competing policies which reflect different ideological stances
- economic issues arising from education authorities' concerns for all pupils
- fundamental differences about the nature of specific learning difficulties, that is whether children with specific learning difficulties form a discrete group, are part of the continuum of all children with reading problems or are individuals whose difficulties are not amenable to any kind of categorisation
- the recognition of specific learning difficulties
- the uncertainty over what constitutes effective provision
- and the conflicts of emotions, particularly between pressure groups and the education sector

It is fair to say that in some educational authorities these issues have been to a great extent resolved or partially resolved. Some authorities have well-established policies in specific learning difficulties/dyslexia and many of these have been developed in consultation with parents and parents' groups (Banks, 1996; Mager, 1996). Additionally, many authorities also support a range of provision from mainstream to discrete provision in the form of units or schools for dyslexic children.

To summarise, there are a number of issues which are of concern to teachers, policy makers, researchers and parents within the field of dyslexia. This book will essentially deal with those relating to classroom practice. Classroom practice, however, is clearly affected by the results and implications of research and indeed the perceptions and policy of the education authority. Although significant progress has been made towards achieving a common understanding of dyslexia, education provision and practice is still characterised by differences in different parts of the country and in different countries. Such differences can be seen in policy, assessment procedures, nature of provision, teaching approaches and training of school staff. This is not necessarily a critical comment, as authorities may well differ in their focus on practice and provision, but can still be governed by a clear rationale resulting in an effective service.

Since the educational needs of dyslexic children are catered for in a variety of different ways, this book presents a range of assessment strategies and teaching approaches. Although some of these may not be appropriate for all teachers, it is hoped that all involved with dyslexic children will in some way benefit from an enhanced awareness of these strategies and approaches.

It is heartening to end this introductory chapter on a positive note. Despite the controversies which exist, there has been significant progress not only in the knowledge which is available on dyslexia, but also in the means of dissemination through journals, texts, working groups and conferences. Such dissemination has helped to restore the confidence of parents and practitioners and has certainly been to the advantage of dyslexic children and adults everywhere.

Chapter 2

The Acquisition of Literacy

WHAT is reading? This question, despite its apparent simplicity, can provide some insight into how reading is perceived by the learner, and some answers as to why, for a significant number, the acquisition of reading skills is an arduous and sometimes deflating process.

Figure 1

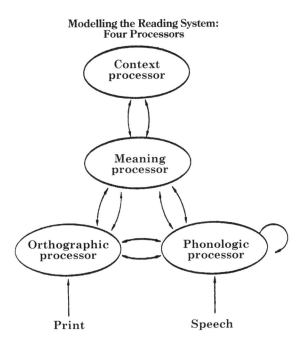

Modelling the Reading System:
Four Processors

(Reproduced from Adams (1990) with permission)

Learning to read requires a number of skills, many are considered pre-reading skills and some develop as a result of reading itself. Being deprived of fluency in reading can therefore further affect the development of many of the reading sub-skills.

Some specific factors which are important in the acquisition of literacy include word attack skills, such as letter recognition, segmentation, blending, phonemic awareness, analogy strategies and grapheme–phoneme correspondence, and word recognition skills, such as recognition of word patterns and the use of visual memory skills. Other factors, such as environmental considerations, development of the concepts of print, development of language concepts and how the whole concept of reading is viewed by the learner, are also important.

These factors underline the view that reading is an interactive and reciprocal process. In other words the more skills the child has access to, the more competent he will become not only in reading as an activity but also in the development of reading sub-skills. The flip side of this also applies – that is, those children who lack competence in the reading sub-skills will not have ready access to reading and are consequently deprived of an opportunity of developing these skills. This is described as the Matthew effect (Stanovich, 1986). This interactive and reciprocal nature of the reading process is also illustrated through the model suggested by Adams (1990) (see Fig. 1). This model of the reading system highlights the interactions between context, meaning, orthography (print) and phonology (speech).

The orthographic processor is responsible for sequencing the letters in a word: the phonological processor for matching those letters to the letter sound; the meaning processor relates to the reader's knowledge of word meaning and the context processor provides an overview of the meaning of the text. These processors work together and receive feedback from each other.

CHILDREN'S PERCEPTION OF READING

How do children perceive reading? This question was put to a sample of children aged between 7 and 10 years (Reid, 1993d) and the responses illustrate the different perceptions and beliefs children hold of reading. Some of the responses include learning words, learning new words, looking at words and saying them, learning about things, finding out about things, stories, words and sentences.

The main distinction which can be drawn from the responses related to aspects of the **task** of reading rather than the **function**. Those who focused on the 'task' highlighted aspects such as the decoding of words and the learning of these words. A typical response from the 'task' group was 'Reading is when you look at words and you say them in your mind'. The 'function' group recognised reading as an activity from which they derived pleasure and the purpose of reading was to obtain meaning from text.

Why do children perceive reading in such vastly different ways? Does the answer to this question lie in the method and strategy used to teach children reading? Or perhaps the answer to this is related more to the child's skills and abilities and how easy and accessible learning to read is for the child. Whichever way one might be inclined to argue, there is something fundamentally amiss if the child perceives reading as an arduous and laborious exercise – a product of classroom routine and relentless practice. If this is the child's perception of reading, then surely the real meaning of reading is lost and books then become a confusing contradiction between the pain and pleasure of acquiring knowledge.

Children with specific learning difficulties/dyslexia seldom have a perception of reading which reveals the pleasure of books and the real meaning of print. They often perceive reading as a dreaded exercise, calling for skills in precision and accuracy – an exercise which appears to stretch their natural and accessible competencies.

This presents a challenge for teachers, that is, to teach the basic fundamental structure and framework for the understanding of print, but at the same time to provide an enriched and meaningful language experience to facilitate and encourage access to books. This can help the child gain some real appreciation of the message and pleasure of books.

READING SKILLS

The skills used in reading are little different from many of the skills used in other aspects of learning.

For example, linguistic, visual and auditory skills are all essential for access to reading. These skills are also used in other learning activities such as speech, listening, creative and visual work. These skills develop independently of reading because they are used in learning activities other than reading. This does not necessarily imply that coaching in reading sub-skills promotes proficiency in the practice of reading. Rather the view could be held that it is the actual practice of reading which fosters reading skills and therefore reading practice is essential to develop skills as a reader (Smith, 1988; Clay, 1985).

Adams (1990), however, suggests that activities designed to develop young childrens' awareness of words, syllables and phonemes significantly increase their later success in learning to read and write. The impact of phonemic training or reading acquisition, Adams suggests, is especially strong when phonemes are taught together with the letters by which they are represented. This suggests an important role for the teacher in the fostering of reading skills.

Adams (1990) further suggests an important role for the three aspects of: language, visual and auditory factors. For example, she suggests independent writing activities can help foster an appreciation of text and its comprehension and that phonic instruction can help with both the sounds of words and the spellings of words; and reading aloud to children according to Adams is perhaps the single most important activity for building the knowledge and skills eventually required for reading.

An examination of these three factors, linguistic, visual and auditory reveals some areas of difficulty encountered by dyslexic children when learning to read (see Figs. 2 and 3).

Figure 2

Language Factors

Reading is messages expressed in language and children have to transpose their understanding of oral language into an understanding of the written language.

This presents difficulties for some children because:
- the flow of oral language does not always make the break between words clear
- of difficulty in breaking messages into words
- of difficulty in breaking messages into their sequences of sounds
- of problems in retaining those sounds in memory
- of difficulty in articulating sounds
- of difficulty in recognising sounds in written form.

Figure 3

Visual Factors

Some of the most important visual factors include:
- recognition of visual cues
- left to right orientation
- recognition of word patterns
- recognition of letter and letter shapes

Auditory Factors

These include:
- recognition of letter sounds
- recognition of sounds and letter groups or patterns
- sequencing of sounds
- corresponding sounds to visual stimuli
- discriminating sounds from other sounds
- discriminating sounds within words

Many of the above visual and auditory aspects of reading do not develop spontaneously in children with specific learning difficulties. These skills need to be taught, and usually in a sensitive and structured manner. Some of the skills, therefore, which are required in reading include, automatic rapid word and letter recognition, phonological and visual skills, knowledge of the concepts of print, vocabulary knowledge, general knowledge, ability to use context as an aid to word recognition and comprehension and analogy skills.

How one decides to prioritise the teaching of these skills within a programme depends to a great extent on the strengths and difficulties of the child. This interaction of skills underlines the multi-faceted nature of reading and the long-standing notion that no one method, medium, approach or even philosophy holds the key to the process of learning to read (Bullock Report, 1975).

Figure 4

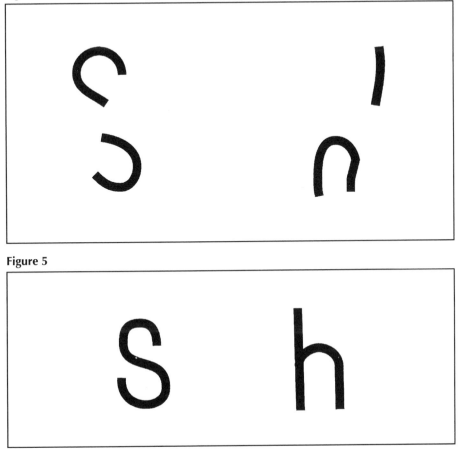

Figure 5

READING DEVELOPMENT

There are clearly a number of important sub-skills which contribute to the reading process. These skills do not all appear at once, but are developing skills relating to a number of factors. Harrison (1994) cites some research evidence suggesting a child's background such as intelligence, prior learning and home background contribute approximately 85% to what is achieved in school, the other 15% to schooling including teacher input and teaching methods. From this it follows, therefore, that the reading skills acquired at an early stage are extremely important – these are skills in language, comprehension and vocabulary. These provide an impetus for the development of reading skills related to print awareness.

Adams (1990) discusses the importance of the visual aspects of print and how this relates to the different types of print young children come across – the sources range from instructions for toys to comic books. She asserts that this visual awareness of print does not develop in isolation, but becomes a component of the developing child's environment. This leads to the child developing concepts of print such as left and right, words, sentences, the back of the book and the front. It is important, therefore, to ensure that the child has a grasp of these basic concepts of print, a point highlighted by Clay (1985) in the Reading Recovery Programme.

Furthermore, Tunmer, Herriman and Nesdale (1988) found that the performances of children on tests designed to measure concepts about print has been found to predict future reading achievement. Adams (1990) suggests that basic knowledge about print is essentially the foundation upon which the orthographic and phonological skills are built.

It is suggested that recognising the visual identities of letters is an important stage in reading development and this skill takes time and practice and necessitates a degree of visual attention (Adams, 1990). Thus the child who becomes familiar with the shapes in Fig 4 will soon recognise and realise that these shapes are part of the letters shown in Fig 5. Adams suggests that the cause of poor readers displaying errors in letter orientation may reflect insufficient knowledge of letter shapes.

It seems, therefore, that the reading process is underpinned by the visual recognition of individual letters and then transposing these letters into their phonological correspondences.

Dyslexic children may well have some difficulties in the visual stage but almost certainly will have difficulty in translating the letters to their phonic equivalents. From the twenty-six letters in the alphabet, hundreds of correspondences can be made.

Teaching programmes in reading should, therefore, recognise this and the difficulties which will confront dyslexic childen if these correspondences are taught in isolation. It is important that a teaching programme integrates the visual, phonic and the context aspects of reading simultaneously at all stages in reading from early development through to competence.

One such programme which achieves this is that developed by Reason and Boote (1994) which identifies three strands: meaning, phonics and fluency at four stages – early development, beginning to read, becoming competent and achieving competence. The three strands are taught simultaneously at all these stages through related activities.

Frith (1985) identifies the following developmental stages in the acquisition of reading skills.

Logographic Stage

The child makes use of visual recognition of overall word patterns – thus he/she is able to recognise words as units. This may not necessarily mean the child can reproduce these words accurately (this would be an alphabetic skill) and as a result the child can easily misspell words they are able to read.

Alphabetic Stage

The child tackles the sound/symbol correspondence and one can identify if children possess this one-to-one correspondence between the letter and the sound.

Orthographic Stage

The child possesses and comprehends knowledge of letter-sound relationship as well as structure and meaning. Thus as well as being aware of rules the child can use cues and context.

It has been argued that children with specific learning difficulties can find the alphabetic stage difficult because the sound/symbol correspondence rests to a great extent on skills in phonics. Before children, therefore, acquire a competent understanding of the relationship between letter units (graphemes) and sound units (phonemes) they need a degree of phonological awareness (Frith, 1980; Snowling, 1987).

Frith (1985) puts forward the view that writing and the desire to write helps to enhance the alphabetic stage of reading because spelling is linked more directly to the alphabetic principle and letter-sound relationships. This view is also supported by the work of Bradley and Bryant (1991) who found that beginner readers in the process of acquiring the skills of the alphabetic stage use visual strategies for reading but phonological strategies for spelling. In their study children read correctly words which were visually distinctive such as 'school' and 'light' but failed to read simpler words like 'bun' and 'sit'. Yet these children tended to spell correctly words they had failed to read such as 'bun' and 'sit' and spell incorrectly words they had read by focusing on the visual patterns (school, light).

The alphabetic reader according to Snowling (1987) may also find difficulty reading words which have inconsistent orthographic patterns but which are pronounced in the same way. Similarly, irregular words are **mis**pronounced e.g. 'island' would be pronounced 'is-land'.

This developmental aspect of reading serves to illustrate the importance of the procedure of error analysis and identifying the type and pattern of errors made by children with difficulties in reading.

READING MODELS AND METHODS

There are two principal models of the reading process. These have come to be known as 'Bottom-up' (i.e. data driven) and 'Top-down' (concept driven) (see Fig. 6).

The 'Bottom-up' model suggests that first we look at the stimulus, i.e. the components of the letters and then move to the meaning.

Figure 6

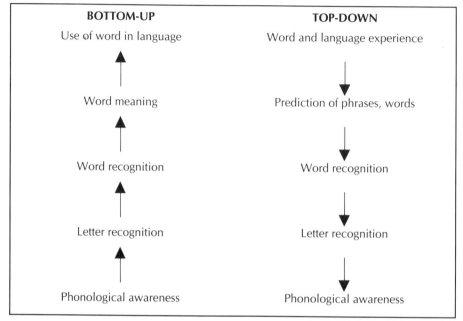

BOTTOM-UP	TOP-DOWN
Use of word in language	Word and language experience
↑	↓
Word meaning	Prediction of phrases, words
↑	↓
Word recognition	Word recognition
↑	↓
Letter recognition	Letter recognition
↑	↓
Phonological awareness	Phonological awareness

This emphasises the need to translate:

- written symbols to sound
- sound to meaning.

'Bottom-up' theorists argue that the brain attends to every bit of available information, thus we read letter-by-letter so quickly that it becomes automatic.

The 'Top-down' model is concept driven. The reader attempts to absorb the meaning of the text from the cues which are available. These cues can include:

- the context of the passage being read:
  this relates to the syntactic context, i.e. the structure of the sentence, and semantic context, i.e. the anticipated meaning of the passage;
- the graphic information available:
  i.e. what the word looks like, the reader anticipates the word or sentence from these descriptive cues (see Fig. 7).

Goodman's model, known as the psycholinguistic guessing game (1976) strongly advocated a top-down approach to reading. This model asserts that good readers make efficient use of hypothesis–formation and prediction in reading and thus make good use of the contextual cues available to the reader. Additionally, the efficiency in prediction of text means that good readers, according to Goodman, will have less need to rely on graphic cues and therefore do not have to process every visual characteristic of text.

Goodman's model of the reading process has, however, been subject to powerful criticism. The main exponents of this criticism are Tunmer (1991), Stanovich

Figure 7

Mac⸱⸱ᵒni blenᴅ with ˈᵉese sauce and mix ᴸᴸ sᵒ⸱ᵉ herbs anᵈ sᵖⁱᵤes

(1988), Adams (1990) and Liberman and Liberman (1992). Essentially the counter arguments to Goodman's model suggest that the central tenet of the model that good readers are dependent on context for word recognition is inaccurate. It is suggested, in fact, that it is poor readers who are dependent on context, good readers do not need to rely on context as they possess efficient word recognition skills, can recognise words effortlessly and can utilise maximum cognitive capacity for comprehension. The effort required for poor readers to recognise words reduces their cognitive capacity for comprehension.

Additionally, there is now considerable evidence (Adams, 1990) that good readers actually fixate nearly every word as they read. This process is achieved rapidly in efficient readers, therefore less cognitive effort is required than for example with poor readers. So even when the word is highly predictable, good readers actually visually process every word.

Lovegrove (1993) highlights the importance of visual factors in poor readers. He comments on the two visual sub-systems – the transient and the sustained systems. The transient system which is sensitive to contrast and more suited to identifying the general form of objects has a fast transmission time, and deals with peripheral vision. The sustained system is sensitive to black and white, detailed stimuli and is slow to change. It has a slow transmission time and deals with the central vision.

The key feature in relation to these systems is that both systems inhibit each other – that means that they do not operate simultaneously. Lovegrove's studies show that poor readers have a weak transient system and a normal sustained one. This results in interference between the two systems and has implications for the processing of visual stimuli in reading, since reading involves the synchronisation of both transient and sustained systems. This may therefore have implications for masking parts of a page which are not being focused on at that time. It certainly has implications for allowing sufficient processing time for poor readers.

Although there may be flaws in the detail of Goodman's model, many of the messages contained within it require consideration such as the view that skilled readers have the ability and the opportunity to make efficient use of context. Additionally, Goodman's emphasis on reading for meaning should not be lost, but requires to be balanced with other reading skills within a teaching programme.

The Interactive Compensatory Model

Both 'Top-down' and 'Bottom-up' models have limitations in terms of an understanding of the reading process because clearly readers draw on both these processes when reading. The Interactive Compensatory Model attempts to explain how these dual processes work.

This model acknowledges that reading involves recognising words based on information provided simultaneously from both the text and the reader, and as proposed by Stanovich (1988) focuses on the following assumptions:

- readers use information simultaneously from different levels and do not necessarily begin at either the graphic (Bottom-up) or the contextual (Top-down) level;
- during their development of reading skills, readers may rely more heavily on some levels of processing than on others, e.g. they may use context to greater or lesser extents;
- the reader's weaknesses are compensated for by his/her strengths.

Stanovich casts doubt on the view that good readers use the Top-down model more than poor readers. Indeed as indicated above good readers pay more attention to graphic detail and poor readers rely more on context. Thus higher level processing of text does not necessarily need the completion of all lower levels of processing. Stanovich's model, therefore, takes account of the fact that many poor readers have developed strategies for compensating for their information processing difficulties.

Models of reading therefore need to take into account the following:

Print

- logographic stage
- alphabetic stage
- orthographic stage

Language

- communicative aspects of print

- structure of language
- meaning

Context

- prediction
- life experiences
- knowledge
- pleasure and purpose

Most models of reading are derivations from the 'Top-down' or 'Bottom-up' processes.

NATURE OF READING

It should be recognised, however, that reading is a holistic activity. This means that in order to engage successfully in the reading process the learner must utilise a range of cognitive and learning skills. Thus reading depends on:

- the use of skills associated with the verbal and auditory domain, such as language knowledge and language use;
- perceptual and spatial domain, in relation to letter and word recognition;
- segmentation of words and sentences;
- contextual factors which may relate to the reader's previous knowledge and cognitive development.

The reader not only reads for meaning and for accuracy, but also reads for 'thought'. This means that aspects including personality, experience and imagination are all related to the holistic learning activity of reading.

For the teacher the implication of this is that the learner needs to be considered as an individual in relation to reading. It is important to ensure that the general context is appropriate and suited to the individual's style and interests. Interest level, organisation of learning and careful balance between group and individual attention are important factors in the development and integration of skills necessary for reading.

The most popular methods used by teachers in the teaching of reading include the following:

- phonic
- look and say
- language experience

Phonic Model

The phonic method highlights the importance of phonology and the sounds of letters and letter combinations.

Figure 8

Phonics Checklist

Consonants

	Initial	Final
s		
m		
r		
t		
b		
f		
n		
p		
d		
h		
c /k/		
g /g/		
j		
l		
k		
v		
w		
z		
c /s/		
g /j/		
qu		
y		

	Final Only
ck	
x	
ss	
ll	
tt	
ff	
bb	
dd	
pp	

Short Vowels

CVC words

a	
e	
i	
o	
u	

Blends

	Initial
bl	
cl	
fl	
pl	
br	
dr	
gr	
tr	
cr	
fr	
pr	
gl	
sl	
sn	
sp	
st	
sw	
sc	
sk	

	Final
ft	
lp	
mp	
nd	
nk	
nt	
pt	
sk	
sp	
st	

Consonant Digraphs

sh	
ch	
th	
wh	
ph	

Long Vowels

CVCe words

a	
e	
i	
o	
u	

y as a Vowel

/e/ (bunny)	
/i/ (by)	

Vowels followed by r

ar	
or	
er	
ir	
ur	

Silent Letters

Initial		Final	
kn		-tch	
wr		-dge	
gh		-gh	
sc		-lk	
gn			

Vowel Digraphs

ai (paid)	
ay (pay)	
oa (boat)	
ee (tree)	
oe (toe)	
oi (join)	
oy (joy)	
ew (chew)	
ou (cloud)	
ou (soup)	
au (haul)	
aw (saw)	
ea (preach)	
ea (deaf)	

Vowel digraphs, cont.

ow (crow)	
ow (cow)	
oo (boot)	
oo (hook)	
ie (pie)	
ie (thief)	
ey (they)	
ey (valley)	
ei (ceiling)	
ui (build)	
ui (fruit)	

Prefixes

dis	
un	
re	
im	
in	
mis	
pre	

Suffixes

-ful	
-ly	
-less	
-ness	
-able	
-ible	
-ion	
-ment	
-er	
-or	
-en	

Vowels in Spelling Patterns

ind (bind)	
ild (wild)	
igh (high)	
old (cold)	
olt (colt)	
ost (host)	
ost (cost)	

Reproduced from Chall and Popp (1996) with permission

There are a number of structured phonic programmes in existence which can teach children to distinguish the 44 phonemes or sound units of English, by using a variety of strategies. These strategies may include colour-coding and marks to indicate short or long sounds.

Although phonic programmes are structured, and structure is beneficial for children with specific learning difficulties, there are also difficulties associated with such programmes. The most important of these include the possibility that:

- they may increase the burden on children's short and long term memories by increasing what the child needs to remember;
- there are still words which need to be taught as sight vocabulary because they do not fall into the 'sound blending' category, such as 'one' and 'many'.

Phonic methods can help children who have an obvious difficulty in mastering and remembering sound blends and vowel digraphs and have difficulty in synthesising them to make a word. At the same time they present additional learning which may be seen to be meaningless and out of context. Some difficulty may be identified in merging the two components, i.e. knowledge of sound and knowledge of language, together to facilitate a meaningful reading experience.

Chall and Popp (1996) emphasise the need to teach phonics and argue that if taught well it is highly meaningful – through phonics children can get close to the sound of a word and through that to the meaning of the word. They suggest a systematic phonics approach from pre-school with related activities set within a total reading programme.

Frith (1995) emphasises the nature of the phonological 'core variable' in literacy learning and particularly how it is associated with dyslexia. The Theoretical Causal Model (Frith, 1995) highlights the distinctiveness of phonological competence by focusing on three levels for assessing phonological difficulties: biological observations about brain functioning; cognitional, in relation to the hypothetical constructs of intellectual ability and phonological processing ability; and at the behavioural level, in relation to performance in assessments such as phonological awareness tests, naming speed tests and non-word, reading and spelling tests.

Support for the phonological core variable model as an explanation of the difficulties associated with dyslexia has led to illuminative research activity and the development of phonological skills training programmes (Reason and Frederickson, 1996; Hatcher, Hulme and Ellis, 1994; Iversen and Tunmer, 1993; Wilson and Frederickson, 1995).

Look and Say Model

Look and say methods emphasise exposure to print on the grounds that children will become familiar with words and build up a sight vocabulary with increased exposure. The emphasis is therefore on meaningful units of language rather than sounds of speech.

Figure 9

THE PHONEMES OF THE ENGLISH LANGUAGE			
Vowels (20)		*Consonants (24)*	
Symbol	*Sound (or value)*	*Symbol*	*Sound (or value)*
aɪ	try - write	b	back - rubber
aʊ	noun - now	d	day - rudder
ɑ	father	dʒ	judge - George - raj
ɒ	wash - odd	ð	this - other
æ	cat - trap	f	few - puff
eɪ	day - steak - face	g	got - bigger
əʊ	go - goat	h	hot
ε	get	j	yet
εə	fair - square	k	car - key - clock - trekked - quay
ɜ	her - stir - word - nurse	l	lip
i	he - see	m	much - hammer
ɪ	ship	n	now - runner
ɪə	hear - here	ŋ	sing
o	force	p	pen - pepper
ɔ	north - war	r	round - sorry
ɔɪ	noise - toy	s	see - missed
u	lunar - pool	ʃ	ship - mission
ʊ	foot - put	t	ten
ʊə	pure	tʃ	church - latch
ʌ	bud - blood - love	θ	three - heath
		v	very
		w	will
		z	zeal
		3	decision - treasure

(Total = 44)

Reproduced from Doyle (1996) with permission

This type of method therefore requires attractive books which can become progressively more demanding. The use of flash-cards and pictures can be used in the initial stages. The method, however, assumes a good memory for shapes of letters and words as well as the ability to master many of the irregularities of spelling and sound-symbol correspondence. This, of course, may be difficult for children with dyslexic difficulties, particularly since their memory may be weak and can rapidly become overloaded. Some elements of the phonic approaches can accompany most look and say methods.

Indeed Chall and Popp (1996) suggest that a good phonics programme needs to pay attention to sight recognition and that fluent reading depends on both automatic sight recognition and the application of phonic knowledge.

Language Experience Model

Language experience methods focus on the use of language, both oral and written, as an aid to learning to read through various modes of language enrichment. This helps the reader develop important language concepts and schemata which in turn help to bring meaning to print. Although the child may have a decoding problem the experience gained in language can help to compensate for this and bring some meaning to the text.

This model engages the child in the process of going from thought to speech and then to encoding in print and from print to reading.

Pre-reading Activities

There is considerable evidence to suggest that pre-reading activities can help facilitate the reading process. Such activities as well as developing pre-reading skills also help to develop essential skills in comprehension and the development of schema. This latter aspect is particularly important as this can provide the reader with a general understanding of the text and help to relate this to previous learning. Mommers (1987) in fact shows that conceptual development is the most powerful predictor of success in reading.

Figure 10 shows how the same piece of text can relate a different message to different readers. It is clearly possible for two readers to extract different meanings from this same piece of text. Both are reading, but they may obtain different messages from the same print. In the process of reading, the reader interprets the text and the text (or the print) relates a message to the reader.

Figure 10

PACKING FOR THE FAMILY HOLIDAY

Everything had to be in the right place – nothing could be forgotten, otherwise mother would be angry. Even the shirts, blouses and bed linen had to be folded. Just as well this does not happen a lot. True, people will be inspecting it but they are not interested in whether the garments are correctly folded. Naturally, everything had to be cleaned and dusted – the whole house from top to bottom and, of course, the whole family would need to be on their best behaviour. Politeness was to be the order of the day, no speaking out of turn. This episode really was going to be fun!

SELLING OUR HOUSE

Everything had to be in the right place – nothing could be forgotten, otherwise mother would be angry. Even the shirts, blouses and bed linen had to be folded. Just as well this does not happen a lot. True, people will be inspecting it but they are not interested in whether the garments are correctly folded. Naturally, everything had to be cleaned and dusted – the whole house from top to bottom and, of course, the whole family would need to be on their best behaviour. Politeness was to be the order of the day, no speaking out of turn. This episode really was going to be fun!

The texts of Fig. 10 serve to underline the interactive nature of reading. This interactive aspect is extremely important as it combines the reader's background experience and previous knowledge with the 'new' text to be read. This interaction provides the reader with meaning and interpretation. Reading, therefore, is an interaction of previous knowledge involving the use of semantic and syntactic cues and accuracy in the decoding of print. It is important that in teaching reading all these aspects are considered. It is likely the child with specific learning difficulties will find this interactive process difficult as his efforts and cognitive capacities are directed to either mechanically decoding the print or obtaining the meaning from print – simultaneous interaction of these processes is not easily accomplished.

Two key elements of reading therefore are the understanding of print and the message (purpose) of the print (Fig. 11). They both have to be carefully considered in the selection and development of reading programmes and strategies for children with specific learning difficulties.

Figure 11:   Reading skills

UNDERSTANDING OF PRINT	PURPOSE OF PRINT
• Alphabet skills • Organisation of letters and words • Visual features of letters and words • Phonological skills • Word rules • Understanding of syntax	• Semantic understanding • Vocabulary skills • Use of inferences • Comprehension skills • Prediction skills • Concept and schema building

THE READING DEBATE

The teaching of reading has been subject to historical debate. Theories and methods have been reviewed and revised often following the revelation of dismal and disappointing attainment scores in national surveys. The 'Head Start Programme' in the United States and the resultant DISTAR approach to the teaching of reading, emanated from such concerns and alarm over low standards of literacy.

The issue of reading standards is still a national concern and a national debate. Turner (1991) cites the concern over reading standards as a phenomenon which can be largely explained by the trend from phonic instruction to that of whole language, language experience and 'real' books. This argument gains some credence from the widely accepted view that beginning readers need to possess at least a basic knowledge of phonological skills, before they can effectively benefit from enrichment through literacy and associated language activities.

Wray (1991), however, challenges this view by arguing that the evidence for suggesting that a decline in reading standards is due to the move towards a whole-language approach is not strong. He suggests that the whole-language movement is not practised widely enough to account for such a decline in reading standards. He further suggests that the criteria for assessing reading attainment needs to be questioned since it raises the fundamental point 'What is reading?'

At the same time it might be argued 'What is whole-language?' Bergeron (1990) attempted to obtain a consensual definition of whole-language from the literature and found whole-language was defined as an approach, a philosophy, an orientation, a theory, a theoretical orientation, a programme, a curriculum, a perspective on education and an attitude of mind. It is difficult either to promote or to criticise a movement when it is so loosely defined.

To attempt to find the positive aspects of this loose interpretation called 'whole-language' one can look for some common factors in Bergeron's responses. Adams (1990) argues that some commonalities include:

- construction of meaning from text
- developing and explaining the functional dimensions of text
- pupil-centred classrooms
- integration of language arts.

These points can be complementary to any education system and might be described as the flip side of the whole-language movement. The other side, promoted by Smith (1971, 1973) and Goodman (1973) suggests that skilful readers do not process individual letters, spelling-sound translations are irrelevant for reading, and it is therefore not necessary to teach spellings and sounds.

Smith (1971) therefore argues that phonics teaching should not be emphasised because the child has to learn phonic rules by himself and can only do this through experience in reading. Thus phonics teaching, according to Smith, can lead to too deliberate decoding and as a result the meaning of the text will be lost. He argues that decoding is a classroom induced behaviour, not a natural one, and that skilled and even beginning readers only use it to a limited extent.

There are considerable arguments against this (Adams, 1990; Turner, 1991) centering on the need for children to read words before they can obtain meaning from a text. Adams (1990) in fact argues that automaticity develops from actually reading words and not by ignoring or guessing them.

This view is supported by researchers and educationalists in other countries. Adamik-Jászó (1995) describes the Hungarian experience as based on reading programmes focusing on the oral language development of the child. This indicates that phonemic awareness is an essential prerequisite of reading instruction. Studies by Johnston, Connelly and Watson (1995) comparing the book experience approach in New Zealand with systematic phonics approach in Scotland showed that children in the phonics programme were significantly better at reading non-words and had significantly superior reading comprehension.

Similarly, in the United States, Ehri (1995) suggests that for sight word reading to develop, learners must acquire and apply knowledge of the alphabetic system. She asserts that a weakness in the whole language approach is the absence of systematic phonics instruction at the early stages. Attention is not paid to the need for young children to master the alphabetic system through learning letter shapes and names, sounds and letter correspondences and blending sounds into words. Many children do not acquire these skills merely through exposure to print.

The situation, however, is not without counter-argument which emphasises the need to engage the beginning reader with a balanced reading programme. For example Stainthorp (1995) reports on a study which suggests that top-down, context-driven strategies can modify performance in reading. She accepts, however, that the beneficial effects of context are partly dependent upon children having developed some decoding skills and the skills required for decoding should not be left to chance. This view is reiterated by Turner (1995), who suggests that children learn to read by being taught, although he suggests that the component skills of reading are initially learned independently.

Smith, (1993), however, illustrates how reading in fact relies on a combination of word-centred and meaning-centred approaches and therefore assessment of reading clearly requires to account for these two aspects, in order fully to assess reading and evaluate reading programmes. Smith in fact contends that the important point is that a reading approach should be clear and have a 'firm sense of purpose'. Teachers should be aware of the approach they are using and why they are using it.

Bryant (1994) contends that both forms of linguistic knowledge, constituent sounds and language experience, play an important part in children's acquisition and development of reading and writing skills. He reports on a longitudinal study in which children's scores in phonological tasks predicted the progress they made in learning about letter-sound associations, and that scores in semantic and syntactic tasks were good predictors of children's ability to use context and decipher difficult words within a meaningful context. Bryant concludes that each form of linguistic knowledge makes an independent and specific contribution to the reading process, particularly since the children's scores in the phonological task did not predict the children's success in the use of context, and similarly scores in the semantic and syntactic tasks were not significant in predicting phonological skills.

Clearly a balanced approach is necessary when looking at the teaching of reading. Both the phonic method and the 'whole-language' movement have many commendable aspects – both should be utilised in relation to the needs of the individual reader.

It should, however, be noted that children with dyslexic difficulties usually have considerable difficulty in phonological awareness and resultantly in acquiring alphabetic and phonic knowledge. This, therefore, needs to be considered in the development of a balanced programme for dyslexic children.

READING STRATEGIES

There are many activities which can be utilised to support a structured phonics programme. Among the most appropriate of these is the use of games and structured activities to reinforce a particular teaching point. Many of these

Figure 12

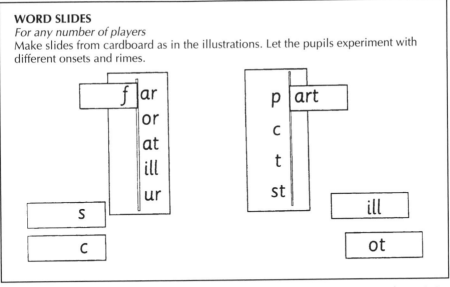

WORD SLIDES
For any number of players
Make slides from cardboard as in the illustrations. Let the pupils experiment with different onsets and rimes.

Reproduced from Gorrie and Parkinson (1995) with permission

games and activities can be developed by the teacher, although there are some excellent examples available commercially. An example of an onset and rime game is shown in Fig. 12.

There is now some evidence of groups of teachers utilising their own resources and developing specific phonological programmes for their own particular context. One successful example of this is the Phonological Awareness Programme for Primary One classes (Hunter, Connelly, Baillie and Thomson 1996). This is a six-week programme which focuses on syllable segmentation, rhyming skills, alliteration and resources. An example of week one is shown in Fig. 13. Other strategies which can be used are those which rely on the use of context.

Readers can utilise two principal types of context

- *Syntactic context* – i.e. the grammatical structure of sentences and clues from prefixes, punctuation, word endings and word order;
- *Semantic context* – i.e. the meaning of words and the meaningful relations between words.

Contextual cues can be of considerable benefit to the learner. Such cues can be seen in the form of syntactic and semantic context.

Syntactic context helps the reader predict the written word. If the child is reading only key words he will not be able to draw on syntactic context for meaning. Fig. 14 below illustrates the importance of syntactic context.

This is how the billboard on the newsagent's street-stand may read. It can be read easily because the vocabulary is simple; but the phrase is lacking in syntactic cues, e.g. does it mean 'two raiders in bank robbery' or 'two banks have been

Figure 13

WEEK ONE
SYLLABLE SEGMENTATION

CIRCLE GAME – It is important to begin at this level to develop listening and organisational skills. The children sit in a circle and the group leader starts the game by clapping once. Each child in turn claps their hands once, progressing round the circle. As the children become more confident the clapping patterns can become more complex.

CLAPPING NAMES – Each child is encouraged to clap the number of syllables in their name. Compare the number of syllables in each child's name. Ensure the children can clap and say the syllables together. If they have all coped with this the leader will clap a child's name without saying whose it is. The children try to identify whose name was clapped and stand up if their name matches the pattern.

RHYMING SKILLS

NURSERY RHYMES – Each child will be given the opportunity to recite a familiar nursery rhyme chosen from a picture. The leader will already have chosen one of the rhymes and written it out with the rhyming words missing. Each of the words should be written on a separate piece of card. The leader then recites the rhyme asking the children to fill in the missing word. Allow the children to draw a picture for the rhyme.

RECOGNISING RHYME – Two objects will be placed on the table and the children have to decide whether they rhyme or not.

(Suggested objects; cat – hat, snake – cake, egg – peg, bear – chair, pie – tie, box – socks, doll – ball, map – cap)

ALLITERATION

FEELY BAGS – In the bag will be pairs of objects which start with the same sound. Each child will take an object out of the bag and say what it is. The group will then decide what sound it starts with. As each child pulls out subsequent objects they will have to decide if it makes a pair with the one they already have. The child with most pairs is the winner.

(Suggested objects for ten pairs: ball – bell, pen – pear, car – cat, game – goose, doll – dice, tape – teddy, fan – fish, sock – soup, money – marble, net – nine)

RESOURCES

Nursery rhymes and pictures. A rhyme written with the rhyming words omitted and cards with these words. Paper & pens. Pairs of objects for recognising rhyme Feely bag and objects

---

robbed'? The lack of syntax may therefore change the meaning. If the reader is not competent at reading all the words, then some of the syntactic cues could be lost. This could result in the reader being deprived of some essential semantic cue, consequently restricting meaning and comprehension.

For many readers, therefore, a sentence from a newspaper article would be easier to process than the headline of the article. This is because:

Figure 14

- the headline would have no developed context to provide the reader with some clues;
- often headlines use 'eye-catching' phrases and do not utilise grammatical structure so the reader cannot rely on syntactic cues.

Semantic context relates to the meaning of words and how they convey messages. This acts as a powerful aid to reading and many readers with poor decoding skills can rely, perhaps too much, on the use of semantic context. Using inferences and even accurate guessing can be a powerful aid to dealing with the written word. It is important, therefore, that learners develop skills in using inferences and identifying the main theme and points in a particular story. Simple exercises such as that in Fig. 15 can help develop semantic context.

Figure 15

THE BLUE BUS DROVE INTO THE G . . . A . . . E.

THE PEN HAD NO I . . . .

In these examples the learner has to infer the correct response from the semantic context.

Context therefore as a reading strategy can be important and is evident in the following ways:

- within the sentence, i.e. before and after the word being read;
- within the text, i.e. before and after the sentence being read;
- within the reader, i.e. entire store of knowledge and experience.

To utilise fully the benefits of contextual reading it is also important for the reader to have a stock of sight words in order that the context can be accurately obtained. It has been argued, for example, by the proponents of the language experience approach, that instead of helping children build up a stock of sight words in order to read, perhaps teaching should be directed to help children read in order to build up a stock of sight words. This would mean that sight words can be built up gradually within the context of reading itself.

It is interesting to note that the 220 words on the Dolch list – that is, the most commonly used words – make up around 75% of the words in primary reading materials (Chall and Popp, 1996).

A classic dilemma is exemplified here between encouraging, indeed insisting on, reading accuracy of all the words, and accepting the accurate reading of the key words, which should be sufficient through the use of semantic cues for comprehension acquisition. The reading of every word, although it may help the reader obtain the full use of the benefits of syntactic cues, can restrict the reader's use of prediction and inferences because attention and concentration are absorbed in accurate decoding. Although accuracy may help aid comprehension, an understanding of the text is possible without full accuracy. Therefore if the child has difficulty with accuracy, it is important that efficient use of semantic context is encouraged, although in the pursuit of this accuracy should not be totally ignored, but carefully considered alongside the need for efficient use of the semantic cues available.

Contextual strategies can be summarised thus:

- words are easier to identify in context than in isolation;
- beginning readers can often identify words in context that they cannot identify in isolation;
- to identify words we use preceding syntactic and semantic cues to predict what might be coming next;
- grapho/phonic cues can help to identify words;
- syntactic and semantic context can help to confirm or correct these identifications.

This chapter has looked at some principles in the acquisition of literacy by focusing on reading and has examined a variety of approaches by discussing some of the problems children with dyslexia may display in relation to reading. Since the concept of dyslexia is essentially a multi-faceted one with neurological, psychological and educational perspectives, it follows that the teaching of reading should be flexible and should consider the child's learning difficulties and preferences, in the educational context. Clearly no one approach can be singled out and a combination of methods involving the teaching of sight words, phonics and context is preferable. At the same time one must also look at what the child brings to the situation and have some knowledge of the child's background knowledge and preferred learning styles and strategies. All of these aspects are important to facilitate the acquisition of literacy.

Chapter 3

Assessment Approaches

AIMS AND RATIONALE

There are a variety of reasons why an assessment should be undertaken. It may be to identify the appropriate level of text and learning materials for the child, or to diagnose a difficulty or perhaps to review progress. Whatever the reason it is important to have clear aims when conducting an assessment.

Fig. 16 highlights some of these aims.

Figure 16

AIMS OF ASSESSMENT

- identification of the learner's general strengths and weaknesses;
- an indication of the learner's current level of performance in attainments;
- an explanation for the learner's lack of progress;
- identification of aspects of the learner's performance in reading, writing and spelling, which may typify a 'pattern of errors';
- identification of specific areas of competence;
- an understanding of the student's learning style;
- an indication of aspects of the curriculum which may interest and motivate the learner.

In many cases the assessment may confirm what the teacher already suspects, as children's strengths and weaknesses may be obvious to the class teacher. The teacher is in daily contact with the child and this ongoing contact provides valuable insights into the child's strengths and weaknesses.

The assessment should, however, also uncover some explanation for children's difficulties and to look for particular patterns, such as errors, which seem to be predominantly due to visual, auditory, motor or memory difficulties. These may be identified as a specific pattern. The unearthing of a pattern of difficulties can help the teacher decide on the nature of the child's difficulty and so can assist in the planning of appropriate programmes of work.

Assessment, however, should aim not only to assess the child, but also to assess the curriculum, to analyse which factors motivate the child and help to promote development in thinking and progress in attainments. Similarly it is important to analyse the child's learning style, looking at how the learner relates to the classroom, the task and the curriculum in general. Key questions, therefore, which need to be addressed before an assessment is undertaken, relate to the what, the why, the how and the effect of assessment.

What?

What is one looking for when conducting an assessment?

In relation to dyslexic children one may be looking for a specific pattern of difficulties such as difficulties in organisation, sequencing, phonological awareness, word recognition and memory problems. At the same time the focus for the assessment could be on the curriculum and one may be looking for an explanation as to why a particular child is having difficulty in a specific area. One may, therefore, be looking for particular strategies or resources which can help to access the curriculum for a particular child.

Why?

Why should an assessment be carried out and what purpose does this serve?

Although there may be a number of different reasons why an assessment is required there are usually some common factors. The assessment may be used for diagnostic purposes in order to provide information which may account for the child's difficulties in learning. At the same time the assessment may be used as a predictive tool – in order to obtain some information which can help the teacher predict how the child will cope with particular aspects of the curriculum. Used in this way, however, the information from the assessment may in fact be misused since it may lead to unnecessary curricular restrictions being placed on the child. This indeed is one of the misuses of IQ tests since the case may arise where a child assessed as having a low IQ is disadvantaged in terms of curricular access and expectation – this of course should be avoided at all costs.

The assessment may be used in a 'normative' way by comparing the child with his peers. Again some caution should be applied, although it may be useful to obtain some kind of data in relation to how the child is progressing in relation to others in the same chronological age range.

If the child has already been assessed, then further assessment can contribute to monitoring and review. This is an important element of any assessment since it assists in measuring the effects of teaching. Assessment should be linked to teaching, and there can be a prescriptive element to assessment in that it may offer some suggestions for teaching approaches or programmes.

If there is a suspicion that the child may have dyslexic difficulties and the assessment is being conducted to discover if this is indeed the case, then feeding back this information, particularly to the parents, can be extremely useful. If the difficulties are to be effectively tackled then it is important that the school, parents and the child should be working collaboratively. Biggar and Barr (1996) suggest in fact that mixed messages and anxieties between parents and the school can be extremely damaging for the child's self-concept.

How?

The issue of how an assessment should be conducted is an important one.

It may be advisable to use a range of assessment strategies and not simply opt for one particular type of assessment. This chapter will provide some examples of the range of assessment strategies which can be used. Clearly, how one tackles the assessment depends to a great extent on the purpose of the assessment. For example, standardised tests, although quite limited in terms of diagnostic information, can provide useful information with which to measure progress.

It is useful to have a battery of strategies prepared or an assessment framework which can be accommodated within the school context. The assessment framework described later in this chapter should provide some guidance in this respect. At all times it is important to link assessment and teaching. Assessment should not be conducted in isolation but within the context of the curriculum and the child's progress within the classroom. It is, therefore, important to look at the process of learning – the strategies used by the child – in addition to the product, that is the actual attainment.

Many forms of assessment which look at attainments can be described as static, in that they test what the child can do without assistance. Assessment, however, can also be provided with an additional dynamic dimension thus allowing the assessment process to be used more flexibly. It has been argued (Campione and Brown, 1989) that when conducting an assessment the teacher should *not* be asking, '*what can the child do?*' but '*what do I need to do to help the child successfully complete the assessment?*' The help which is necessary to facilitate the correct response from the child should be noted. Thus the teacher is focusing on the process of the assessment not the product or the outcome of the assessment.

Effect

A consideration throughout the assessment process is the effect of the assessment – the assessment outcome. It is important to ensure that the assessment provides information which can be readily linked to a teaching programme or which can be used to help the child cope more effectively with the curriculum.

It is also important to bear in mind that a formal assessment, by necessity, provides a 'spotlight' on a particular child and the child understandably, quickly becomes aware of this. The assessment, therefore, should be implemented judiciously in order that the child is not exposed to any feelings of failure additional to those already resulting from his/her particular difficulties. The assessment should uncover data which will help in the development of a teaching programme.

The identification and assessment of specific learning difficulties is of crucial importance, since a full assessment will facilitate the planning of appropriate intervention which will help to prevent the child from becoming engulfed by a feeling of learned helplessness. Preventing, or at least minimising, such failure removes the threat that intransigent learning difficulties will become so deeply embedded that they not only penetrate the affective domain but also result in inappropriate reading styles embedded within the child's learning pattern.

Clearly, therefore, assessment should consider the child's self-concept. Every effort should be made to ensure that the difficulties displayed by the child and the underlying problems do not detract from the development of skills in learning and in access to the curriculum.

It is vital that the approaches and strategies selected provide the data and information to facilitate an effective teaching programme, preferably within the context of the classroom and the curriculum. Careful preparation and planning are necessary before embarking on assessment and the questions relating to what, why, how and effect must be addressed at this planning stage and reviewed throughout the assessment.

APPROACHES AND STRATEGIES

It is necessary, therefore, to use a broad range of assessment strategies in order to ensure that adequate attention is given not only to the student's learning and cognitive profile but also to the process of learning itself and the context within which learning takes place.

Assessment for specific learning difficulties should consider three aspects – difficulties, discrepancies and differences. The central **difficulty** is clearly related to the decoding or the encoding of print, and this may be the result of different contributory factors. For example, some difficulties may include phonological processing, memory problems, organisational and sequencing difficulties, motor coordination, language problems, or perceptual difficulties of an auditory or visual nature.

The **discrepancies** may be apparent in comparing decoding and reading/ listening comprehension, between oral and written responses, and in performances within the different subject areas of the curriculum.

It is also important to acknowledge the **differences** between individual learners, including dyslexic children. An assessment, therefore, should also consider learning and cognitive styles. An appreciation of this can help to effectively link assessment and teaching, which should be a principal aim in assessing for specific learning difficulties.

A wide range of assessment strategies can be used to help recognise the **difficulties, discrepancies** and **differences** displayed by learners.

The range which will be discussed in this chapter is outlined in Fig. 17.

Figure 17

ASSESSMENT APPROACHES AND STRATEGIES

STANDARDISED
- Weschler Intelligence Scale (WISC III)
- Weschler Objective Language Dimensions (WOLD)
- Weschler Objective Number Dimensions (WOND)
- Weschler Objective Reading Dimensions (WORD)
- British Ability Scales
- New McMillan • Neale Analysis
- Aston Index

DIAGNOSTIC
- As above
- Miscue Analysis
- Bury Infant Check
- Reading Assessment for Teachers (RAT Pack)

DIAGNOSTIC SPELLING TEST
- Boder Test of Reading and Spelling Patterns
- Slingerland
- Adult Assessment (Klein, 1993)

SCREENING
- Cognitive Profiling System (COPS)
- Dyslexia Screening Test (Fawcett and Nicolson, 1996)
- Quest Reading and Number Screening Tests
- Bangor Dyslexia Test
- Checklists

PHONOLOGICAL
- Phonological Assessment Battery (PhAB,1996)
- Sound Linkage (Hatcher, 1994)
- Phonological Awareness Procedures (Gorrie and Parkinson, 1995)
- Lindamood Auditory Conceptualisation Test (LAC Test)
- Phonological Abilities Test (Muter, Hulme and Snowling, 1997)

COMPONENTS APPROACH
- Decoding/listening comprehension
- Non-word Reading (Snowling)

OBSERVATIONAL
- Observational Survey/Running Record (Clay)
- Observational Framework (Reid, 1994)

METACOGNITIVE
- Assisted Assessment (Campione and Brown)
- Pass Model (Das *et al.*, 1994)
- Portfolio Assessment
- Multiple Intelligences Approaches (Lazear, 1994)

STANDARDISED AND DIAGNOSTIC

This form of assessment consists of standardised or norm-referenced tests which provide some form of score or measure which is compared with the average scores of a standardised sample. From this type of test one can obtain, for example, a reading age or IQ score. As well as providing an indication of the pupil's progress in relation to his peers, these tests can also provide information which can be used diagnostically and prescriptively. Important factors in standardised tests are the aspects of validity and reliability. Standardised tests must have a high **validity** and **reliability** so that the teacher can use the data from the test with confidence.

- **Validity:** This refers to the design of the test and whether the test actually measures what it was designed to measure, e.g. IQ, decoding, verbal comprehension, etc.
- **Reliability:** This refers to the reliability in obtaining the same responses from the test if repeated under similar conditions. Clearly the reliability of a test is limited by its validity.

Wechsler Intelligence Scale

One such standardised test in widespread use for the assessment of children who may have specific learning difficulties/dyslexia is the Wechsler Intelligence Scale for Children. This test was originally devised as an assessment tool for psychologists and psychometricians. It provides both an IQ and sub-test profile. It was revised and re-standardised in 1974 and a new version with more modern and appropriate test materials was produced in 1992 (WISC III).

The WISC-III consists of six verbal sub-tests – information, similarities, arithmetic, vocabulary, comprehension and digit span – and seven performance (non-verbal) tests – picture completion, coding, picture arrangement, block design, object assembly, symbol search and mazes. In addition to verbal and performance IQ scores, the tests can yield index scores relating to verbal comprehension, perceptual organisation, freedom from distractibility and perceptual speed. These can provide very useful information in a diagnosis of the child's strengths and weaknesses.

Cooper (1995) suggests that the WISC series of test are probably the best validated and most widely accepted measures of children's intellectual functioning in the world.

The use of ability measures such as the WISC according to Siegal (1989) rests on all or some of the following assumptions:

- that tests of ability or IQ are valid and reliable measures, so that there is some virtue in examining discrepancies between ability and achievement;
- particular sub-tests are valid instruments in the assessment of specific cognitive sub-skills;
- distinctive patterns may emerge which can be reliably correlated with specific learning difficulties;
- that IQ and reading share a causal dependency with IQ factors influencing reading ability.

Siegal, however, argues that the evidence in relation to these points is inconsistent. She argues that IQ tests do not necessarily measure intelligence, but in fact measure factual knowledge, expressive language ability, short-term memory and other skills related to learning. The implication of this for children with dyslexia, is that because of the nature of their difficulty,their scores in relation to factual knowledge, expressive language and short-term memory will provide an artificially depressed IQ score. This view is in fact supported by Miles (1996) who suggests that the concept of global IQ for dyslexic children is a misleading one because it will not provide a valid reflection of their real abilities.

This assertion clearly undermines the view that the sub-tests and even sub-test patterns can reveal useful information in the assessment of specific learning difficulties. Yet factor analytic studies of the WISC-R (Lawson and Inglis, 1984–85) show that verbal skills can be isolated as a discrete factor. Interestingly, the sub-tests which had a high loading value for the factors Arithmetic, Coding, Information and Digit Span are those sub-tests which present problems for children with specific learning difficulties. This is consistent with the 'ACID' profile which identified the same set of sub-tests and provides some evidence for a distinctive dyslexic cognitive profile (Thomson, 1984). Miles (1996) also suggests that the WISC can reveal patterns of strengths and weaknesses which can be useful in a diagnosis of dyslexia.

Wechsler Dimensions

In addition to the WISC there are a number of other related assessments which focus on particular dimensions of learning. These include the Wechsler Objective Reading Dimensions (WORD), Language Dimensions (WOLD) and number dimensions (WOND). The combined subscales of the WORD, WOLD and WOND produce the measures obtained from the Wechsler Individual Achievement Test (WIAT).

The WORD assesses reading and spelling abilities from ages 6 years to 16 years 11 months. It consists of three sub-tests and basic reading, spelling and reading comprehension.

The WOLD focuses on language attainment and the subtests are listening comprehension, oral expression and written expression.

The WOND provides assessment in numerical attainment and the subtests are called mathematics reasoning and numerical operations.

The WIAT provides a screening of potential achievement difficulties by using the subscale scores from the dimensions tests described above.

British Ability Scales

The British Ability Scales (BAS II; Elliott *et al.*, 1996) may be used as an alternative to the WISC.

The BAS II is divided into two batteries, the Early Years Battery, which consists of cognitive scales, and the School Age Battery, which comprises both cognitive and achievement scales. Some of the scales and a summary of abilities are are shown overleaf.

Summary of abilities measured by the BAS II scales

Scale	Abilities measured
Block building	Visual–perceptual matching, especially of spatial orientation, in copying block patterns.
Copying	Visual–perceptual matching and fine-motor coordination in copying line drawings.
Early number concepts	Knowledge of, and problem-solving using, pre-numerical and numerical concepts.
Matching letter-like forms	Visual discrimination among similar shapes.
Matrices	Inductive reasoning: identification and application of rules governing relationships among abstract figures.
Naming vocabulary	Expressive language; knowledge of names.
Number skills	Recognition of printed numbers and performance of arithmetic operations.
Pattern construction	Non-verbal reasoning and spatial visualisation in reproducing designs with coloured blocks.
Picture similarities	Non-verbal reasoning shown by matching pictures that have a common element or concept.
Quantitative reasoning	Inductive reasoning: detection and application of rules concerning sequential patterns in dominos and relationships between pairs of numbers.
Recall of designs	Short-term recall of visuo-spatial relationships through reproduction of abstract figures.
Recall of digits forward	Short-term auditory memory and oral recall of sequences of numbers.
Recall of digits backward	Working memory and oral recall of reversed sequences of numbers.
Recall of objects	Short-term and intermediate-term verbal and visuo-spatial recall of a display of pictures.
Recognition of pictures	Short-term visual memory measured through recognition of objects.
Speed of information processing	Quickness in performing simple mental operations.
Spelling	Knowledge and recall of spellings.
Verbal comprehension	Receptive language: understanding of oral instructions involving basic language concepts.
Verbal similarities	Verbal reasoning and verbal knowledge.
Word definitions	Expressive language: explanation of work meanings.
Word reading	Recognition (decoding) or printed words.

(Reproduced from Elliott et al., (1996) with permission of NFER Nelson)

Clearly some of these sub-tests and scales can be very appropriate in assessing the cognitive strengths, weaknesses and progress in attainments of dyslexic children

There is, however, strong evidence to dispute the assertion that IQ and reading ability share a causal dependency. Stanovich (1992) argues that the key to reading disability is related to the problem of phonological processing. This notion has indeed widespread support, Frith (1995). Stanovich further argues that phonological processes are independent of intelligence and are not measured or directly taken account of in IQ tests.

The difficulty known as hyperlexia (Aaron, 1989; Healy, 1992) can be used as evidence to dispute any valid association between IQ and reading attainment. Hyperlexia has been described as affecting those children with good decoding skills but poor comprehension indicating a low general IQ.

Siegal (1990) cites the existence of a hyperlexic group as further evidence of the need to disassociate IQ and reading attainment. It has been argued that listening comprehension correlates more highly with reading ability than IQ. The evidence from studies of hyperlexia (Healy, 1992) therefore suggests that children with low IQ scores can be good mechanical readers. This clearly indicates that a causal relationship between IQ and reading ability is a doubtful one.

Aston Index

The Aston Index was developed by Aston University in Birmingham. It consists of a series of tests which claim to be able to:

- identify children with potential language associated problems early in their education. (It can therefore be used as a screening device);
- be used to analyse and diagnose reading and language difficulties displayed by children who are experiencing difficulties in coping with basic attainments.

The Aston Index produces a pupil profile based on a number of tests.
The tests are divided into:

- General Underlying Ability and Attainment
- Performance Items.

The 'General Underlying Ability' section consists of tests on:

- picture recognition
- vocabulary
- Goodenough draw a man test
- Copying geometric designs
- Grapheme/phoneme correspondence
- Schonell reading test
- Spelling test.

The Performance Items consist of tests on:

- Visual discrimination
- Child's laterality
- Copying name
- Free writing
- Visual sequential memory (pictures)
- Auditory sequential memory
- Sound blending
- Visual sequential memory (symbolic)
- Sound discrimination
- Graphomotor test.

The tests within the Aston Index help the teacher diagnose the nature of the problem which may be preventing the child from achieving a satisfactory level in basic attainments. The Aston Index, however, has been the subject of criticism in relation to weaknesses in both construction and standardisation. There is also some doubt as to the potential of the test to discriminate between various groups of children experiencing specific learning difficulties (Pumfrey and Reason, 1991).

The Aston Portfolio Assessment Checklist is essentially a development from the Index and consists of assessment cards, checklists and teaching cards which help the teacher identify specific difficulties associated with attainments and suggest possible methods of dealing with this difficulty.

Edwards Reading Test

This test, although providing data relating to a reading range, can be used diagnostically. It has the clear advantage of assisting in the assessment of reading skills using a range of criteria. Thus in addition to the Quick Word Screen Test there are also tests on oral reading, silent reading and listening comprehension. Scores can be recorded for comprehension, accuracy and speed. All the reading passages are graded in year level and recommended satisfactory scores for the year levels are provided.

The interesting and useful aspect of the Edwards Reading Test (1981) is that it enables the teacher to compare the child's performance in the decoding of single words free from context, with comprehension from passages read both orally and silently. This can provide useful information which may highlight discrepancies in a child's reading skills and performances.

Neale Analysis of Reading Ability

This revised edition (1989) consists of a set of graded passages for testing reading rate, accuracy and comprehension of oral reading, and can be used as an attainment test and a diagnostic test. A demonstration cassette is also included which provides useful extracts from test sessions. The test material has an appealing format – a brightly coloured book with pictures accompanying each of the graded passages.

There is also a Diagnostic Tutor Form with extended passages for further error analysis and Supplementary Diagnostic Tests focusing on discrimination of initial and final sounds, names and sounds of the alphabet, graded spelling and auditory discrimination and blending, which can provide very useful information to help the teacher both diagnose and prepare teaching programmes.

Diagnostic Tests

All the standardised tests described above can and should be used diagnostically. Clearly with some tests it is easier to obtain diagnostic information than with some others. The tests described below can provide diagnostic information quite readily.

The Boder Test of Reading and Spelling Patterns

This test was constructed by Elena Boder, Professor of Paediatrics, University of California and Sylvia Jarrico, Research Psychologist. It is intended to fulfil the need for a practical, direct diagnostic screening procedure that can differentiate developmental dyslexia from non-specific reading disorders. It attempts to classify dyslexic readers into one of three subtypes on the basis of their reading-spelling patterns. The unique feature of the test is that it jointly analyses reading and spelling as interdependent functions.

The key features of the test include:

- reading and spelling tests with equal numbers of phonetic and non-phonetic words;
- a reading test based on sight vocabulary and phonic attack skills;
- an individualised written spelling test based on the results of the oral reading test.

The authors claim that it is beneficial to examine two basic components of the reading-spelling process – the Gestalt and the analytic function. These correspond to the two standard methods of initial reading instruction – the whole word (look-say) method, which utilises visual/Gestalt skills, and the phonics method which relies on the student's ability to analyse words into their phonic components.

Furthermore, the authors argue that the strengths and deficits of the Gestalt and analytic functions of dyslexic children are displayed within three characteristic reading-spelling patterns. These are:

- The dysphonetic group. This type of reader has difficulty integrating written words with their sounds. Thus he/she will display poor phonic word analysis and decoding skills. Typical misspellings are phonetically inaccurate and misreadings are word substitutions, which can be semantic, e.g. 'bus' for 'car' and 'tree' for 'wood', or might be Gestalt substitutions, e.g. 'bell' for 'ball'. This category – the dysphonetic – is likely to be the largest among the dyslexic readers.

- The dyseidetic group. This group displays weaknesses in visual perception and memory for letters and whole word configurations. They may have no difficulty in developing phonic skills, but will have a weakness in the visual/Gestalt area. Their typical misspellings are phonetically accurate and can be decoded, e.g. 'wok' for 'walk', and their misreadings are good phonetic attempts and non-phonetic words such as 'talc' for 'talk'. Visuospatial reversals can also be seen in this group, e.g. 'dab' for 'bad' and 'for' instead of 'of'.
- Mixed dysphonetic and dyseidetic patterns. This group has difficulty in both the development of sight vocabulary and phonic skills.

Clearly, if learners from the dysphonetic group are identified, then their strengths will be on the visual side rather than phonic analysis skills. The implications of this for teaching may be a preference for a visual whole-word approach to help build a sight vocabulary before tackling the difficulty with phonics which will be very evident.

Dyseidetic readers are unable to perceive whole words as a visual entity. Although it is important to build up a sight vocabulary with this type of learner, reading skills can be more readily attained through a phonics programme.

For children who have difficulty with both visual and auditory stimuli, learning can be provided through the third channel – tactile-kinesthetic. Both phonic programmes and whole word techniques can be supplemented with an emphasis on the tactile-kinesthetic.

Teaching Reading through Spelling

This programme produced by teachers at the Reading Centre at Kingston upon Thames (Teaching Reading Through Spelling) contains a very useful booklet on diagnosis of specific learning difficulties (Cowdery, McMahon, Morse and Prince, 1983).

The programme provides a very comprehensive diagnosis and assessment but both the time and the expertise required for such comprehensive assessment is likely to be outwith the scope of the class teacher. Some of the strategies, however, particularly in relation to informal testing and diagnosis can be readily utilised by the class teacher.

The assessment objectives outlined by the authors include compiling a case profile, obtaining sample data of the problems, obtaining criterion-referenced and diagnostic information and obtaining age-related data. The objectives are achieved through interview with parents and the child; observation; informal testing and diagnosis and standardised testing and diagnosis.

Each of the stages has a specific function. For example, the interview conducted in a 'relaxed and supportive manner' attempts to provide an initial estimate of the child's abilities and parent's perception of the problem. Observation can take account of aspects such as directional confusion, coordination, movement, attention span, eye movements and general level of activity.

The informal testing involves noting conversational and listening skills, noting errors, omissions and difficulties in conversation. Mispronunciation of words and asking for questions to be repeated or clarified can also be noted. In addition to conversational and listening skills, sequencing skills such as reciting days of the week, and months of year can be recorded as well as aspects of dominance – eye, ear, hand and foot – and directional aspects such as knowledge of left and right, below and above, and ability to mix laterality such as being able to touch the left ear with right hand.

Further information may be derived from observation of classroom activities by noting competencies in using different types of materials such as scissors, paints and paste, and observations can be made in physical education by noting general movement skills and motor coordination. The diagnostic programme provides some useful activities which the teacher can provide for the child in order to obtain further data, including threading a needle, dealing cards, throwing and catching a ball, kicking a ball, screwing a lid on a jar, tying a shoelace and doing up buttons.

The programme also provides pointers to the assessment of language skills by noting the child's word finding difficulties, vocabulary range, expressive difficulties, receptive language skills, phonological difficulties (such as the confusion of sounds), grammatical errors and articulation difficulties.

Slingerland

The Slingerland Assessment (1974) is a diagnostic assessment which can provide data relating to both the child's skills in learning and preferences in learning style in relation to language and literacy.

The test has three components, each applicable to a different stage – Test A is directed at infants, Test B to middle primary and Test C to upper primary. The tests can be administered to a group or individually. There are nine sub-tests in the assessment and the tests can be administered over several sessions. There are also pre-reading screening procedures (1977) which can highlight auditory, visual and kinesthetic difficulties. These difficulties can be due to short attention span, faulty perception and recall of visual or auditory symbols and fine motor difficulties. As in other Slingerland tests this screening pack also attempts to highlight, for classroom teachers, the 'strengths and weaknesses of the learning modalities of their pupils'. As well as a pupil assessment booklet, the test also contains a teacher observation sheet. This observation sheet focuses on attention span, behaviour and social relations, general maturity and indications of mental growth, language factors, coordination in terms of gross movement and fine motor control and general information in relation to activity of modality preferences.

In the screening procedures test each of the sub-tests performs a different function but can be used to cross-check on data to confirm diagnostic opinions. For example, in Test A, Sub-test 1 focuses on the visual-kinesthetic area. It involves copying from the blackboard and can help to identify children with perceptual motor difficulties and visual scanning; because it is a visual coping task, it can also provide data on the linking of the child's visual-kinesthetic skills.

Sub-test 2 performs a similar task, except the 'model' is closer and comparisons between the results of this test and the previous one can be drawn.

Sub-test 3 looks at visual perception, visual discrimination and memory. It involves displaying a card with a written word to the child, then distracting him before asking him to identify the word from a number of words on the test sheet.

Sub-test 5 is similar, except that the child has to reproduce the word in writing, thus associating visual memory with the kinesthetic channel.

The other sub-tests focus on auditory memory, which involves listening to the word, then selecting it from the test sheet; visual discrimination and linking the auditory and visual channels through listening and looking activities to identify words.

The Slingerland Test has no norms. Its use, therefore, is diagnostic and the insight provided by the test into the student's strengths, weaknesses, modality preferences and modality integration can help the teacher identify appropriate teaching materials for the student.

Miscue Analysis during Oral Reading

The strategy known as miscue analysis is based on the 'Top-down' approach to reading which has developed from the work of Goodman (1972). Goodman argued that the reader first has to make predictions as to the most likely meaning of the text. Such predictions were based on how the reader perceived the graphic, syntactic and semantic information contained in the text. The reader, therefore, according to Goodman, engages in hypothesis testing to either confirm or disprove the prediction – this he named the 'psycholinguistic guessing game'.

It was, therefore, assumed that miscues occur systematically and occur whether reading is silent or aloud, and that the degree of sense the child makes of the material reflects his use of prior knowledge.

The marking system which is usually adopted in miscue analysis is indicated in Fig. 18.

It is important to observe whether the miscue is self-corrected, the graphic or phonemic similarly between the expected response and the observed response (what the child actually says) and whether the miscue produces syntactically or semantically acceptable text.

It is, therefore, possible to obtain useful data on the child's reading pattern by observing the reading errors and noting the significance of these oral errors (see Fig. 19).

There are some specifically designed assessment materials to use with the miscue analysis strategy. Arnold (1984) has developed a series of graded passages which have been specially prepared with miscue analysis in mind. The graded passages range from reading levels 6 to 12 years. They vary in length and are written in autobiographical, narrative and informational styles.

Figure 18

	MARKING ERRORS OR 'MISCUES'
Reversals:	Indicate reversals of word or phrase by Z e.g. 'will Z you' should be 'you will'
Omissions:	Circle all omissions, either of letters or whole words, e.g. he saw (the) car.
Insertions/Additions:	Use this sign ∧ if a word is inserted into the text.
Substitutions:	Cross out any word for which another is incorrectly substituted and write in the substituted word, e.g. above about
Repetitions:	Draw a wavy line under any word that is repeated ⁓‿‿‿
Hesitations:	Insert a diagonal slash when this occurs, i.e. /.
Non-response:	Indicate by dashed line beneath the word at which the child halts. -----------

The manual, as well as outlining the theoretical viewpoint and rationale for miscue analysis, provides a number of illustrative case studies with comments and suggestions of follow-up action.

Arnold (1992) has also produced a diagnostic reading record. This also contains case studies which highlight assessment through the use of miscue analysis. It also includes a teacher's handbook and pupil profile sheets and focuses on observations of reading behaviour and an examination of oral reading through discussion in order to obtain the child's level of understanding of the passage.

This can be a useful resource for the teacher and the reading passages are contained in photocopyable masters.

PHONOLOGICAL ASSESSMENT

Essentially phonological assessment focuses on the question arising from what specific learning difficulties are rather than what they are not. This is supported by the work of many researchers in this area critical of the use discrepancy or exclusionary definitions of specific learning difficulties/dyslexia (Stanovich, 1991;

Figure 19

THE SIGNIFICANCE OF ORAL ERRORS

● **Omissions**
These may occur in relation to reading speed - for example, when the child's normal silent reading speed is used when reading orally. As the child progresses in reading ability and reading speed increases, omissions may still be noted as they tend to increase as reading speed increases.

● **Additions**
These may reflect superficial reading with perhaps an over-dependence on context clues.

● **Substitutions**
These can be visual or semantic substitutions. In younger readers, substitutions would tend to be visual and in older readers contextual. In the latter case they may reflect an over-dependence on context clues.

● **Repetitions**
These may indicate poor directional attack, and perhaps some anticipatory uncertainty on the part of the reader about a word to be read.

● **Reversals**
These may reflect the lack of left-right orientation. Reversals may also indicate some visual difficulty and perhaps a lack of reading for meaning.

● **Hesitations**
These can occur when the reader is unsure of the text and perhaps lacking in confidence in reading. For the same reason that repetitions may occur, the reader may also be anticipating a different word later in the sentence.

Self-corrections
These would occur when the reader becomes more aware of meaning and less dependent on simple word recognition.

Frith, 1995; Gallagher and Frederickson, 1995; Reason and Frederickson, 1996). Additionally early intervention studies have shown that phonological skills training facilitates the acquisition of reading skills (Blachman, Ball, Black and Tangel, 1994), and that even within a comprehensive literacy programme phonological skills training has enhanced the progress of children with reading difficulties (Hatcher, Hulme and Ellis 1994). In view of this convincing evidence of a relationship between phonological processing and reading skills it is of some importance that a detailed phonological assessment should be conducted. Some examples of such assessment are described below.

The Phonological Assessment Battery (PHAB)

This battery is based on the Theoretical Casual Model (Frith, 1995) which provides convincing support for a phonological 'core variable' in literacy difficulties and highlights the view that phonological competence is distinct from general cognitive ability. The battery consists of five measures

- Alliteration test
- Rhyme test
- Naming speed test
- Fluency test
- Spoonerism test

Each of these tests seem to be ideally suited to assess dyslexic difficulties. There is good evidence that dyslexic children have difficulty with rhyme and alliteration and some researchers have indicated that naming speed is in itself a significant feature of dyslexic difficulties (Wolf, 1991, 1996; Nicholson and Fawcett, 1995). This battery offers some advantages over other tests which aim to assess dyslexic difficulties. Both the content of the battery and the clear theoretical rationale which underpins it are impressive.

Sound Linkage

This is essentially a teaching approach (Hatcher, 1994) but is introduced by a test of phonological awareness. The test aims to measure the extent to which young children can manipulate sounds within words. As it is linked to the teaching programme it is possible to measure progress at various intervals. The test consists of

- Syllable blending
- Phoneme blending
- Rhyme
- Phoneme segmentation
- Phoneme deletion
- Phoneme transposition

Each of these areas are covered in the programme, contained within appropriate activities.

Phonological Awareness Procedures

This programme (Gorrie and Parkinson, 1995) essentially has three components – assessment, games and resources. The assessment section provides a very detailed analysis of the child's phonological awareness. The assessment covers the following areas:

- Polysyllabic word/non word repetition and recognition
- Syllable segmentation, deletion of prefixes and suffixes and deletion of syllables (see Fig. 20)
- Intra-syllable segmentation such as detection of onset and rime at rhyme judgement and production
- Phoneme segmentation such as blending, detection and deletion of initial and final phonemes

Figure 20

DELETION OF SYLLABLES - POLYSYLLABIC WORDS

METHOD: Say each word aloud and ask the pupil to delete the syllable in bold type. Words may be repeated only once.

Practice Items: 'If I take **car** away from **car**pet, what have I got left?' (pet)
'Now take **tur** away from **tur**ban' (ban)
'Take **net** away from mag**net**' (mag)
'Take **bin** away from ro**bin**' (ro)

table	(ble)	. . . .
win**dow**	(win)	. . . .
number	(ber)	. . . .
famous	(mous)	. . . .
chim**ney**	(chim)	. . . .
pa**per**	(pa)	. . . .
pillow	(low)	. . . .
den**tist**	(den)	. . . .
acorn	(corn)	. . . .
trumpet	(pet)	. . . .

Total Score=

These procedures provide a straightforward method to help the teacher obtain useful information in relation to the child's phonological awareness.

Lindamood Auditory Conceptualisation Test (LAC Test)

This highly acclaimed procedure (Clark, 1988) was developed to measure phonological awareness (Lindamood and Lindamood, 1979). The test consists of a procedure in which coloured blocks are used by students to represent sounds heard in words.

The Lindamoods found strong correlations between students' performances in this test with word recognition, reading comprehension and spelling.

SCREENING

The screening of children, at virtually any stage in education, is an issue which has aroused considerable debate and controversy. Three main questions can be raised in relation to screening:

- What is the most desirable age (or ages) for children to be screened?
- Which skills, abilities and attainments in performances should children be screened for?
- How should the results of any screening procedures be used?

Additionally, the benefits of screening need to be weighed against the costs in terms of staff and resources which are necessary to implement effective screening procedures. This raises the issue as to whether screening should be for all children, or only for those who do not appear to be making satisfactory progress. Some screening strategies are described below.

Bangor Dyslexia Test

This is a commercially available short screening test developed from work conducted at Bangor University (Miles, 1983a). The test is divided into the following sections:

- left-right (body parts)
- repeating polysyllabic words
- subtraction
- tables
- months forward/reversed
- digits forward/reversed
- b–d confusion
- familiar incidence

It is important to note that this test is only intended as a screening device to find out whether the subject's difficulties are or are not typically dyslexic and may therefore offer a contribution towards an understanding of the subject's difficulties. It should not therefore be seen as a definitive diagnosis.

Dyslexia Screening Test (DST)

The authors of this test (Fawcett and Nicolson, 1996) claim it was developed due to both the wider theoretical understanding of dyslexia, particularly since the publication of the earlier Bangor Dyslexia Test, and the changes in the British educational system, particularly relating to the formal procedures for assessing whether children have special educational needs. It may also have a use, according to the authors, of assessing whether some children should have concessionary extra time in examinations.

The screening instrument can be used for children between 6.6 to 16.5 years of age, although there is also an alternative version developed by the same authors for younger children, Dyslexia Early Screening Test (Nicolson and Fawcett, 1996). There was also a feasibility study conducted by the same authors on a Dyslexia Screening Test for Adults (Nicolson, Fawcett and Miles, 1993).

The norms for the Dyslexic Screening Test were the result of extensive testing involving over 1000 children. The test consists of the following attainment tests;

- one minute reading
- two minute spelling
- one minute writing

and the following diagnostic tests;

- rapid naming
- bead threading
- postural stability
- phonemic segmentation
- backwards digit span
- nonsense passage reading
- verbal and semantic fluency.

These tests are consistent with the current theoretical standing of dyslexia, particularly in relation to the phonological core variable and the rapid naming hypotheses. As in all screening tests there is some limit on the value of the information but the wide range of factors considered in this test does enhance its value as a screening device.

Cognitive Profiling System for (COPS1)

This computerised screening programme represents an exciting breakthrough in this area (Singleton, 1996a and b). The programme constitutes a user-friendly package, complete with facilities for student registration, graphic report and print out of results. The COPS suite has undergone extensive piloting and has also been converted to several languages.

COPS benefits from the advantages associated with computer programmes such as greater provision in presenting assessment tasks and greater accuracy in measuring responses. The programme can be administered with only the minimum of training and generally provides a greater degree of objectivity than some other forms of screening.

The developers of COPS1, which has an age range of 4 years to 11 years 8 months, are currently working on a similar suite of materials aimed for ages 9 to 15 years (COPS2) and for adults (COPS3). They have also developed additional computerised tests to assess reading, spelling, number skills, motor coordination and intelligence. These materials, known as baseline assessment, represent the only fully computerised objective baseline assessment scheme which provides the teacher with a baseline profile of each child. This kit has the potential therefore to fulfil an important function, particularly in curriculum planning for children with dyslexia difficulties.

Quest – Screening, Diagnostic and Support Kit (Second Edition, 1995)

This updated version of Quest consists of group screening tests and individual diagnostic tests. The responses from the diagnostic test together with the associated workbooks can help in the planning of learning support programmes for pupils with difficulties in language and mathematics.

The screening is related to Key Stage 1 of the National Curriculum in England and Wales and Key Stage 1 of Standards of Attainment in the National Curriculum in Northern Ireland as well as level A of the 5–14 curriculum in Scotland.

Essentially the materials aim to identify pupils at the beginning of the third year of schooling who may require support in learning. The materials, reading and number screening tests and reading and number diagnostic tests are accompanied by a series of workbooks, reading quest, looking quest, writing quest and number quest and a teacher's quest manual.

These materials represent a comprehensive list which can identify children's difficulties early and offer a good example of materials which effectively link assessment and teaching. Examples of the test descriptions in the Quest Diagnostic Reading Test are shown below.

- pre-reading
- auditory discrimination
- auditory sequential memory
- visual discrimination
- visual sequencing
- visuo-motor coordination

Word search skills

- sight vocabulary
- letter recognition (sounds)
- simple blends
- beginnings and endings
- digraphs, silent 'e' rule and silent letters
- word building
- reading comprehension

Checklists

There are many variations of checklists for identifying dyslexia. This in itself highlights the need to treat checklists with considerable caution. Checklists are not, in any form, a definitive diagnosis of dyslexia and are therefore of fairly limited value, except perhaps for a preliminary screening to justify a more detailed assessment. Some checklists can, however, provide a range of information which may produce a picture of the child's strengths and weaknesses, such as the one shown in Fig. 21. Even these, however, are still very limited and no substitution for a full assessment.

Figure 21

CHECKLIST ON READING			
READING:	SEVERE	MODERATE	NO DIFFICULTY
Sight vocabulary	_____	_____	_____
Sound blending	_____	_____	_____
Use of contextual clues	_____	_____	_____
Attempting unknown vocabulary	_____	_____	_____
Eye tracking	_____	_____	_____
Difficulty keeping the place	_____	_____	_____
Speech development	_____	_____	_____
Motivation in relation to reading material	_____	_____	_____
Vocabulary	_____	_____	_____
Naming deficit	_____	_____	_____
Use of associative words	_____	_____	_____
Omit words	_____	_____	_____
Omits phrases	_____	_____	_____
Omits whole lines	_____	_____	_____

Figure 21 (cont.)

CHECKLIST FOR WRITTEN WORK			
WRITTEN WORK:	*SEVERE*	*MODERATE*	*NO DIFFICULTY*
Directional configuration	_____	_____	_____
Difficulty in associating visual symbol with verbal sound	_____	_____	_____
Liability to sub-vocalise sounds prior to writing	_____	_____	_____
Bizarre spellings	_____	_____	_____
Poor handwriting	_____	_____	_____
No joined handwriting	_____	_____	_____
Poor organisation of work on page	_____	_____	_____

This form of assessment can provide some general data on the broad areas of difficulty experienced by the child. For example, the teacher may decide the child has a pronounced difficulty in the use of contextual cues, but this does not provide information as to why this difficulty persists and the kind of difficulties the pupil experiences with contextual cues. Does the child use contextual cues on some occasions, and under certain conditions? Clearly, this type of assessment, though useful, is limited and the teacher would be required to carry out further investigations to obtain a further picture of the difficulty.

Bonar and Lowe (1995) have developed a structured observation checklist for early intervention. Although not specifically aimed at identifying dyslexic children the checklist, due to its comprehensiveness, can be extremely useful. The comprehensive nature of this checklist can be seen from the areas it examines. These include medical, attendance, general ability, language, fine motor, general coordination, motivation, learning style, social adjustment, parents' support and attainments. The checklist is not used in isolation but is a component in a process of early identification which includes planning meetings, meetings with parents, monitoring forms and implementation and review meetings. Utilising a checklist within this type of structured framework can provide useful information to identify and monitor the child's progress.

METACOGNITIVE ASSESSMENT

Metacognition refers to the child's self-knowledge of learning. It examines the quality of the learning process – the structure and organisation of the learner's knowledge base, of mental models (schemata) and efficiency of student self-monitoring. Metacognitive knowledge therefore involves both content and process knowledge.

Most traditional forms of assessment look only at the content base, and what the child can and cannot do becomes the product of the assessment. Glaser, Lesgold and Lejoie (1987) recommended developing tests which examine the process of learning and how the child's knowlege base changes with learning.

It is important that a preoccupation with identifying the nature of the dyslexic difficulties should not prevent an assessment of the child's learning processes as this has considerable linkage with appropriate teaching and how materials should be presented.

There are a number of ways of assessing the metacognitive strategies of dyslexic children. Some of these are described below

Assisted Assessment

Campione and Brown (1989), dissatisfied with the limited information which can be obtained from normative procedures, have developed a soundly researched model for assisted or dynamic assessment, focusing on the task and the process of learning. They have also linked this form of assessment with the intervention model known as Reciprocal Teaching (Palincsar and Klenk, 1992).

The focus of Campione and Brown's work relates to aspects of learning and transfer; the information obtained provides an indication of the nature and amount of help needed by the child, rather than the child's level of attainment or improvement. This can be revealed through 'prompts', memory tasks and help with developing learning strategies.

Campione and Brown argue that there should be a link between assessment and instruction. They argue that traditional tests are intended to be predictive and prescriptive BUT fail on both counts. Their argument rests on the assertions that children can be too readily mis-classified and that traditional tests do not really provide a clear indication of what is really required for instruction.

Campione and Brown argue that the context of assessment is important and divide assessment into two aspects:

Static tests. In these the child works unaided on sets of items and is given but a single chance to demonstrate his/her proficiency. Thus:

- no aid is provided;
- social interaction between the tester and the child is minimised;
- objective scoring systems can be readily implemented;
- norms can be available.

Although such tests may fulfil a purpose they have considerable shortcomings.

- They say nothing about the processes involved in the acquisition of the responses.
- Some children may get the right answer for the wrong reason.

- Students may be mis-classified because they have not yet acquired the competence but are in the process of acquiring it.

Dynamic tests. Dynamic type tests emphasise the individual's potential for change. Such tests do not attempt to assess how much improvement has taken place, but rather how much **help** children need to reach a specified criterion and how much help they will need to transfer this to novel situations. Such tests are therefore metacognitive in that they can provide information on how the child is learning. By noting the cues necessary to facilitate the correct response from the child, the teacher can obtain some information on how the child thinks and learns. Such information can be relayed back to the child to illustrate how he or she managed to obtain the correct response. Thus assessment is **a learning experience, not a testing one.**

There are a number of different forms of dynamic assessment models, such as Feuerstein's Learning Potential Assessment Device (LPAD), which is inextricably linked to the Intervention Model – Instrumental Enrichment. The LPAD battery includes both verbal and non-verbal tasks, analogical reasoning, numerical reasoning, memory strategies, and conceptual categorisations; it also utilises Raven's Progressive Matrices as one of the measures. Extensive training is required to develop proficiency in the administration of the LPAD, although it has been described as the 'most comprehensive and theoretically grounded expression of dynamic assessment' (Lidz, 1991).

Elliott (1996) maintains that dynamic assessment offers considerable promise by providing valuable information about children's true potential and can be used to help develop educational intervention programmes. He also argues, however, that because dynamic assessment research is in its infancy, and it represents more of a general concept than a specific technique, it does not readily fit into 'western models of professional thinking'. This thinking, according to Elliott, is characterised by the perseverance with familiar techniques because of time demands and the increasing number of formal assessments professionals need to undertake to assist in decision making regarding placements and resources. It is, however, unfortunate if the need for quantitative data overburdens professionals at the expense of developing and disseminating qualitative strategies, which can provide a real insight into students' learning skills and development.

Pass Model

Das, Naglieri and Kirby (1994) offer a model which highlights planning skills as an indicator of metacognition. This model, the PASS model (Planning, Attention, Simultaneous and Successive processes) focuses on *how* information is processed, not *what* is processed. This model conceptualises the brain as concerned with three major interconnected systems which relate to strategies:

- attention – maintains alertness, motivation and arousal
- information – receives, processes, stores information using simultaneous and successive information processing
- planning – regulatory, use of strategies, approaches to tasks

With this model, skills in successive and simultaneous processing can also be detected. The dyslexic child may have difficulty with successive processing where items are processed linearly and logically in sequential fashion. Simultaneous processing, however, involves dealing with information holistically and integrating and synthesising information into a meaningful whole.

The third dimension of the PASS model, planning, represents an important aspect of metacognition. This relates closely to strategy development in problem solving. Ayres (1994) argues that planning is accompanied by a number of functions which relate to metacognition, such as the ability to form plans of action, to regulate behaviour so that it conforms to the planned outcome, and to evaluate performance. Few existing tests actively measure planning – although the Mazes sub-test of the WISC-III relates to this in some way through visual planning and digit span backwards involves planning processes as the child endeavours to convert the digits backwards.

Das *et al.* (1994) in fact argue that 'planning' discriminates good from poor readers of comparable IQ. Poor planners perceive a page in a disorganised manner, choose incorrect targets, often impulsively, make more errors and fail to change their strategy if it is inefficient.

Multiple Intelligences Approaches

Lazear (1994) by utilising Gardner's theory of multiple intelligences (Gardner, 1985) has contributed greatly to a new assessment paradigm consisting of multiple intelligences approaches. Though the author quite rightly argues that a multiple intelligences assessment should grow out of a multiple intelligences curriculum, some significant insights can be gained for assessment in general by utilising the approach advocated by Lazear.

The basic premise of Lazear's assessment paradigm emerges from the implications of Fig. 22. This suggests that assessment should be comprehensive and consider a number of different elements. Lazear contends that assessment should be used to enhance students' learning and particularly to experience their ability to transfer learning to other areas and indeed beyond formal schooling. Lazear further contends that because there are no standard students, instruction of testing should be individualised and varied. Lazear's model lends itself to curriculum-based assessment. Assessment therefore should be occurring simultaneously with learning and should therefore be an inbuilt factor within the curriculum. Curriculum-based assessment, particularly using a multiple intelligence approach, ensures that the assessment process is relevant to the actual curricula work with which the student is involved. This helps to clearly identify teaching and learning aims, it establishes criteria for success, and tasks

Figure 22

Logical-Mathematical Intelligence
Deals with inductive and deductive
thinking, numbers, and abstract
patterns; sometimes called scientific
thinking

Verbal-Linguistic Intelligence
Deals with words and language,
both written and spoken

Visual-Spatial Intelligence
Relies on sense of sight
and ability to visualize;
includes ability **to create**
mental images

*7 Ways of Knowing**

Intrapersonal Intelligence
Relates to self-reflection,
metacognition, awareness
of internal states of being

Bodily-Kinesthetic Intelligence
Relates to physical movement
and the wisdom of the body;
uses brain's motor cortex, which
controls bodily motion

Interpersonal Intelligence
Has to do with person-to-person
relationships and communication

Musical-Rhythmic Intelligence
Deals with recognizing tonal patterns,
sounds, rhythms, and beats

* Adapted *from Seven Ways of Knowing: Teaching for Multiple Intelligences* by David Lazear
(Palatine, Ill.: Skylight, 1991).

can be matched to pupils previous experiences of particular abilities (Weedon amd Reid, 1998. While the above points are commendable it should be emphasised that assessment should not necessarily dominate the teaching and learning process.

A Components Approach

The limitations of discrepancy models of assessment such as intellectual/ attainment discrepancies have led to the development of alternative criteria and procedures to assist in the differential diagnosis of reading difficulties.

One such approach, known as the 'components approach' (Aaron, 1989, 1994; Aaron and Joshi, 1992), examines the components of the reading process.

The main aims of the 'components approach' to assessment are:

- to distinguish the dyslexic child from the 'slow learner' child who displays reading difficulties;
- to distinguish the dyslexic child from the child who has a comprehension deficit in reading;
- to adapt the assessment for classroom use, to make it available for the teacher and psychologist;
- to allow for a complete diagnostic procedure which would be comprehensive enough to include quantitative as well as qualitative information that is relevant to the reading process.

The main strands of the components approach are:
- the identification of the factors which determine performance;
- a description of the components of reading;
- an evaluation of the child's functioning in relation to these components.

Aaron (1989) describes four main components of reading:

- Verbal comprehension;
- Phonological awareness;
- Decoding speed;
- Listening comprehension.

It can be argued that decoding and comprehension are the two most important components of reading, representing visual and auditory processing skills together with meaningful comprehension. (This simultaneous processing involving decoding and comprehension may require hemispheric integration and justify the claim that reading is a holistic activity).

In normal readers, decoding and comprehension are consistent and complementary. Thus as a child reads (decodes the print) meaning is simultaneously expressed.

Research suggests that:

- COMPREHENSION is a controlled process, i.e. is attention-demanding, with limited capacity.

- DECODING is an automatised process, i.e. not attention-demanding, and does not require reader's conscious control.

It is known that for dyslexic children decoding does not readily become auto-matised (Fawcett, 1990) and therefore requires:

- attention-demanding operations;
- conscious control from the reader.

These are also factors in comprehension and hence it is argued that dyslexic readers, when decoding, draw on some of the capacities which should be focus-ing on comprehension and thereby weaken their potential for comprehension while reading. This suggestion is supported by work on visual imagery in reading (Bell, 1991a) which claims that the decoding process weakens the dyslexic child's gestalt (right hemisphere) and consequently comprehension.

Aaron (1989) suggests that differences in reading achievement are due to factors associated with either decoding or comprehension or a combination of both. To differentiate between these two abilities, it is necessary to assess them independently. Thus reading comprehension has to be assessed without involv-ing the decoding of print.

Some researchers suggest that reading comprehension and listening com-prehension share the same cognitive mechanisms and that the two forms of comprehension are related. Palmer (1985) obtained a highly significant correla-tion between these two forms of comprehension and states that 'reading com-prehension can be predicted almost perfectly by a listening measure – therefore a test of listening comprehension can be used as a measure of reading com-prehension.' It is suggested however that although the correlation may still be significant it may be lower than some studies have shown (Bedford-Feuell, Geiger, Moyse and Turner, 1995).

Certainly in the early reading stages there seems to be a close relationship between decoding and reading comprehension, so one can use a decoding assess-ment procedure in the early years. One must, however, attempt to use a task which is closely related to decoding but not influenced by environmental or contextual factors.

A components approach to assessment which can be readily carried out by the teacher can include the following:

- decoding test (non-words reading test);
- word reading test;
- phonological awareness test;
- listening comprehension test;
- reading comprehension test.

Aaron (1989) has indicated four different categories of reading disorders (see Fig. 23).

An interesting difference is drawn here between hyperlexic readers and dys-lexic readers. Hyperlexic readers are those who can decode and are therefore

Figure 23

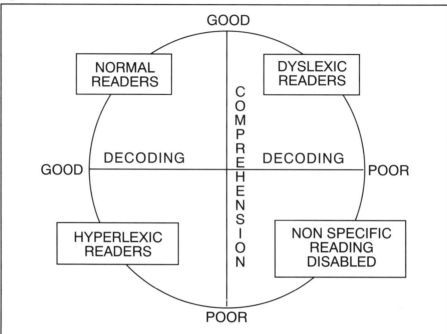

Reproduced with permission from P. G. Aaron (Aaron, 1989)

good at mechanically reading while dyslexic readers are poor at decoding and read inaccurately but can perform better in reading comprehension tasks.

This emphasises that the key components of the reading process which are to be assessed are:

- decoding;
- listening/reading comprehension.

The components approach is a diagnostic procedure which does not rely solely on norm-referenced, standardised tests, but can be applied with locally developed assessment materials from which programmes can be developed in the context of the curriculum and the classroom activities.

Aaron and Joshi (1992) contend that a measure of listening comprehension is more appropriate in diagnosing reading difficulties than, for example, an IQ measure. Listening comprehension tests do not possess the same drawbacks as IQ measures (Siegal, 1989) and the diagnostic findings can link directly to teaching procedures. The components approach therefore gains support from the view that reading comprehension and listening comprehension are highly correlated and reading is made up of two components, comprehension and decoding.

Research (Gough and Tunmer, 1986), suggests that the reading difficulty of a subject who has good listening comprehension but lower reading comprehension can be attributed to poor word recognition skills. A formal diagnostic procedure involving decoding and listening comprehension would therefore seem to be an appropriate one.

OBSERVATIONAL ASSESSMENT

There are a number of different forms of observational assessment.

These can provide important data and also offer some pointers as to appropriate teaching strategies.

An observation schedule or framework should be constructed before an assessment. A number of benefits of observation schedules can be identified, for example they can be flexible, adaptable to different situations, and can be used within the context of the learning situation. Hopefully a 'natural' response will then be recorded free from the influence of 'test contamination' factors.

Throughout the observation it is important to record not only what the student does or can do but how the response is achieved – the cues required, level and extent of the assistance needed at the stages the student needs to go through to solve a problem or obtain a response.

With increased importance being placed on early identification and metacognitive aspects of learning, procedures such as observational criteria can have an important role to play in the assessment process.

Observational Framework

In this framework one is looking at a broad range of areas which can relate to some of the difficulties experienced by children with specific learning difficulties/ dyslexia.

It is important to gather information which relates to the child, the learning situation and context. The aim is not just to find out how or why the child is having difficulty, but to gain some insight and understanding into the strategies and processes of learning for that child.

A framework for observational assessment for specific learning difficulties can therefore include the areas listed below.

Attention
- Length of attention span?
- Conditions when attention is enhanced?
- Factors contributing to distractability?
- Attention/distractability under different learning conditions?

Organisation
- Organisational preferences?
- Degree of structure required?
- Organisation of work, desk, self?

- Reactions to imposed organisation?

Sequencing
- Able to follow sequence with aid?
- General difficulty with sequencing: work; carrying out instructions; words when reading; individual letters in written work?

Interaction
- Degree of interaction with peers, adults?
- Preferred interaction – one-to-one?
                               small groups?
                               whole class?
- How interaction is sustained?

Language
- Expressive language?
- Is meaning accurately conveyed?
- Spontaneous/prompted?
- Is there appropriate use of natural breaks in speech?
- Expressive language in different contexts, e.g. one-to-one, small group, class group?
- Errors, omissions and difficulties in conversation and responses, e.g. mispronunciations, questions to be repeated or clarified?

Comprehension
- How does the child comprehend information?
- What type of cues most readily facilitate comprehension?
- Use of schema?
- What type of instructions are most easily understood – written, oral, visual?
- How readily can knowledge be transferred to other areas?

Reading
- Reading preferences – aloud, silent?
  Type of errors:

Visual, e.g.
- Discrimination between letters which look the same?
- Inability to appreciate that the same letter may look different, e.g. 'G' 'g'?
- Omitting or transposing part of a word (this could indicate a visual segmentation difficulty)?

Auditory, e.g.
- Difficulties in auditory discrimination?
- Inability to hear consonant sounds in initial, medial or final position?
- Auditory sequencing?

- Auditory blending?
- Auditory segmentation?

Motivation/initiative
- Interest level of child?
- How is motivation increased, what kind of prompting and cueing is necessary?
- To what extent does the child take responsibility for own learning?
- What kind of help is required?

Self-concept
- What tasks are more likely to be tackled with confidence?
- When is confidence low?
- Self-concept and confidence in different contexts?

Relaxation
- Is the child relaxed when learning?
- Evidence of tension and relaxation?

Learning preferences
These include the following learning preferences:
- Auditory?
- Visual?
- Oral?
- Kinesthetic?
- Tactile?
- Global?
- Analytic?

It is important, therefore, to note in observational assessment the preferred mode of learning. Many children will of course show preferences and skills in a number of modes of learning. Multi-sensory teaching therefore is crucial in order to accommodate as many modes as possible.

Learning context
When assessing the nature and degree of the difficulty experienced by the child, it is important to take into account the learning context. This context, depending on the learner's preferred style can either exacerbate the difficulty or minimise the problem (Reid, 1992 and 1994). The contextual factors below should therefore be considered.

- classroom
- role of teacher
- task
- materials/resources.

Observation and assessment therefore needs to adopt a holistic perspective i.e.:

- observing components within a framework for learning;
- observing some factors within that framework associated with specific learning difficulties/dyslexia;
- observing preferred styles of learning;
- acknowledging the importance of the learning context.

Systematic Observation

Structured systematic observation can yield some important information in relation to the student's strengths, difficulties and actual performances in the classroom context. Perhaps the most sophisticated of the systematic observation strategies are those devised for the Reading Recovery Programme. Clay (1993) provides a detailed analysis of systematic observation choosing to refer to observation tasks designed to make a teacher attend to how children work at learning in the classroom. Although the Clay observation tasks were designed to develop a 'running record' for use with the Reading Recovery Programme some of the general principles can be utilised for use with dyslexic children.

Clay (1993) suggests that to observe systematically one must:

- observe precisely what children are saying and doing;
- use tasks which are closely related to the learning tasks of the classroom;
- observe what children have been able to learn;
- identify from this the reading behaviour they should now be taught;
- focus the child's general reading behaviour to training on reading tasks rather than on specific sub-skills such as visual perception or auditory discrimination.

In order to achieve the above Marie Clay has developed a 'diagnostic survey' (The Running Record) which looks at directional movement, motor coordination, reading fluency, error behaviour, oral language skills, letter identification skills, concepts about print and writing skills.

This latter aspect is particularly important as writing skills may provide some indication of any reading problems, e.g. a poor writing vocabulary may indicate the child is taking very little notice of visual differences in print. The weakness in visual discrimination may be because the hand and eye are not complementing each other and this is an important aspect of early writing. Additionally, in writing, other factors such as language level and message quality are also important to note. In writing, children are required to pay attention to details of letters, letter sequences, sound sequences and the links between messages in oral language and messages in printed language.

Other useful aspects of Clay's model involves the 'concepts of print test' which addresses vital aspects relating to the childs knowledge of print and familiarity with books. Questions of whether the child can distinguish the front from back of the book, left from right, recognise errors in print, distinguish between capital and lower case and locate first and last letters are all addressed. This provides crucial information at this early stage of reading – information which certainly should be gathered for children who are at risk of failing in literacy.

Clay's observation approach also focuses on strategies for decoding. The teacher therefore records different strategies the child uses in relation to location and movement, language, how the child deals with difficulties, e.g. seeking help, searching for further cues, and the extent of self-correction. Self-correction according to Clay is an important aspect of reading progress and needs to be accurately recorded.

SUMMARY

A vast array of approaches have been described in this chapter. To recap, these include standardised, diagnostic, phonological assessment, components of reading assessment, metacognitive, screening and observational. Clearly, no one approach can provide both sufficient data to identify and assess dyslexia and provide a sufficient and effective linkage with teaching. Different factors need to be taken into account and all assessment procedures discussed in this chapter have considerable merits. The factors which determine what approach or approaches should be used relate to the reasons for the assessment and the purposes for which the information is to be put. It is, however, important to bear in mind that different children may well display different profiles and still meet the criteria for specific learning difficulties/dyslexia. Ideally, the assessment should link with teaching and if this is a successful outcome of the assessment, then it will indeed have been a valuable and worthwhile exercise.

Chapter 4

Assessment Process

The previous chapter provided a description of many of the assessment approaches and strategies suitable for use for students with specific learning difficulties (dyslexia). This chapter will attempt to organise these approaches into a framework or process which can be adapted to accommodate to different educational contexts.

One of the key issues in the assessment process is that of early identification. How such identification should take place and when it can most effectively, and most sensitively, be conducted are matters of some debate. This is clearly an important aspect of the assessment process and it is important that schools have procedures in place to meet the needs of early identification. Other aspects also need to be considered, such as whole school policy, role of other professionals, linkage with teaching, role of parents and professional development and training. These will be briefly described below.

Early identification

- When should this take place, how should it be conducted and by whom?
- What criteria should be used at this early stage for a diagnosis?

Whole-school involvement

- What are the advantages of whole-school involvement?
- How can this be successfully and effectively conducted?

Multi-professional assessment

- How can the different professions coordinate their roles in relation to assessment?
- What are the roles of the speech therapist, educational psychologist, school medical officer, specialist teacher and class-teacher?

Linkage with teaching

• How can identification and assessment be most effectively related to teaching and in particular the curriculum?
• How appropriate is assessment outwith the context of the curriculum?

Role of parents

• How can the school most effectively communicate with parents?
• The importance of parents contributions to the assessment process should not be overlooked.

Professional Development

• The importance of training in relation to assessment must be emphasised. Training should not only be provided for a small number of specialists, who are subsequently over-stretched because of the demands being placed on them. Training needs to be provided for all professionals involved in assessment, particularly the class teacher.

MODELS OF IDENTIFICATION

Pumfrey (1990) contends that the concept of diagnosis and treatment is based on a medical model and is not therfore appropriate to the education context. Teachers, Pumfrey asserts, ought to be wary of moving down the classification escalator, which he describes as moving from individual differences to deviations, difficulties, disabilities, deficits and eventually to defects.

Yet while this 'classification escalator' is clearly something which ought to be avoided, and something which underlines the inherent dangers of hasty diagnosis or perceiving lack of attainments as a within-child difficulty which requires diagnosis, it is still beneficial to implement early identification procedures, despite these risks. It has been well argued that the intricacies of the reading process result in significant numbers of children adopting ineffective reading strategies which need to be identified and modified by the teacher lest the error behaviour becomes too entrenched thus placing a restriction on further progress (Clay, 1989; Pumfrey, 1990). To ensure, however, that a medical diagnosis-treatment model is not perceived as the principal assessment strategy, it is important that assessment is undertaken by the class teacher, using informal strategies, and that this assessment is linked to teaching and the curriculum. This type of model has some advantages over formal assessment by specialist teachers, but if difficulties do persist there is a definite role for utilising the expertise of specialist teachers.

Assessment has been described as 'hypotheses generation followed by intervention' (Pumfrey, 1990), but before hypotheses can be generated in even a vague way, a high degree of awareness and training is necessary. This makes it possible for assessment procedures and models of identification to be encapsulated into the context of the curriculum and the classroom. It is also important that such models and training should be included in the training of other professionals, such as speech therapists and educational psychologists.

The focus for this model is the school, not necessarily the child, and it can be illustrated in the following way:

Figure 24:   The whole-school interactive model

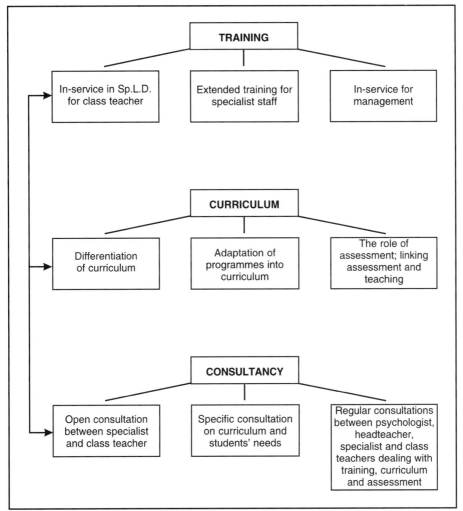

The above model may enable the philosophies concerning individual needs and whole-school approaches to interact effectively, minimise the role conflicts and misconceptions between professionals and provide appropriate and effective support for children with specific learning difficulties, teachers, parents and other professionals.

This model can be viewed as one which is interactive and involves the whole school, because it emphasises the need for staff training, awareness of the curriculum and teaching implications, and regular consultancy. Key aspects include initial early warning signs, assessment and consultancy, and monitoring and review. These are described below from the perspective of the class teacher.

Initial early warning signs

- The class teacher may identify coordination difficulties, difficulties with pencil grip, immature use of language, sequencing or organisational difficulties **prior** to the teaching of reading skills. These difficulties can be highlighted through classroom observation, discussions with parents and diagnostic assessment.

Assessment/consultancy with management team

- To discuss the difficulties and possible materials and resources which can be used. This is an important aspect and time should be specifically allocated for this.

Close monitoring of progress when reading skills are taught, looking for:

- difficulties with **phonological awareness,** e.g. awareness of rhyme, syllabification, natural breaks in speech and written language;
- **auditory discrimination** recognising and repeating sounds;
- **visual difficulties** such as failure to recognise letters, comparison between visually similar letters, missing lines when reading confusing picture cues;
- **sequencing difficulties** such as confusing order of letter or words or digits;
- **organisational difficulties** such as directional confusion, laterality problems and sequencing difficulties;
- **memory** – inability to follow instructions, particularly when more than one item is to be remembered;
- **motor difficulties** – for example, poor pencil grip, awkward gait, poor coordination, difficulty doing two simple tasks simultaneously.

Monitoring/review meeting

- This would probably be with school management and nursery staff to discuss the necessity of a fuller assessment and how this should proceed. Some suggestions for teaching to support the teacher needs to be made at this stage. Discussions with parents are also important here.
- Suggested revisions to teaching may be carried out, during which time teacher records progress and difficulties.
- School management review with parents to discuss progress and further action if necessary, for instance the involvement of other professionals such as educational psychologists and speech therapists.

AN ASSESSMENT FRAMEWORK

In order to establish some form of assessment process within the school it is useful to develop an assessment framework which will include the kind of procedures, tests and strategies which can be utilised within the particular school context in which the teacher is working.

An example of one possible framework is shown below. The framework was devised in response to the needs of mainstream and specialist teachers for some re-assurance and control in the identification and assessment of specific learning difficulties/dyslexia (Kettles, Laws and Reid, 1996)

- Sensory assessment
- Word recognition test
- Non-word reading test
- Spelling test
- Phonological assessment
- Miscue analysis
- Reading/listening comprehension test
- Free writing
- Curriculum information
- Observational assessment
- Additional relevant information

1. Difficulties

Word Reading Test   Test Used:

Date	Chronological Age	Reading Age	+/–Discrepancy (mths)

Spelling Test   Test Used:

Date	Chronological Age	Spelling Age	+/–Discrepancy (mths)

Phonological Skills

The Phonological Assessment Battery (PhAB) covers this aspect comprehensively (see Chapter 5). Additional information can however be obtained from the following:

1. Ask child to give each letter name and corresponding sound; to offer a word beginning with each sound; and to write the letter corresponding to each sound.

Letter	a	m	t	s	i	f	d	r	o	g	l	h	u
Name													
Sound													
Word													
Writes													

Letter	c	b	n	k	v	e	p	w	j	y	x	q	z
Name													
Sound													
Word													
Writes													

2. Child reads aloud CVC words containing letters from the full alphabet.

Errors										

3. Child reads aloud words with common final consonant blends (tick if read).

Blend	st	mp	nk	nd	ft	sk	ck	nt	ng
Response									

4. Child reads aloud words with common initial blends (tick if read).

Blend	fl	fr	sl	sm	sn	sw	sk	sp	st	bl
Response										
Blend	br	cl	cr	dr	gl	gr	pl	tr	tw	pr
Response										

5. Child reads aloud words with magic 'e' pattern (tick if read).

Pattern	a – e	i – e	o – e	u – e	e – e
Response					

6. Child reads aloud words with the following letter combinations (tick if read).

Letters	sh	ch	th	aw	oo	ou	ow	ai	ea	oa	ay	ee	oi	or
Response														

Non-Word Reading Test

Attached is a list of items containing regular spelling patterns which vary in syllable length and complexity. Children should be asked to read aloud each list from 1 to 8. The tester should tick correct responses, record any errors and indicate non-responses (NR) where applicable. Note whether child is affected by syllable length.

List 1	List 2	List 3	List 4
bof	zavil	snep	fomp
cug	cogat	clag	rilt
jid	jefum	drin	hent
kem	radun	twud	jang
wex	woxib	flom	yuld
naz	hesik	bret	zelk
yol	yupog	grap	wilp
hap	nimep	plog	yump
vus	felat	swid	lond
rit	mabup	smug	bamp

List 5	List 6	List 7	List 8
brant	dramep	bamosp	brafeld
clemp	flegom	levunk	clonusp
dwilk	grifut	rudalg	prinalt
frolt	plonad	fonemp	twugimp
glund	swulig	higald	frekont
prand	twapon	vadipt	swalupt
swemp	bletud	donisk	glatong
twing	crovin	gupont	smideng
blomp	smiron	jerupt	pludint
crulk	dwuzet	kalomp	crogamp

2. Discrepancies

Tests such as the New Macmillan Reading Analysis or Neale Analysis of Reading Ability can be used to complete systematic observation of the child's reading behaviour as well as to identify any discrepancy between reading and listening comprehension skills. Administer chosen test as instructed in the manual, completing miscue analysis and recording child's responses to comprehension questions.

Reading Comprehension   Test Used:

Date	Chronological Age	Comprehension Age	Discrepancy (mths)

Using an alternative form of the same test (e.g. Form B of the New Macmillan Reading Analysis) read the passages slowly to the child and record his/her responses to the comprehension questions as before.

Listening Comprehension   Test used:

Date	Chronological Age	Comprehension Age	Discrepancy (mths)

Writing Skills

Arrange for the child to complete a short piece of independent writing. Allow 5 to 10 minutes for completion. Analyse this in relation to the factors below:

Fluency	**Comments**
Speed (Words per Minute)	
Punctuation	
Sentence Structure	
Choice of Words	
Spelling	
Pencil Grip	
Letter Formation	
Size and Spacing	
Attitude to Task	

National Curriculum Attainments*

English									
Speaking and Listening	w	1	2	3	4	5	6	7	8
Reading	w	1	2	3	4	5	6	7	8
Writing	w	1	2	3	4	5	6	7	8
Spelling	w	1	2	3	4	5	6	7	8
Handwriting	w	1	2	3	4	5	6	7	8
Mathematics	w	1	2	3	4	5	6	7	8
Using and Applying Maths	w	1	2	3	4	5	6	7	8
Number and Algebra	w	1	2	3	4	5	6	7	8
Shape, Space and Measure	w	1	2	3	4	5	6	7	8
Handling Data	w	1	2	3	4	5	6	7	8
Science									
Experimental and Investigative Science	w	1	2	3	4	5	6	7	8
Life Processes and Living Things	w	1	2	3	4	5	6	7	8
Materials and their Properties	w	1	2	3	4	5	6	7	8

Comments

*Note: This can be adapted from the 5–14 Curriculum in Scotland and for any aspect of the school curriculum.

3. Differences

Research on learning styles highlights the need to asssess the process by which learning takes place, not just the actual performance in attainments. It is important to note individual differences in cognitive and learning style by commenting on general strengths and weaknesses as well as on aspects of the curriculum which interest and motivate the learner.

Observational Assessment (Reid, 1992)

The following framework is **not** a checklist but a guide to the type of factors which should be observed in identifying learning strategies, strengths and weaknesses. When completed, this framework should provide you with an overview of the child's learning skills within the context of the classroom.

Interaction   **Comments**
Pupil/Teacher Interaction
Interaction with Peers?

Attention/Concentration
Focus on Task
Major Sources of Distraction
Concentration Span in Different
   Tasks

Organisational Aspects
Sequence of Activities
Organisational Strategies
Materials and Desk in Order
Teacher Direction

Motor Factors
Handwriting Skills
Body Posture
Colouring
Tracing
Copying

Learning Style
Reliance on Concrete Aids
Memory Strategies
Listening/Auditory Skills
Oral Skills
Visual Approaches
Learning Sequentially
Learning Globally

Emotional Factors
Self-Esteem
Confidence
Motivation
Signs of Tension

This framework can be accommodated within the school process. An example
of such a process is shown below (Jackson and Reid, 1997)

Assessment Process

Criteria

Pre-School—Developmental History

Assessment strategy

- Speech and language
- Co-ordination
- Problem solving skills
- Interest in activities

—Parental discussion
—Observation
—Screening
—Consultation with nursery/kindergarten staff

- Attention/concentration
- Social skills

—Observation

Primary 1–4 criteria

Assessment strategy

- Phonological difficulties
- Sequencing problems
- Laterality
- Auditory sequential memory; visual discrimination
- Reading/listening comprehension

- Oral and written work

—Phonological Assessment Battery
—Observation
—Observation
—Cops 1; Bury Infant Check; Aston Index

—Non-word reading tests/ listening comprehension passage
—Comparison of performances; observation

Primary 5–7 criteria

Assessment strategy

- Organisational strategies
- Writing/copying

- Persistent phonological difficulties

- Memory

- Concepts/schema

- Persistent spelling difficulties

- Self-esteem

—Metacognitive assessment; observation
—Assessment on task
—Visual/kinaesthetic assessment
—Integrated phonological assessment/ teaching programme (e.g. Sound Linkage)
—Aston index, digit span
—Mind mapping strategies
—Problem solving assessment
—Thinking skills
—Study skills
—Diagnostic spelling test
—Unscrambling spelling (spelling strategies)
—Behavioural objectives (i.e. target words, goal, objectives)
—Masterly learning
—Learning styles

Secondary school criteria

Assessment strategy

- Adjustment difficulties
- Persistent reading and spelling difficulties
- Preparation for examination

—Shadow in different subjects/ observation
—Miscue analysis
—Learning styles
—Study skills
—Visualisation approaches
—Mind mapping
—Organisational strategies
—Learning styles

IDENTIFYING EMERGING LITERACY SKILLS

It is important to establish an assessment framework which can fit into a whole school assessment process. There may also be some merit in establishing a more detailed analysis and process at very early stages of literacy development. Weedon *et al.* (1996) have developed a battery of sub-tests which seek to profile a wide range of emerging literacy skills and sub-skills. These tests have been used to specifically identify potential dyslexic children (Reid and Weedon, 1997), through administering the test to a complete class group at the same time. Athough this research is ongoing, early signs are that, with further refining, it should be possible to develop an instrument which has more sophistication than a screening test but can still be used on a large scale for the complete year group of six-year-olds.

The 18 sub-tests in the original design were refined and reduced to thirteen after piloting. The summary of skills tested and a description of the sub-tests are shown below:

Test	Sub-tests method	Skills tested
Text comprehension—reading	The pupils read silently then answer questions by ringing Yes/No/Doesn't Say options	Silent reading comprehension, factual and inferential
Text comprehension—listening	The pupils listen to a passage then answer questions from teacher by ringing Yes/No/Doesn't Say options	Listening comprehension, factual and inferential
Sight word spelling	The teacher reads phonically regular words, and pupils write them	Visual strategies in spelling
Spelling of phonically regular words	The teacher reads phonically regular words, and pupils write them	Phonic strategies in spelling
Single word reading—sight words	The teacher speaks phonically irregular words, and pupils identify and ring their choice from a choice of visually similar options	Sight vocabulary and visual strategies in reading
Single word reading—phonically regular words	The teacher speaks phonically regular words, and pupils identify and ring their choice from a choice of other words and misspellings	Phonic strategies in reading
Phonological awareness	The teacher speaks groups of words and non-words. The pupils ring Yes/No to indicate whether they are the same	Phonological skills of rhyme, segmentation and discrimination

Non-word spelling	The teacher speaks and the pupils spell non-words	Phonological effectiveness in spelling
Non-word reading	The teacher speaks a non-word, and the pupils ring their choice of the correct spelling from a set of options	Phonological effectiveness in reading
Verbal memory	The pupils listen to a list of items, then ring as many as they can from a set of pictures that includes those items	Retention of verbal information in memory
Visual perception	The pupils are shown non-letter symbols, then identify and ring their replicas from choices of visually similar symbols	Ability to perceive visual differences, and visual perception
Visual memory	Abstract shapes are displayed briefly, then pupils ring those seen from a choice of their response sheets	Ability to hold visually received information in working memory
Abstract visual logic	The pupils select from a choice of abstract visual symbols to complete a sequence of visual symbols	Ability to perceive logical visual pattern

Further research involving the dyslexic sample (Reid and Weedon, 1997) made it possible for the sub-tests to be ranked, from those presenting greatest difficulty through to those presenting least difficulty. A distinction was also made between dyslexic readers and those children who had global learning difficulties (globally less effective readers) (see the table below).

Rank order of skill and sub-skill difficulty for the two groups of readers, from tasks presenting greatest difficulty through to those presenting least:

Dyslexic readers	**Globally less effective readers**
Non-word spelling	Listening
Reading comprehension	Reading comprehension
Regular reading	Segmentation
Non-word reading	Verbal memory
Regular spelling	Visual perception
Auditory discrimination	Blending
Sight spelling	Non-word reading
Blending	Sight reading
Sight reading	Sight spelling
Visual perception	Visuo-motor skills
Letter/sound correspondence	Visual memory
Visuo-motor skills	Letter/sound correspondence
Rhyme	Non-word spelling

Verbal memory	Regular spelling
Segmentation	. . . *mean for whole sample.* . .
. . . *mean for whole sample.* . .	Regular reading
Visual memory	Rhyme
Listening	Auditory discrimination

The dyslexic readers presented a distinctively different profile. They are less effective than the other group in almost all the phonological skills or sub-skills that contribute towards literacy – yet they achieve a level of reading comprehension similar to that of the other group. The results from this research also suggests that the discrepancy between listening comprehension and reading comprehension is a useful piece of data to help in the identification of literacy difficulties at this early stage.

Another useful example of a process which can be accommodated within the whole school can be seen in the document 'Partnership, Pupils, Parents and Professionals' (Fife Education Authority, 1996). The document consists of a set of guidelines which offers teachers advice on 'identification', what to look for, information gathering, instruction, and the role of school management. These guidelines also attempt to establish a uniform process for registering concern, implementing action and reviewing progress – a summary of intervention. This summary provides the class teacher with a structure within which some of the assessment strategies described thus far can be implemented. It is useful to record and maintain such a summary and this can be particularly helpful to teachers and parents of children with dyslexic difficulties.

This chapter has sought to contextualise the previous chapter on assessment approaches and strategies. The actual detail of the examples of the process described here is not so important as the principles which it seeks to establish. Those principles include the need to have some form of school-based process for assessment and for staff to be provided with support, awareness and training to feel competent to implement those procedures. The vast array of assessment strategies for helping to identify dyslexia can result in confusion and uncertainty on the part of the teacher, It is therefore of the utmost importance that assessment is not left to one specialist, but should be an integral and continuous component of school policy and practice.

Chapter 5

Teaching Approaches

This chapter will describe some of the most popular and appropriate teaching approaches for use with dyslexic children. It divides teaching approaches into four broad areas: individualised approaches; support approaches; assisted learning and whole-school approaches. This latter aspect will be dealt with in the next chapter on curriculum access.

In determining the most appropriate programmes and strategies for children with specific learning difficulties, a number of factors must be considered, the most important of which are:

- the context
- the assessment
- the curriculum
- the learner.

THE CONTEXT

The context relates to the classroom, the school and the teaching situation. The issue of one-to-one tuition and that of mainstream provision for children with specific learning difficulties is an ongoing issue of debate.

In many schools, specialist teachers work cooperatively with class teachers, and clearly intervention in this case may be of a different nature to that where specialist teachers withdraw children for individual tuition. Both these systems can be effective. It is important therefore that the teacher uses the context to its maximum benefit through the provision of materials and teaching programmes that can be effectively adapted to different teaching situations and contexts.

ASSESSMENT AND THE CURRICULUM

One of the objectives, perhaps the principal objective, of an assessment is to provide some guidance to help in the development of teaching programmes. It is important therefore to find out which teaching programmes and strategies have been used to determine which teaching approaches should be implemented for that student.

It is important to examine the assessment findings in a holistic manner by looking at all aspects of the assessment, such as strengths, weaknesses, self-concept, interest and learning preferences and to link these factors to an appropriate teaching programme.

THE LEARNER

It is important to adopt a holistic perspective, looking not only at the learner's strengths and weaknesses, but the preferred learning style, i.e. under what conditions would the child be most likely to learn. Which approaches may be preferred by the learner? In what way would these approaches help to maintain the learner's interest and motivation as well as enhancing self-esteem?

These questions must be considered before deciding on appropriate intervention and teaching programmes. Although children with specific learning difficulties have some common core difficulties they do not represent an identical discrete entity with identical profiles. Therefore intervention and teaching programmes will be tailored to the profile of needs of the individual learner and this will vary depending on the preferred learning style and cognitive profile of each dyslexic child. The knowledge of the learner which can be most readily recorded by the class teacher is, therefore, of extreme importance in order to successfully match the needs and learning style of the child with the teaching and the requirements of the curriculum.

PROGRAMMES AND STRATEGIES

The various types of programmes and strategies which can be used are outlined below.

Individualised programmes

- These are highly structured, can be seen as essentially free-standing and form a central element of the overall strategy for teaching children with specific learning difficulties.

Support approaches and strategies

- these may utilise the same principles as some of the individual programmes, but can be used more selectively by the teacher thus making it possible to integrate them more easily within the normal activities of the curriculum.

Assisted learning techniques

- These strategies utilise different and various methods but a central, essential component is the aspect of learning from others. These programmes could therefore involve either peer or adult support and interaction and utilise some of the principles of modelling.

Whole-school approaches

- These recognise that dyslexic difficulties are a whole-school concern and not just the responsibility of individual teachers. Such approaches require an established and accessible framework for consultancy, whole-school screening, and monitoring of children's progress. Early identification is a further key aspect of a whole-school approach.

Some examples of these programmes and strategies are shown below in Fig. 25.

It is important to consider the rationale for using particular programmes and strategies. Within the areas described here of individualised learning, support approaches and strategies, assisted learning and whole-school approaches, many quality and effective means of dealing with the dyslexic-type difficulty are at the teacher's disposal. Therefore the criteria for selection – the context, the

Figure 25

1 INDIVIDUALISED APPROACHES	2 SUPPORT APPROACHES AND STRATEGIES
Alphabetic Phonics	Aston Portfolio
Alpha to Omega	Simultaneous Oral Spelling
Bangor Dyslexia Teaching System	Counselling Approaches
DATAPAC	** Phonic Codecracker
DISTAR	Microcomputer Software Programmes
Hickey Language Course	Neuro-Motor Programmes
* Letterland	Special Needs Manual – Reason and Boote
Reading Recovery Programme	Study Skills
* Spelling Made Easy	Quest Materials
Slingerland	Visual Acuity Activities
Orton-Gillingham Method	
Sound Linkage	
Skill Teach	
3 ASSISTED LEARNING PROGRAMMES	**4 WHOLE-SCHOOL APPROACHES**
Apprenticeship Approach	Counselling Strategies
Paired Reading	Literacy Projects
Peer Tutoring	Study Skills Programmes
Reciprocal Teaching	Thinking Skills
Cued Spelling	Consultancy

*   These can also be used as the main teaching programme for the whole class.
**   This can also be used as an individualised programme.

assessment, the curriculum and the learner – must be carefully considered. These factors are as influential in the selection of teaching approaches as the actual programme or strategy itself.

INDIVIDUALISED PROGRAMMES

Most individualised programmes incorporate some, or all, of the following principles and approaches.

- multisensory
- over-learning and automaticity
- highly structured and usually phonically based
- sequential and cumulative

Multisensory methods utilise all available senses simultaneously. This can be summed up in the phrase 'hear it, say it, see it and write it'. These methods have been used for many years and have been further refined by Hornsby and Hickey in phonic structured programmes which incorporate multisensory techniques.

Over-learning is deemed necessary for children with dyslexic difficulties. The short- and long-term memory difficulties experienced by dyslexic children mean that considerable reinforcement and repetition is necessary.

The structured approaches evident in programmes of work for dyslexic children usually provide a linear progression, thus enabling the learner to complete and master a particular skill in the reading or learning process before advancing to a subsequent skill. This implies that learning occurs in a linear developmental manner. Although there is evidence from learning theory to suggest this may be the case, there is still some doubt in the case of reading that mastery of the component sub-skills results in skilled reading. In reading, a number of cognitive skills such as memory and visual, auditory and oral skills interact (Ellis, 1989). This interaction is the key feature so it is therefore important that the skills are taught together and purposefully with the practice of reading as the focus.

Sequential approaches are usually appropriate for children with specific learning difficulties because it may be necessary for them to master sub-skills before moving to more advanced materials. Hence a sequential and cumulative approach may not only provide a structure to their learning, but help to make learning more meaningful and effective.

Many of the individual programmes, however, have been evaluated fairly positively. For example Hornsby and Miles (1980) conducted a series of investigations examining 'dyslexia-centred teaching' programmes with the aim of evaluating how effective these programmes were in alleviating dyslexia. This study and a follow-up study (Hornsby and Farmer, 1990) indicate that the programmes did result in an improvement in terms of pupils' reading and spelling ages.

PROGRAMMES IN PRACTICE

Below is a survey of some of the individualised programmes which may be utilised for children with specific learning difficulties/dyslexia.

Letterland

Letterland, developed by Lyn Wendon, consists of many different elements. The materials are extremely useful for teaching reading, spelling and writing, and for developing and sustaining motivation. The programmes are internationally renowned as well over fifty per cent of all primary schools in England and Ireland rely on this programme (Letterland International, 1997).

Letterland encompasses a number of teaching elements based on recognised and essential components of the teaching of reading. The major elements are language, with an emphasis on listening, speaking and communicating; phonic skills; whole word recognition skills; sentence awareness; comprehension; reading and spelling connections and preliminary skills in creative writing. The materials consist of teachers' guides, friezes, code cards, flashcards, word books, cassettes and songbooks, copymasters, workbooks, games and resources, software, videos and materials specifically designed for use at home.

The programme may also be seen as a preventative approach since it is appropriate for early intervention and may also facilitate the reinforcement of important developmental concepts in learning such as object constancy.

The Letterland system essentially grew out of close observations of failing readers and the materials reinforce the importance of a reading for meaning orientation to print. The system encourages motivation and exploration of written language and results in schools. Wendon (1993) suggests that Letterland can account for a measurable decrease in the number of children in schools requiring extra help with reading and spelling.

Letterland focuses on letters and sounds and by using pictograms encourages children to appreciate letter stages and sounds, thereby reinforcing both shape and sound of letters and words. Integrated within this, however, are the programmes and exercises on whole word recognition, reading for meaning, spelling and creative writing. Spelling is not presented as a series of rules but instead through a story approach, focusing on the Letterland characters.

Progress through the Letterland programme is by a series of steps. These steps can provide the teacher with choice and flexibility and the programme can be implemented to the whole class, in small groups or individually.

There are a number of aspects about Letterland which make it useful for some children with specific learning difficulties. These include the use of pictograms – which can be particularly beneficial to the learner with difficulties in phonological awareness and auditory skills. The use of the story approach to reading and spelling which encourages the processing of information using the long-term memory, is particularly beneficial to dyslexic children whose short-term memory

Figure 26

Reproduced from Wendon (1996), with permission

Figure 27

Reproduced from Wendon (1996), with permission

Figure 28

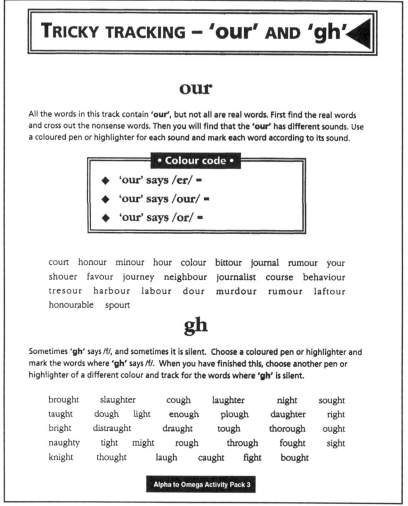

TRICKY TRACKING – 'our' AND 'gh'◀

our

All the words in this track contain '**our**', but not all are real words. First find the real words and cross out the nonsense words. Then you will find that the '**our**' has different sounds. Use a coloured pen or highlighter for each sound and mark each word according to its sound.

• Colour code •

◆ 'our' says /er/ =

◆ 'our' says /our/ =

◆ 'our' says /or/ =

court honour minour hour colour bittour journal rumour your shouer favour journey neighbour journalist course behaviour tresour harbour labour dour murdour rumour laftour honourable spourt

gh

Sometimes '**gh**' says /f/, and sometimes it is silent. Choose a coloured pen or highlighter and mark the words where '**gh**' says /f/. When you have finished this, choose another pen or highlighter of a different colour and track for the words where '**gh**' is silent.

brought	slaughter		cough	laughter		night	sought
taught	dough	light	enough	plough		daughter	right
bright	distraught		draught	tough		thorough	ought
naughty	tight	might	rough	through		fought	sight
knight	thought		laugh	caught	fight	bought	

Alpha to Omega Activity Pack 3

Illustration reproduced by kind permission of the publishers (Hornsby and Pool, 1989)

is generally weak. The range of activities which incorporates different approaches allows the learner to develop imagination and creativity in the use of letters and words. Other useful aspects include the focus on the context aspects of reading and the use of syntactic and semantic cues.

Alpha to Omega

Alpha to Omega is a phonetic, linguistic approach to the teaching of reading and can be used as a programme or as resource material. It is highly structured and follows a logical pattern of steps which promote the acquisition of phonological and language skills.

There is an emphasis on learning the 44 phonemes from which all English words are composed. These consist of the 17 vowel sounds and the 27 consonant sounds. There is also an emphasis on the acquisition of language structure, focusing on content words – nouns, verbs, adjectives and finite words – prepositions and participles. There is, therefore, an emphasis on using words in the context of a sentence. The programme provides a highly structured format for the teaching of sentences and for grammatical structure.

There are also three accompanying and very useful activity packs designed for different stages. These packs provide appropriate back-up exercises to reinforce the teaching programme (see Fig. 28). There is also an extremely useful programme of learning games – before Alpha – which can be used with children under five. These games are in a series of structured stages, are multisensory and aim to foster language development and other pre-reading skills such as visual and auditory perception and discrimination, fine motor control, spatial relationships and knowledge of colour, number and directions.

Orton–Gillingham

Programmes based on this approach have become a central focus for multisensory teaching. The programmes offer a structured, phonic-based approach which incorporates the total language experience and focuses on the letter sounds and the blending of these sounds into syllables and words. The approach rests heavily on the interaction of visual, auditory and kinaesthetic aspects of language.

Orton–Gillingham lessons, according to Henry (1996) always incorporate card drills, spelling and reading and usually include activities such as

- card drills – this involves the use of commercial or teacher-made cards containing the common letter patterns to strengthen the visual modality: phonemes (sounds) for auditory and kinaesthetic reinforcement and syllables and whole words to help develop blending skills
- word lists and phrases
- oral reading selection – this involves the teacher first reading the passage, then the student
- spelling of phonetic and non-phonetic words
- handwriting – with attention being placed on pencil grip, writing posture and letter formation. This would also include tracing, copying and practice and making cursive connections such as *br*, *bl*.
- composition – encouragement to develop writing sentences, paragraphs and short stories.

According to Clark (1988) the introduction of letters is a carefully sequenced procedure and is carried out in the following way:

- to begin with ten letters are taught – two vowels (a,i) and eight consonants (f,l,b,j,h,m,p,t);

- each of the letters is introduced with a key word;
- the difference between vowels and consonants is taught together with the position of the mouth in the pronunciation of the sounds (different coloured cards are used for vowels and consonants).

Once the child has mastered the letter name and sound, the programme then advances to introduction of blending the letters and sounds. This begins with simple three-letter words and the child repeats the sounds until the word is spoken without pauses between the constituent sounds.

The visual-kinaesthetic and auditory-kinaesthetic associations are formed by the pupil tracing, saying, copying and writing each word.

Reading of text begins after the pupil has mastered the consonant–vowel–consonant words to a higher automatic level, i.e. when the pupil can recognise and use these words.

The initial reading material is taken from the programme and contains words the pupil has learnt from the teacher's manual.

The programme gives considerable attention to the learning of dictionary skills as well as development of written language from pictographs to ideographs and eventually to the alphabet.

The programme does appear to be more suited to a one-to-one situation and it would be difficult to integrate the programme within the school curriculum. As in many of the programmes derived from the Orton–Gillingham approach, the key principles of over-learning, automaticity and multisensory approaches are very apparent and these principles *can* be utilised within the classroom curriculum.

Hickey Multisensory Language Course

The Hickey Multisensory Language Course (Augur and Briggs, 1992) recognises the importance of the need to learn sequentially the letters of the alphabet. The dyslexic child, however, will usually have some difficulty in learning and remembering the names and sequence of the alphabetic letters as well as understanding that the letters represent speech sounds which make up words.

The programme is based on multisensory principles and the alphabet is introduced using wooden or plastic letters; the child can look at the letter, pick it up, feel it with eyes open or closed and say its sound. Therefore the visual, auditory and tactile-kinaesthetic channels of learning are all being utilised with a common goal.

The programme also suggests some activities to help the child become familiar with the alphabet. These include:

- learning the letters sequentially;
- positioning of each letter of the alphabet;
- naming and recognising the shape of the letters.

These programmes involve games and the use of dictionaries to help the child become familiar with the order of the letters and the direction to go, e.g. he needs to know that 'I' comes before 'K', the letters in the first half of the alphabet and those letters in the second half. The alphabet can be further divided into sections, thus it will be easier for the child to remember the section of the alphabet in which a letter appears, for example:

A B C D
E F G H I J K L M
N O P Q R
S T U V W X Y Z

The Hickey language course includes activities related to sorting and matching the capital, lower-case, printed and written forms of the letters; practising sequencing skills with cut-out letters and shapes; and practising positioning of each letter in the alphabet in relation to the other letters (this involves finding missing letters and going backwards and forwards in the alphabet).

The course also indicates the importance of recognising where the accent falls in a word since this clearly affects the spelling and rhythm. The rhyming games can be developed to encourage the use of accent by placing the accent on different letters of the alphabet. This helps to train children's hearing to recognise when a letter has an accent or is stressed in a word.

The course includes reading and spelling packs which focus on securing a relationship between sounds and symbols. This process begins with single letters, and progresses to consonant blends, vowel continuations and then to complex letter groupings.

The reading packs consist of a set of cards; on one side the lower-case letter is displayed in bold with an upper-case (capital) letter shown on the bottom right-hand corner, in order to establish the link between the two letters. The reverse side of the card indicates a key word which contains the sound of the letter with the actual sound combination in brackets. Rather than providing a visual image of the key word, a space is left for the child to draw the image. This helps to make the image more meaningful to the child and also utilises and reinforces visual and kinaesthetic skills.

The spelling pack is similar in structure to the reading pack. On the front of the card the sound made by the letter is displayed in brackets, while the back contains both the sound and the actual letter(s). Sounds for which there is a choice of spellings will in time show all the possible ways in which the sound can be made. Cue words are also given on the back as a prompt, in case the child forgets one of the choices.

Spelling is seen as being of prime importance by the authors of the programme since they view it as an 'all round perceptual experience'. The multisensory method used involves the following process:

• the child repeats the sound heard;

Figure 29

Example worksheet 23.1: short vowel discrimination (ĭ) or (ă)

Suggestions for teachers

Put in the missing vowels (ĭ) or (ă). Read the words. Use SOS to spell, *cover*, write and check the words.

pan		🍳	p.n		🍌
.nt		🐜	t.n		🪣
t.p		🚰	sn.p		✂️

Example worksheet 23.2: picture words

The first letters of these objects make a word. Can you find two words?

Reproduced from Augur and Briggs (1992), with permission

- feels the shape the sound makes in the mouth;
- makes the sound and listens;
- writes the letter(s).

This process involves over-learning and multisensory strategies.

Bangor Dyslexia Teaching System

The Bangor Dyslexia Teaching System (Miles, 1989) is a structured, sequential teaching programme developed for teachers and speech and language therapists involved in supporting children with dyslexia.

A useful aspect of this programme is the division between primary and secondary pupils. Although it is acknowledged that some secondary pupils are still 'beginning' readers and need to go through the same initial stages of acquiring literacy as beginning readers in the primary school, the programme makes some special provision and adaptations for secondary students. This helps to make the secondary material more age appropriate.

The basic philosophy of the programme is not unlike that of other structured, phonic programmes for dyslexic children. It centres around the issue of phonological difficulties and the problems dyslexic children have in mastering the alphabetic code. The programme attempts to provide children with some competence, at the earliest stage possible, in recognising and categorising speech sounds. Miles (1989) argues that it is not possible for children to benefit from 'top down' language experience approaches to reading if they have not mastered the basic principles of literacy. Some of these principles, which the programme for primary aged children focuses on, include: the teaching of basic letter sounds and the structure of words, long vowels, common word patterns, irregular words, alphabet and dictionary skills, grammatical rules and silent letters.

The programme attempts to acknowledge that dyslexic children may have difficulties with both visual and auditory processing. The issue of auditory processing, particularly relating to the acquisition of phonic skills, is well documented (Frith, 1985; Stanovich, 1991; Rack, 1985) and a study by Stein (1995) has helped to reawaken the debate on visual aspects of reading and the difficulties some dyslexic children may have in picking out visual letter patterns.

The programme shares the same principles as that utilised by other similar programmes for dyslexic children. It is highly structured and the teacher has to proceed systematically through the programme. The aspect of over-learning is acknowledged to be important and therefore revision of material already learned occupies an important place in the implementation of the programme.

One of the difficulties inherent in following the principle of over-learning is the aspect of boredom, which may result from repetitive revision of material already learnt. This programme acknowledges that pitfall, and suggests ways of overcoming it through the use of games and other adapted materials.

The multisensory teaching element is also crucial in this programme. Some of the exercises attempt to engage all the available senses simultaneously, thus acknowledging the accepted view that dyslexic children benefit from multisensory learning.

The programme also utilises the particular benefits of mnemonics for dyslexic children as well as the notion of reading and spelling as an integrated activity. Some emphasis is also placed on encouraging dyslexic children to use oral language to plan their work. It is felt that such verbalisations help children clarify their thoughts and planning before embarking on a course of action There is also a useful appendix containing guidance on handwriting, alphabet and dictionary skills.

The secondary component of the programme provides useful advice on dealing with the problem of teaching basic literacy to older students. Miles suggests that the material for older pupils should include words of more than one syllable, even though the student is at the early stages of literacy. Some effort is made to ensure that the student is familiar with polysyllabic words in order that the potential for creative writing is not unduly restricted. At the secondary stage the aspect of reading for meaning is of great importance in order to ensure sustained motivation. The Bangor Dyslexia Teaching System acknowledges this and suggests a range of techniques which can help to support the student through the decoding difficulty in order that maximum meaning and pleasure can be derived from the text. Such suggestions include: supplying difficult words; introducing the story and the book's background and characters; pointing out clues such as capital letters and titles; encouraging fluency by reading from one full stop to the next; omitting words which are difficult, thus encouraging the use of context to obtain meaning; practice; and reading rhymes and limericks which aid sound and syllable awareness.

The programme for secondary students, although less structured than that for primary, includes sections on syllabification and stress, plurals, short and long vowel patterns, silent letters, prefixes and suffixes.

The Bangor Dyslexia Teaching System clearly attempts to teach the dyslexic child the basic rules of literacy and the English language. Although the programme can stand on its own, it would be advisable for the teacher to attempt to integrate and relate the programme within the child's class work. This can be possible by selecting aspects of the programme which are most useful and would be particularly appropriate for secondary students of whose learning priorities Miles acknowledges the teacher would need to take into account.

Alphabetic Phonics

The key principles found in the majority of individualised programmes for dyslexic children – multisensory techniques, automaticity and over-learning – are all found in the Alphabetic Phonics programme. Additionally, the programme also recognises the importance of discovery learning. Opportunities for discovery learning are found throughout this highly structured programme.

The programme, which stems from the Orton–Gillingham multisensory approach, was developed in Dallas, Texas, by Aylett Cox. She has described Alphabetic Phonics as a structured system of teaching students the coding patterns of the English language (Cox, 1985).

Cox asserts that such a phonic based programme is necessary because around 85% of the 30,000 most commonly used English words can be considered phonetically regular and therefore predictable. Thus learning phonetic rules can allow the child access to the majority of the commonly used words.

Alphabetic Phonics provides training in the development of automaticity through the use of flash cards, and over-learning through repetitive practice in reading and spelling until 95% mastery is achieved.

Figure 30: Alphabetic Phonics

1. An alphabetic activity, which emphasises sequence and directionality.
2. Introduction of a new element or concept, which begins with discovery and is reinforced with multisensory techniques.
3. Training in automatic recognition of letter names, through flashcard presentation (Reading Decks).
4. Training in recognition of letter sounds, by having students pronounce the sounds for a letter or letters presented on flashcards (Spelling Decks) and then naming and writing the letter or letters.
5. Practice in reading and spelling (10 minutes allotted for each). Each task is continued until student reaches 95 percent mastery, as measured by the Bench Mark measures.
6. Handwriting practice.
7. Practice in verbal expression, first oral and later written, focusing on various skills (e.g., sequencing ideas, creative expression, vocabulary, syntax).
8. Listening to good literature and building comprehension skills, while reading instruction focuses on decoding skills.

Reproduced by kind permission of publishers (Cox, 1985)

The programme also incorporates opportunities to develop creativity in expression and in the sequencing of ideas.

The programme is highly structured with daily lessons of around one hour. Lessons incorporate a variety of tasks which help to keep the child's attention directed to the activities and prevents tedium or boredom. A typical lesson may include the activities outlined in Fig. 30.

In this programme reading comprehension instruction does not begin until the student has reached a minimal level of accuracy in relation to decoding skills. Cox, however, does recognise that children will learn and retain new vocabulary more effectively and efficiently through experiential learning, and that this is particularly applicable to dyslexic children.

Although a number of studies have claimed impressive results using the Alphabetic Phonics Programme (Ray, 1986; Frankiewicz, 1985) it has been asserted that the research methodology used and the lack of effective control groups somewhat diminish the impressive results of these studies (Clark, 1988). Additionally, in order to teach the programme effectively, it has been maintained that 480 hours of teacher training is required, based on knowledge of the structure of the English language, knowledge of phonetic rules and patterns in spelling and integration of these activities into a structured, hierarchical curriculum. An accompanying text (Cox, 1992) *Foundations for Literacy* does however provide an easy to follow lesson guide for the teacher (see Fig. 31).

In the programme Cox suggests a number of linkages between multisensory activities and the letter such as association of cursive shape, speech sound, graphic symbol and kinaesthetic memory. An example is provided in Fig. 31.

The principles and practices of this programme, such as structure, multisensory technique, emphasis on automaticity, emphasis on building comprehension skills, experiential learning and listening skills, and in particular recognition of letter sounds, can have desirable outcomes. These can readily be adapted and

Figure 31:   Multisensory introduction of a letter

Linkage 2 – Association of student's kinesthetic memory of letter's cursive shape (in hand and arm) with its name. Teacher demonstrates already learned approach strokes in the same order daily. Student chooses the one that fits best. All letters begin on baseline and are written left-to-right.

1. Teacher prints a three-inch 'reading' letter on board and writes cursive letter over it, showing the relationship of 'writing' letter to 'reading' letter. The letter is then erased.
2. Teacher places small arrow at starting point and writes large cursive letter carefully on board (one to three feet high) while describing strokes and rhythm. Student observes closely. Leave model on board.
3. Student sky-writes letter several times in the air (facing chalk-board), naming letter just before writing it every time. He always points his index finger toward the arrow and names letter before he starts. Teacher emphasises stop to promote rhythm. Right hander begins sky-writing at mid-line and moves toward the right. Left hander begins to the left of the body and moves toward mid-line.
4. Student traces large model of letter several times on paper (first with finger tip) until he has the 'feel' in his muscles. He always names letter aloud before he begins to write its approach stroke.
5. Student copies letter once with model in view.
6. Student writes large letter twice from memory, always naming letter first.
7. Student writes large letter twice with eyes closed or averted, each time 'telling his hand' the letter's name before beginning the approach stroke. He develops independent follow-through without the need for teacher's oral directions.

Reproduced by kind permission of publishers (Cox, 1992)

implemented into teaching programmes devised for different needs and contexts.

The Slingerland Programme

The Slingerland Programme is an adaptation of the Orton–Gillingham Programme. Essentially, the programme was developed as a screening approach to help minimise the difficulties experienced by children in language and literacy. The Slingerland Screening Tests accompany the programme and are usually administered in the early stages of education.

The programme shares similar features with other programmes. Multisensory teaching permeates the programme which begins by introducing letters of the alphabet.

The programme follows the format below.

Writing

This is the first step and usually uses the following order:

● tracing
● copying
● writing in the air
● simultaneously writing from memory and saying the letter

Letter sounds

This involves naming the letter then the key word associated with the letter and then the letter sound.

Blending

This is introduced with oral activities and may involve repetitive use and blends with kinesthetic support to reinforce the material being learnt.

Decoding

In decoding, students begin with three letters c-v-c, e.g. words such as 'bay' and 'way'. They are required to:

- pronounce the initial consonant
- then the vowel
- then blend the two
- and pronounce the final consonant
- and say the whole word

Vowel digraphs and vowel–consonant digraphs are taught as units, although Slingerland maintains that consonant blends are usually learnt more easily.

Reading for meaning

Once decoding has been sufficiently mastered a whole-word approach is encouraged in the reading of text. Initially, students undergo a 'preparation for reading' lesson when some time is spent producing, recognising and reading words and the students become familiar with the image of the word. There is also some emphasis on teacher modelling by reading aloud. To foster reading comprehension skills, the teacher cues in appropriate clues into the questioning technique, e.g. which seven words tell us where the house was – 'it was built on a high hill'.

The Slingerland Programme is highly specific and highly structured and contains some useful strategies and ideas (see Fig. 32).

Research into the effectiveness of the Slingerland Programme indicates that it can produce significant gains in a number of language aspects, such as listening comprehension, punctuation, grammar, syntax, spelling and study skills. Gains have also been noted in vocabulary and the use of inference in reading (Wolf, 1985; McCulloch, 1985).

Project Read

This programme shares similarities with the Reading Recovery Programme (Clay, 1985). It attempts to provide effective reading instruction for those students who are not progressing adequately with reading.

Figure 32:   An example of an activity from the Slingerland Programme

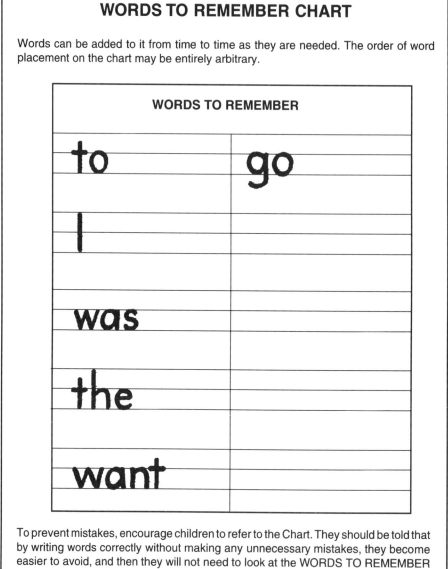

Reproduced by kind permission of the publishers (Slingerland, 1993)

Devised by Enfield and Greene, who now consider the programme an alternative approach to the teaching of reading as well as one which provides remediation (Enfield and Greene, 1981), it is designed essentially for the classroom teacher.

The programme is divided into three phases – phase one highlights the use of phonics; phase two looks at reading comprehension, and phase three concentrates on written expression. The programme also incorporates the principles of multisensory learning, over-learning and automaticity.

Phase one

Phase one focuses on the systematic teaching of phonic skills. Multisensory strategies are used: for example, whilst saying the letter children trace it in the air or on a table, then identify the picture which contains the letter. Attention is also given to mouth positions in the voiced and unvoiced sounds.

Over-learning occurs through a review of previously learned material at the beginning of each lesson, and automaticity is encouraged through the use of flash cards for letter sounds and the writing of the letter symbols in response to the teacher saying the sound.

Sounds are introduced in a structured manner, and usually the student will be familiar with a sound, the letter symbol and the use of the letter symbol and sound in a word before embarking on a new sound.

In order to provide some success, 'reinforcement reading', which consists of students reading texts which contain in the main phonetically regular words, is included in the programme.

Phase two

Phase two focuses on reading comprehension and vocabulary development. The programme presents a sequence of comprehension skills which include identifying the subject of the text; selecting and explaining the meaning of unfamiliar words; identifying aspects of punctuation and the reasons for those particular aspects; noting the nature of the text material (for example, whether it is fiction, non-fiction); the use of inferences contained within the text; the conclusions which one could draw from the text; and the organisation of the text.

Students are encouraged to look for clues in the text which can help to support the conclusions which are drawn from the inferences made from the content. The teacher, therefore, makes a statement which contains inferences and asks students to find clues which can support this inference. Models are provided for demonstrating the structure of a story plot, such as the conflict, preliminary activities prior to the action, the action, the aftermath of the action and the conclusion.

Phase three

Phase three looks at written expression. It focuses on the teaching of sentence structure and paragraph development. Considerable attention is given to creative writing experiences and the identification of ideas and concepts which are found in creative writing.

The Project Read programme appears to possess some interesting elements. The focus on creative writing for example, is an aspect which can sometimes be lost in the quest to ensure that children with dyslexia are taught the essential decoding skills.

DISTAR

DISTAR (Direct Instruction System of Teaching Arithmetic and Reading) was originally designed for socially disadvantaged children in the United States as part of the Project Follow Through scheme launched by the government in 1968. The programme is orientated to achievement in basic attainments and tasks and skills to enhance effective learning.

Some of the features of DISTAR include the transfer of learning from specific examples to general concepts; continual, positive reinforcement to enhance motivation and success; and the monitoring of progress through the use of criterion-referenced assessment. In addition to reading skills, the current DISTAR programme covers language, spelling and arithmetic (Engelmann and Bruner, 1983, SRA).

The reading programme, which commences at pre-school level, incorporates both decoding and comprehension lessons. The programme includes elements of pre-reading skills, pronunciation of letter sounds, different types of sounds, oral blending activities, rhyming activities, sound associations and sequencing skills. The individual lessons utilise a variety of teaching methods including games. These games aim to develop various strategies to help in the retention of letter sounds.

The programme is interspersed with activities to monitor progress in relation to reading accuracy, speed and comprehension.

Evaluation studies display impressive progress in attainments among students undertaking the DISTAR programme – results which appear to continue through to secondary education (Meyer, 1984). Some criticism, however, has been raised that the teacher's manual is too prescriptive and places too much restriction on teachers (Becker, 1977). The focus of the programme on transferring skills from the specific to the underlying general task concepts is indeed commendable and can make the DISTAR materials a useful resource.

Reading Recovery

Reading Recovery is an early reading and writing intervention programme, developed by Marie Clay, which focuses on children who after one year at school have lagged significantly behind their peers in reading and writing. Marie Clay originally introduced the programme in New Zealand, but it has now been shown that the programme can be successfully transferred to other countries and contexts (Pinnell et al., 1988a, 1988b, 1991; Wright, 1992).

The programme aims to boost the reading attainments of the selected children over a relatively short period, around twelve to twenty weeks, with specially trained teachers carrying out the programme, seeing children on an individual basis for thirty minutes daily. The programme centres around the individual child's strengths and weaknesses as assessed by the actual reading programme. It is not, therefore, structured around a set of principles and practices to which the child has to be accommodated, but rather the programme adapts itself to the child's specific requirements and needs. It utilises both bottom-up and top-down reading approaches and therefore encourages the use of decoding strategies through the use of phonics, and awareness of meaning through an awareness of the context and language of the text.

The programme aims to produce 'independent readers whose reading improves whenever they read' (Clay, 1985). There is an emphasis, therefore, on strategies which the reader can apply to other texts and situations, and there is evidence that gains made in the Reading Recovery programme will be maintained over time.

For some children the Reading Recovery programme may need to be supplemented by additional sessions which could include:

- re-reading familiar books
- taking a running record
- reinforcing letter identification
- writing a story, thus learning sounds in words
- comprehension of story
- introducing new book

It is also important that the child is helped to develop a self-improving system. This would encourage the child to:

- be aware of his own learning
- take control and responsibility for his own learning

The goal of teaching reading is to assist the child to produce effective strategies for working on text, and according to Clay this can be done through focusing on the practices of self-correcting and self-monitoring.

The main components of the programme include:

- learning about direction
- locating and focusing on aspects of print
- spatial layout of books
- writing stories
- learning sounds in words
- comprehension and cut-up stories
- reading books
- using print as a cue
- sound and letter sequence
- word analysis

- fluency

A typical Reading Recovery lesson would include the analysis of the child's decoding strategies, the encouragement of fluent reading through the provision of opportunities to link sounds and letters, the reading of familiar texts and the introduction of new books.

Identification

Since the programme provides an intensive input to those children lagging in reading, it is vitally important that the identification procedures are sound in order to ensure that the children who receive the benefits of this programme are those who would not otherwise make satisfactory progress.

The lowest achieving children in a class group, after a year at school at around six years of age, are admitted into the programme. Clay believes that by the end of the first year at primary school it is possible to identify children who are failing. She suggests that this can be achieved through systematic observation of children's learning behaviour, together with a diagnostic survey.

The systematic observation takes the form of noting precisely what children are saying and doing in relation to reading, so the focus is on reading tasks rather than specific sub-skills such as visual perception or auditory dissemination. In order to identify the child's reading behaviour Marie Clay has developed a diagnostic survey which involves taking a 'Running Record' of precisely how the child is performing in relation to reading. This type of analysis of children's errors in reading can provide clues in relation to children's strengths and weaknesses in reading.

The diagnostic survey includes directional movement (which looks at general directional concepts, including motor coordination, impulsivity and hesitancy), error behaviour (focusing on oral language skills, speed of responding and the use of semantic and syntactic context), the use of visual and memory cues, the rate of self-correction, and the child's preferred mode of identifying letters (alphabetic, sound or cueing from words). The survey also includes details of the child's writing skills. This is particularly important since it may provide some indication of any reading problems as well as language level and message quality.

Evaluation of the Reading Recovery

Much of the research evidence which examines the effectiveness of this programme is impressive. The participating children appear to display gains which allow them to reach average levels of performance in reading within a relatively short period (Wright, 1992). There are, however, a number of studies which are critical of the programme.

Meek (1985) argues that the programme is rather restrictive in that it does not allow for children's reading preferences in relation to choice of material, and Adams (1990) observes that the phonics element in Reading Recovery is not systematic and does not emphasise structures such as 'word families'. The programme, according to Topping and Wolfendale (1985), does not make adequate allowance for the effective role which parents can play in enhancing literacy skills, and Glynn *et al.* (1989) argue that many of the gains made by children who have participated in the Reading Recovery Programme have disappeared after a year. Johnston (1992) feels that programmes such as Reading Recovery are only necessary because of the trend from phonics-focused programmes, and she concludes that 'rather than wait until children fail in a non-phonics programme, it would be very much better for them either to be taught routines in a reading programme which emphasises phonics as well as reading for memory, or for the class teacher to have such a scheme available for those who are making very slow progress'.

Dombey (1992), arguing on behalf of the National Association for the Teaching of English, puts forward some doubts about the efficacy of Reading Recovery because it focuses on one particular age group – six-year-olds – and because it requires intensive training of a few specialists with little opportunity for dissemination of the skills of these specialists so that the effects of the programme do not fully percolate into mainstream classes.

Dombey further argues that it could be more cost-effective to study the existing provision for the teaching of reading, and to identify ways in which this could be improved, for example by ensuring that all teachers of young children have the time needed to teach reading thoroughly, and to provide those teachers with adequate training in the teaching of reading for all children.

The introduction of the Reading Recovery programme in Surrey has shown that the programme can be readily adapted to the UK classroom context. Wright and Prance (1992) provide an illustrative case study of one six-year-old girl, the lowest progress reader in the class group. At the start of the programme this girl displayed 75–97% accuracy in reading three one-line caption books and was able to write accurately thirteen of the thirty-seven words on a dictation passage. By the end of the programme the girl had progressed to 98% accuracy on more demanding readers and scored full marks on the dictation passage. In addition the girl displayed considerable gains in the full battery of reading tests administered at the end of the programme. Wright and Prance also acknowledged some qualitative improvements in the girl's reading behaviour, for example she began to recognise similar patterns between words. This is a good example of the application of word knowledge which could be transferred to other contexts – a difficulty, in fact, which seems to pervade children with dyslexia and prevents effective transfer of word knowledge to other contexts. The general monitoring of her own work appeared to improve, something which was highlighted by the increase in her self-correction rate and in the use of the strategy of scanning the print before summarising to read aloud.

Longitudinal studies in Ohio and New Zealand showed that the gains made by children after three to six months of the programme were maintained: the former Reading Recovery pupils were still functioning within the average band at age nine (Clay, 1985; Delford *et al.*, 1987).

A further evaluation conducted by Wright (1992) showed that in Surrey, the gains made by children participating in the Reading Recovery programme were impressive. Ninety-six of those participating reached average levels of attainment in literacy after around seventeen weeks of the programme.

The study did reveal marked differences between schools, which reflected the difficulty some teachers had in seeing the pupils every day.

Only three of the 82 children taken into the programme did not achieve average levels for their classes after twenty weeks. This appears as an impressive statistic when it is considered that at the start of the programme the participating children were only able to read their names or a short sentence, displayed poor recognition of letter names or sounds, and could write only five words unaided in ten minutes. The results are broadly similar to those gains achieved in the New Zealand and Ohio studies (Clay, 1985; Pinnell *et al.*, 1988a, 1988b) and Wright therefore concludes that the Reading Recovery programme was successfully imported to the Surrey context. Indeed, the Surrey children made greater gains than the New Zealand children in all areas except sight vocabulary, although the former did remain in the programme on average several weeks longer than the New Zealand children. Clearly, further research needs to be carried out to assess whether the gains made are maintained in the same manner as those made by the New Zealand children.

Teaching Reading through Spelling

This programme produced by staff at the Kingston Reading Centre (Cowdery *et al.*, 1984–88) provides a very detailed and comprehensive analysis of the diagnosis of specific learning difficulties and programmes of remediation.

It is based on the original Orton–Gillingham Programme and follows the same basic principles as those adopted by other specific programmes recommended by the British Dyslexia Association. The programme is, therefore, phonically based, structured and cumulative. These principles ensure that the programme has a coherent organisation and a progression through alphabetic knowledge to sounds, leading to sound/symbol correspondence. The programme also develops multisensory strategies in teaching and learning. Repetition is also built into this programme as the authors acknowledge the value of automaticity for dyslexic children.

The Teaching Reading Through Spelling programme is essentially a psycholinguistic approach because, although it recognises the importance of phonic knowledge, particularly for dyslexic children who may not obtain full benefit from 'look and say' approaches, it also emphasises articulation and speech training. Linguistic competence, performance and linguistic concepts are therefore guiding principles of this programme.

The authors of the programme appreciate that spelling, being a recall skill (as opposed to reading which is a recognition skill), can present more serious difficulties for the child and therefore the programme attempts to develop an understanding of the spelling system as an aid to developing the processing skills necessary for reading.

The programme is structured in units aimed at different activities. For example there are units on the foundations of the programme, the early stages, later stages, spelling, activity for infants and beginners and a handwriting copy book.

Section one of the foundation programme begins with alphabet work and includes the use of a variety of strategies to help the child become familiar with and retain the letters of the alphabet. Games such as alphabet bingo, alphabet dominoes, mazes and crosswords introduce some variety and enjoyment in this section of the programme.

The early stages programme proceeds through sound–symbol relationship (auditory), sound–symbol relationship (visual), short vowels, voiced and un-voiced consonants, initial and final consonant blends, syllables, syllable division for reading and spelling, grammatical rules and suggested lesson plans for teaching letters and sounds.

The later stages programme develops the work of the early stages and in addition, looks at word families and elaborates on the use of the reading and spelling pack.

The Teaching Reading Through Spelling programme is very detailed and thorough in its approach to phonic and linguistic aspects of teaching reading and spelling. Such a structured approach may easily lend itself to monotony and dullness, particularly since it incorporates the essential aspects of over-learning and automaticity. The programme authors, however, have attempted to overcome this by introducing a variety of stimulating games and strategies which help to provide enjoyment to children, as well as reinforcing the central aspects of the programme (see Fig. 33).

In general the programme provides a good, clear structure and can be readily utilised by the class teacher.

The range of individualised programmes for children with dyslexia is impressive and this section has provided summaries of some of the main approaches.

Some of the principles of the programmes and the methods advocated by their authors, such as 'multisensory', 'structured' and 'cumulative' approaches can provide useful pointers in the development of support materials for dyslexic children. Ideally, for a programme to be of maximum benefit to teachers, it should not only be easily understood and implemented, but also flexible and adaptable to different contexts and types of dyslexic difficulties. The next section, on 'Support Approaches', emphasises the benefits of such flexibility and adaptability.

SUPPORT APPROACHES AND STRATEGIES

In addition to the impressive number of individualised programmes available for children with dyslexia, there is also an abundance of support materials which can be utilised by teachers to complement teaching programmes and curriculum

Figure 33:   Teaching Reading through Spelling

THE (i) GAME

A reading game that reinforces the different spellings of the sound (ī). Suitable for all pupils that have covered the programme to <u>igh</u> and had <u>buy</u> and <u>height</u> pointed out as exceptions, should the teacher wish to include them. This game can be adapted to teach the choice of <u>l</u> and <u>ll</u>; <u>ble</u> and <u>bble</u>, <u>ble</u> and <u>nel</u>.

Aim: To consolidate the use of the (ī) spelling card.

Materials: A pack of cards. On each card write the beginning or end of a word with the sound (ī) in it. About 32 cards will be required to make the game playable.

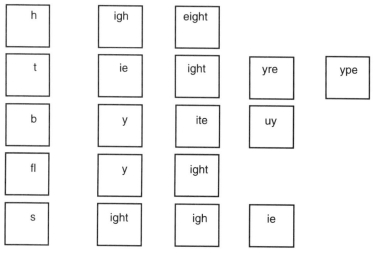

METHOD
1.   Shuffle the cards and deal 7 cards to each player.
2.   The players then look to see if they can make any words with their cards.
3.   They put the completed word/s on the table and read them.
4.   The remaining pack is put face down in the middle of the table and one card is turned face up.
5.   The player on the left of the dealer has a choice of taking the exposed card that has been turned face up or the top card of the remaining pack, to see if s/he can make a word with the cards in his/her hand.
6.   If the first player can make a word s/he puts it on the table and reads it clearly, then throws out a card and the second player has a turn.
7.   The winner is the first player to use all the cards in his/her hand.

Reproduced by kind permission of the publishers (Cowdery et al, 1988)

approaches. Conceptually most of the individualised programmes have much in common, emphasising aspects such as structure, multisensory aspects, over-learning and automaticity. Support materials, however, do not necessarily pro-vide an individual programme, but rather can be used by the teacher to help the child develop some competencies to allow access to the full range of curriculum activities.

Some of these support materials and approaches are discussed below.

Phonological Awareness Approaches

There is strong evidence to suggest that phonological factors are of considerable importance in reading (Ellis and Large, 1988; Stanovich, 1991; Rack, 1994; Wilson and Frederickson, 1995). Children with decoding problems appear to be considerably hampered in reading because they are unable to generalise from one word to another. This means that every word they read is unique, indicating that there is a difficulty in learning and applying phonological rules in reading. It therefore emphasises the importance of teaching sounds/phonemes and ensuring that the child has an awareness of the sound/letter correspondence. Learning words by sight can enable some children to reach a certain standard in reading, but prevents them from adequately tackling new words and extending their vocabulary.

If children have a phonological awareness difficulty they are more likely to guess the word from the first letter cue and not the first **sound**, i.e. the word 'KITE' will be tackled from the starting point of the letter 'K' and not the sound 'ki' so the dyslexic reader may well read something like 'KEPT'. It is important, therefore, that beginning readers receive some structured training in the grapheme/phoneme correspondence; this is particularly necessary for dyslexic children who would not automatically, or readily, appreciate the importance of phonic rules in reading.

Descriptions of some structured programmes are given below.

Sound Linkage

Sound Linkage (Hatcher, 1994) is an integrated phonological programme for overcoming reading difficulties. In addition to a section on assessment it contains ten sections on teaching, each dealing with a specific aspect of phonological processing. For example, Section Three deals with phoneme blending, Section Five deals with identification and discrimination of phonemes, and some other sections deal with phoneme segmentation, deletion, substitution and phoneme transposition.

Although Sound Linkage can be used as an individual structured programme, each section contains a series of activities which can be used to support mainstream curriculum work with dyslexic children. An example from Section One, 'Identification of Words as Units within Sentences', is shown in Fig. 34. The activities are clearly presented and no complex instructions are necessary. Many of the activities are, however, not new, and many teachers will be aware of the importance of them. To have all these activities in a methodical package, linked

Figure 34

PRODUCTION OF INITIAL, FINAL AND MEDIAL WORDS IN SENTENCES OF
TWO TO FOUR WORDS

Materials needed: photocopiable record sheet

Instructions
Explain that you are going to say some words. You want the children to tell you one
of the words. The word you want might be at the beginning, the end or the middle.

Ask them to say:
  My name is [child's name].

Ask:

  What was the word at the beginning? [**my**]
  What was the word at the end? [**child's name**]
  What was one of the middle words? [**name** or **is**]

Say:

  Now listen to this and tell me the word at the beginning. Wake up [**wake**]

Use a similar format for the following:

Middle	It is snowing (**is**)	[ ]
End	Shall we go out? (**out**)	[ ]
End	Stop shouting (**shouting**)	[ ]
Middle	Here comes mum (**comes**)	[ ]
Beginning	Now you've done it (**Now**)	[ ]
Beginning	Good morning (**Good**)	[ ]
Middle	How are you? (**are**)	[ ]
End	Breakfast is nearly ready (**ready**)	[ ]
Total		[ ]/6
Beginning	Hello Fred (**Hello**)	[ ]
Middle	Are you better? (**you**)	[ ]
End	You seem to be (**be**)	[ ]
End	Daffy duck (**duck**)	[ ]
Middle	Laid an egg (**an**)	[ ]
Beginning	'Quack, Quack', she said (**Quack**)	[ ]
Beginning	Saturday morning (**Saturday**)	[ ]
Middle	Time to play (**to**)	[ ]
End	Let's feed the horse (**horse**)	[ ]
End	Stop thief! (**thief**)	[ ]
Middle	Catch that man! (**that**)	[ ]
Beginning	He's stolen my radio (**He's**)	[ ]
Total		[ ]/12

Reproduced from Hatcher (1995) with permission

to assessment, with a clear overall rationale is an appealing feature of the programme.

Section Ten, which contains phonological linkage activities, and Appendix 1 can be related to the child's work in the classroom. Indeed there is no reason why all the activities cannot in some way be transferred to curriculum activities.

The section on phoneme transposition would be difficult for younger children, particularly the activities related to spoonerism (e.g. 'mouse' 'cat' becomes 'cause' 'mat'). Walton and Brooks (1995) however suggest that spoonerisms are attractive items in an assessment and programme for phonological awareness because they offer an alternative which is more appropriate for older children than rhyming and alliteration and not be too contaminated by any difficulties the child may have with reading and writing. Brooks (1990) however suggested the use of semi-spoonerisms as he found full spoonerisms too difficult in a programme for 11- to 14-year-olds. Hatcher attempts to overcome this in the programme Sound Linkage by describing activities which can introduce the child to the use of spoonerisms. One such activity involves pictures of a cow, dog, horse and fish, each cut into two parts, i.e. head and body. The teacher then explains that as well as changing heads we could change the first sounds of the name and get two funny words. The two examples below are then presented to the child.

This comprehensive programme of activities, linking assessment and teaching can be a useful addition to the support materials available to enhance the phonological skills of dyslexic children.

Phonological Awareness Procedures

The useful and easily accessible series of activities to promote phonological awareness (Gorrie and Parkinson, 1995) also begins with an assessment section. Following this the remainder of the programme is in the form of game activities designed to develop specific areas of phonological development. For example there are game activities on syllable segmentation, rhyme judgement, rhyme production, alliteration, onset and rime and phoneme segmentation games. These games provide an excellent resource for the teacher and are suitable for children at different stages of phonological development. An example more suitable for children at a more advanced stage, is shown in Fig. 35.

Phonic Code Cracker

Phonic Code Cracker is a set of materials sub-divided into twelve units, each unit covering a different aspect of teaching literacy, e.g. Unit 3 deals with initial and final consonant blends, Unit 5 deals with common word endings (see Fig. 36) and Unit 9 deals with common silent letters.

Phonic Code Cracker (Russell, 1993) is a very comprehensive and teacher friendly set of materials. The scheme has been devised to provide intensive

Figure 35

RHYMING LOTTO
For two to four players.
NOTE: This is probably the most difficult game to play and should only be tried when pupils have a reasonable grasp of rhyme judgement.
Make a set of Lotto cards each with six or eight different pictures of common objects. Have cards with words which rhyme with the pictures on the Lotto cards. There should be several rhyming words for each picture. Provide each pupil with one Lotto card and six or eight counters or blank cards which can be used to cover their pictures.
Call out each word in turn. If a pupil has a rhyming picture on his/her Lotto board, s/he can cover it with a counter or blank card. The winner is the first person to cover all the pictures on their Lotto board.

WORDS		
look rook crook took	lock flock rock sock	
gate rate date eight	hurt shirt dirt curt	
log frog cog fog	sole mole dole goal	

Reproduced from Gorrie and Parkinson (1995) with permission

phonic practice for children who have been having difficulty acquiring basic literacy skills. It has been successfully used with children with specific reading difficulties in mainstream primary and secondary schools.

Essentially the scheme consists of support material and can be successfully used in combination with other schemes. Precision teaching methods are used, but no timescale is recommended as the author acknowledges that each child will have a different rate of learning. Assessment of the pupil's progress is measured through the use of pupil record skills. There are also fluency tests, time targets, accompanying computer software and – very important for building self-esteem – a mastery certificate which the child can retain as a record of his/her achievement.

Spelling

In relation to spelling, Liberman and Shankweiler (1985) have shown that a clear difference exists in the performance in phonological tasks between good and poor spellers. This implies that successful spelling is related to children's awareness of the underlying phonological structure of words. This is supported by

Figure 36

---- s and ---- es

Plural means more than one. We add s or es.

1 cat	2 cats	1 box	2 boxes
1 peg	4 pegs	1 fox	3 foxes
1 tin	6 tins	1 bus	4 buses
1 crab	3 crabs	1 kiss	8 kisses
1 bed	2 beds	1 glass	5 glasses
1 van	5 vans	1 cross	2 crosses
1 stamp	8 stamps	1 dress	7 dresses

FLUENCY TEST – TIME TARGET 20 SECONDS

vans	buses	legs	foxes
tins	crosses	glasses	pigs
boxes	stamps	kisses	tops

	sec.	sec.	sec.	sec.	sec.

Level 5 4

Reproduced by kind permission of Sylvia Russell (Russell, 1993)

Rohl and Tunmer (1988) who found that good spellers were better at phonemic segmentation tasks than older children matched for spelling age.

Furthermore Bradley and Bryant (1991) showed that measures of rhyme judgment and letter knowledge in pre-school children were a good predictor of subsequent performance in spelling. Thus children who can recognise words

Figure 37

SIMULTANEOUS ORAL SPELLING

1. Have the word written correctly, or made with the letters.
2. Say the word.
3. Write the word, spelling out each letter as it is written, using cursive script.
4. The child needs to – see each letter
                  – hear its name
                  – receive kinesthetic feedback through the movement of the
                    arm and throat muscles.
5. Check to see if the word is correct.
6. Cover up the word and repeat the process.

    Continue to practise the word in this way, three times a day, for one week. By this time the word should be committed to memory. However, only one word will have been learned.

7. This step involves the categorisation of the word with other words which sound and look alike. So if the word that has been learned is 'round' the student is then shown that s/he can also spell 'ground' 'pound' 'found' 'mound' 'sound' 'around' 'bound' 'grounded' 'pounding' etc. That is s/he has learned six, eight, or more words for the effort of one.

Reproduced by kind permission of Lynette Bradley (Personal Communication, 1994)

which sound and look alike would tend to have a good memory for spelling patterns. Indeed Bradley and Huxford (1994) show that sound categorisation in particular plays an important role in developing memory patterns for spelling. Bradley (1989a, 1990) has shown that rhyming is a particularly useful form of categorisation for developing spelling skills and that practice in sound categorisation through nursery rhymes and rhyming word games in early language play helps spelling.

Many children have problems remembering 'chunks', such as 'igh' in 'sight', and 'fight'. If children cannot do this, then every word will be unique. Irregular words can also be learnt using the multisensory techniques indicated in Fig. 37.

Clearly phonological aspects are important in the development of reading and spelling skills. This seems to have considerable importance, particularly for dyslexic children who do not automatically relate the sounds to the visual images of print. Exercises in phonological awareness are therefore of great importance, not just to assist with reading but also to help with spelling, by allowing children to learn and understand sound patterns and to recognise how these are transposed into print.

Quest – Screening, Diagnostic and Support Kit (Second Edition, 1995)

This kit is described in Chapter 3, 'Assessment Approaches' since it is a screening and diagnostic test, but one which provides excellent guidance to link the assessment with teaching. A learning support programme can be developed and implemented, from the results of the diagnostic tests, using the relevant Quest workbooks.

Reason and Boote

Reason and Boote (1994) in their special needs manual 'Helping Children with Reading and Spelling', provide the teacher with a comprehensive teaching kit including a structured framework for teaching reading, spelling and handwriting, activities which can be readily utilised by the class teacher and case studies complete with teaching plans.

The model of literacy learning which underpins this book, provides a superb illustration of the importance of both bottom-up and top-down approaches to reading. The main themes in the literacy learning model cover meaning, phonics and fluency. This is described in an integrative manner which emphasises a holistic view of literacy learning. This interconnecting approach shows the importance of meaning, phonics and fluency at all stages of reading development from the earliest stage to one where basic competence has been mastered.

As well as a step-by-step teaching approach, the book contains a number of activities on aiding the development of phonics, spelling and writing, and the last section of the book illustrates how these ideas can be applied to the classroom. It is important upon selecting a teaching programme that every effort is made to link the activities contained within the programmes to the child's curriculum in the mainstream setting. Reason and Boote in this manual, accomplish exactly that and also provide a plethora of ideas and constructive guidance for the classteacher.

Aston Portfolio

The Aston Portfolio consists of teaching strategies which provide some framework and direction for the teacher. The Portfolio can be used in conjunction with the Aston Index (see Chapter 3) an assessment which highlights areas of strengths and difficulties. Once such information has been obtained, the teacher can then locate the appropriate teaching technique card in the Portfolio box. Each card provides specific remediation exercises and areas on which the teacher should focus.

The teaching technique cards in the Portfolio include: reading–visual skills; reading–auditory skills; spelling; handwriting; comprehension and written expression. The reading–visual skills section, for example, contains cards relating to teaching, sequence, discrimination, reversals, memory, sight vocabulary and word structure. It also contains lists of materials which can be used by the teacher to help the child develop visual reading skills. The Portfolio box also contains a handwriting checklist.

Although the Aston Portfolio can be useful in helping to direct the teacher to appropriate teaching areas and can also be used selectively by the teacher, it does possess some drawbacks. Clearly the size of the cards, by necessity, restrict the amount of information which can be provided; therefore the information is presented more as a collation of helpful 'tips' than as a structured programme of teaching. Yet the cards do have a tendency to be prescriptive and, because of the nature of the Portfolio, overlook the individuality of children. Perhaps a closer link between the Index and the Portfolio could have helped to overcome this.

Although the handbook indicates that the teaching technique cards can be used to help to construct an individual programme for the child, this may in fact be rather difficult without extensive reference to other appropriate resources and strategies. If the teacher is to use the Portfolio, it can only be to provide some 'ignition' to help identify other appropriate resources.

Counselling Approaches

Impressive data (Hales, 1990b; 1995; Biggar and Barr, 1993; Miles and Varma, 1995), support the view that teachers need to appreciate the emotional needs of children with specific learning difficulties. In a number of studies, Hales showed that even very young children are adversely affected by the realisation of their difficulty with literacy. Indeed Hales also provided evidence for the persistence of personality traits of inadequacy among dyslexic people. His study of a group of adult male dyslexics showed they had a preference to be 'people who were unconventional, individualist and more likely to be rejected in group activities'.

Hales therefore suggests that considerable scope exists for personal counselling of the dyslexic individual. This would allow people with dyslexia the opportunity of talking through their fears, and some attempts could be made to help to match 'self image' with reality since often dyslexic children have a self-image which presents a distorted and unrealistic picture of themselves. Although Hales points out that while there is no specific personality disorder which affects dyslexic children independently of other factors, there is still a strong case for considering closely the individual and personal aspects of children and adults with dyslexia. Indeed he argues that it may be important to consider counselling and social support of the 'dyslexic person' before dealing with the 'dyslexic difficulty'. He further emphasises (Hales, 1995) that effective provision for dyslexic employees in the work situation can reduce potential stress in the workplace, but also facilitate the performance of a large number of competent and experienced individuals to work up to their full potential.

This view is reinforced by Newby et al. (1995) who provide first-person accounts of the effects on the individual of being dyslexic. For example, Newby asserts that 'our depths of feelings usually derive from childhood experiences. At school such negative comments led me to truant frequently' (p. 105). Another dyslexic person in the same chapter suggests, 'I personally believe today that the overwhelming levels of anxiety created by the daily ignominies and embarrassments of being a dyslexic person . . . fuelled my abusing myself with prescribed medication and alcohol' (p. 116).

These views are reinforced by Biggar and Barr (1993, 1996) who reported how children with specific learning difficulties seemed acutely aware of their failure to develop literacy skills in a similar fashion to their peers, and how they would attempt to deal with this by concealing or denying their difficulty. The research conducted by Biggar and Barr indicated that factors such as inappropriate attributions, disagreement between adults, and teasing and verbal abuse hindered emotional development. They suggested the following strategies to help facilitate the emotional development of the child:

- ensure that the child's difficulties are accurately described in order to remove doubts, anxieties or prejudices;
- ensure agreement between the significant adults in the child's life, such as parents and teachers;
- ensure the child has a voice, is understood and has a trusting relationship with those adults.

This research places some emphasis on the adult and teacher to attempt to appreciate how it may *feel* for the child to have this type of difficulty.

There is also considerable evidence which shows the positive correlation between self-esteem and scholastic achievement (Burns, 1979; Bar-Tal, 1984). Clearly, therefore, it is particularly important to recognise the value of counselling, sensitivity and success for children with specific learning difficulties.

Furthermore research has shown (Lawrence, 1985) that counselling, in addition to specific teaching programmes, can not only enhance the self-esteem of children, but also enhance their reading attainments to a level in excess of children who received only the teaching programme. In his study, the teaching programme used was DISTAR (see Chapter 5) and counselling continued for twenty weeks, once a week, and was conducted by non-professionals.

Lawrence suggests certain curriculum subjects have the potential to be particularly enhancing in terms of self-esteem. These include music, art, drama and creative writing. Clearly, therefore, this offers scope for the teacher to optimise the confidence of children with specific learning difficulties since art and drama have less of a reliance on literacy. Music and creative writing may well be skills which are well developed among children with specific learning difficulties, but the degree of literacy difficulties which they possess may well prevent them from gaining full access and full success from those areas. This, however, should not be the case! Supporting and encouraging the creative writing and musical ability of children with specific learning difficulties is of great importance, just as is for example the development of phonological awareness.

The case for a dual approach to the teaching of reading, incorporating counselling, seems in the case of children with specific learning difficulties very strong. Lawrence draws the distinction between the teacher's view of children with severe reading difficulties as 'potentially improving readers' and that of the children who may continue to see *themselves* as 'permanently retarded readers'.

It seems therefore that some children have internalised their reading failure, so that irrespective of the benefits of an approach or programme, success will be either superficial or minimal.

Counselling itself, therefore, can perform a dual role – it can be utilised as a mode of interaction with children to create the correct therapeutic environment and state of mind to aid the fostering of skills in learning, in order to maximise the child's potential; it can also be seen as integral to the implementation of a teaching programme and conducted simultaneously with teaching. This may be seen as a counselling approach and conducted more informally than planned and progressive individual counselling.

There are some excellent self-esteem programmes available which can also be successfully utilised for dyslexic children. These include the Mosley (1996) 'circle time' activities and the White (1991) 'self-esteem' activities. These will be discussed in the next chapter, 'Curriculum Access'.

Visual Aspects

It may be useful for the teacher to consider the influence of visual aspects in the development of literacy skills. Although the research appears to lean towards phonological and linguistic areas as the principal difficulty relating to dyslexia (Stanovich *et al.*, 1997; Snowling and Nation, 1997), there is a body of opinion which highlights the visual areas and recommends strategies to help deal with such difficulties (Lovegrove, 1996; Stein, 1991, 1994; Wilkins, 1995; Irlen, 1983, 1989).

Research has been conducted on eye dominance and binocular control (Stein and Fowler, 1993) and eye tracking has also been the subject of some research (Blau and Loveless, 1982). Pavlidis (1990a) suggests that children with dyslexia have less efficient control over eye movements.

Research evidence relating to the visual magno-cellular system, which consists of large cells used for depth perception, indicates that these cells appear to be more disorganised and smaller among dyslexics (Galaburda, 1993). This would mean that stimuli would need to be delivered more slowly in order to be accurately processed.

Stein and Fowler (1993) and Stein (1994) argue that a number of children with dyslexia have binocular instability and suggest that this can be remedied through short-term use of monocular occlusion.

Bishop (1989) argues that practice in reading can develop binocular stability, but Stein and Fowler (1993) suggest this is *not* the case and that short-term use of monocular occlusion will result in binocular stability and should thus help promote significant gains in reading.

Furthermore, Cornelissen *et al.* (1994) found that children who experienced visual confusion of text during reading, because of unstable binocular control, were less likely to incorporate visual memories for letter strings into their spelling strategies, relying instead on sound-letter conversion rules, thus spelling words phonologically. This supports the view, therefore, that unstable binocular control not only affects how children read, but also how they spell.

Irlen (1990) has made claims for a scotopic sensitivity syndrome which can affect the child in terms of light sensitivity, the ability to see print clearly without distortions, the ability to perceive groups of words at the same time, and the ability to sustain focus for a period of time.

Irlen recommends the use of coloured perspex overlays or tinted lens treatment to help overcome these difficulties. The research to support this is, however, fairly patchy. Rosner and Rosner (1987) reviewed the majority of studies of the tinted lens treatment and found significant problems in experimental design and Moseley (1990) found that any significant effect of coloured overlays was due to the reduction in light rather than due to any specific colour. Studies, however, by Richardson (1988), and Wilkins (1990 and 1993) have shown some significant improvement in children using overlays and lenses, particularly in visual activity and muscle balance – and subsequent reading attainments.

Kyd, Sutherland and McGettrick (1992) used the Irlen overlays for children with specific learning difficulties and found significant improvements in reading rate. They are currently involved in follow-up studies examining the effect of the overlays on reading comprehension and accuracy. The results of this study are consistent with the preliminary findings from a project in Norfolk (Wright, 1993), which also provides impressive data for reading rate progress. Wilkins (1993, 1995), following extensive research, has developed a set of materials called Intuitive Overlays which can be used both in assessment and learning situations.

Furthermore Wilkins et al. (1996) have developed a Rate of Reading Test designed to assess the effects of coloured overlays. It is claimed this test has some advantages over conventional tests, which actually test the linguistic and semantic aspects of reading at least as much as the visual. Additionally with conventional tests performance is limited by a reader's vocabulary. The Rate of Reading test therefore seeks to minimise the linguistic and semantic aspects of reading and maximises the visual difficulties.

The same fifteen common words are used in each line in a different random order. The words were selected from the 110 most frequent words in a count of words in children's reading books. The text is printed in small typeface at an optimal level for visual distortion. The test is scored by noting the total number of words in the passage read correctly and calculating the average number correctly read per minute.

Wilkins et al. (1996) found the test both reliable and valid and it successfully predicted the individuals who when offered a coloured overlay continued to use it. They also show that the use of the overlays had an effect on reading speed, and did so immediately. The authors also report on a study by Wilkins et al. (submitted) in which 93 children in primary school, and 59 in the first year intake of a secondary school reported an improvement in perception of text with a particular colour and the 22% of the sample who continued to use them for ten months demonstrated a mean improvement of 14% in reading speed with their overlay (p < 0.02). This improvement was not seen in children who had failed to persist in using the overlay.

Mailley (1997), however, suggests that the present system of vision testing in school and community does not address the diversity of the difficulty. It seems therefore that a comprehensive visual screening procedure is necessary to identify those children at risk.

The Use of Visual Skills

It has been argued (Bell, 1991a) that although programmes directed at enhancing alphabetic and phonological skills are essential, one has to be wary of the 'cognitive cost' of such programmes – a cost which is reflected in a weakening of the gestalt, right hemispheric skills. The gestalt hemisphere is usually associated with visual imagery, creativity and comprehension.

The stress and effort which is necessary for children with dyslexia to fully engage their cognitive resources and to develop phonological skills is so great, according to Bell, that a weakening of the gestalt hemisphere results as resources are diverted from the right hemispheric functions to concentrate on the left hemispheric skills of decoding and phonological processing. Not only does this result in a restriction in the use of visual imagery but also in a stifling of the development of skills in comprehension and perhaps in creativity.

Bell has developed a programme 'Visualizing and Verbalizing for Language Comprehension and Thinking (see Fig. 38). This programme provides a comprehensive procedure for the use of visualising to promote and enhance reading and comprehension. The stages outlined by Bell include picture imagery, word imagery, single sentence, multiple sentence, whole paragraph and whole page. Additionally, the programme provides an understanding of the functions of the gestalt hemisphere and useful strategies for classroom teaching.

Motor Aspects

Russell (1988) has developed a set of graded activities for children with motor difficulties which is a very teacher-friendly text containing clearly illustrated activities. The programme consists of fourteen sections including gross motor, balancing, catching, throwing, kicking and jumping, directional orientation, visual-motor coordination and handwriting activities. These activities, though essentially directed to children with motor problems, can be extremely useful for a number of dyslexic children.

Nash-Wortham and Hunt (1993) have developed an extremely comprehensive book which contains pointers on different areas of motor difficulty such as timing and rhythm, sequencing and laterality followed by a series of exercises for each of the six pointers described.

Figure 38

SUMMARY OF WORD IMAGING

Step 3.

Objective: The student will be able to visualize and verbalize, with *detail*, a single word.

1. **Object Imaging** (optional)
   a. Object imaging is for students who have difficulty understanding what it is to image.
   b. The student looks at an object, closes eyes, recalls and describes image.

2. **Personal Imaging** (not optional but only do one or two)
   a. The student recalls images, and describes something personal but simple such as a pet, room, toy etc.
   b. The teacher questions with choice and contrast.
   c. The structure words are checked through for details and reverbalization.
   d. The teacher gives a verbal summary using the phrase: *'Your words made me picture . . .'*

3. **Known Noun Imaging** (not optional)
   a. The student visualizes and verbalizes a noun. The word should be familiar as well as high in imagery.
   b. The teacher questions specifically with choice and contrast to develop detailed imagery.
   c. The structure words are checked through for details and reverbalization.
   d. If student has been given a choice, have the student describe the image to be sure not restating or paraphrasing.
   e. Request gesturing.
   f. Conclude session with a verbal summary using the phrase: *'Your words made me picture . . .'*
   g. Practise this step until very confident.

4. **Fantasy Imaging** (optional)
   a. Begin with a 'known noun' image and interact to create fanciful, humorous images.
   b. Encourage student to create own fantasy images.

5. **Group Instruction:**
   Apply this step to small groups of 3 to 5 students. Give one word to be described by all individuals in the group. Set the task as: *All students will help create one composite image, not separate images.* Each student will take a turn visualizing and verbalizing different aspects of the word to the group. The teacher will question, choose individuals to go through 3 or 4 structure words at a time, visualize, and summarize the composite image.

---

from *Vizualizing and Verbalizing for Language Comprehension and Thinking.* (Bell, 1991b). Reproduced with kind permission

The inhibition of primitive reflexes

Blyth (1992) found that 85% of those children who have specific learning difficulties that do not respond to various classroom intervention strategies have a cluster of aberrant reflexes. He argues that as long as these reflexes remain undetected and uncorrected the educational problems will persist.

These reflexes should only be present in the very young baby and would become redundant after about six months of life. But if these reflexes continued to be present after that time, Blyth argued, the development of the mature postural reflexes is restricted and this will adversely affect writing, reading, spelling, copying, maths, attention and concentration.

Blyth and colleagues have developed a programme for assessing the presence of these reflexes, with a Reflex-Inhibition movement programme to control the primitive reflexes and release the postural reflexes. This view regarding the affect of uninhibited primitive reflexes on learning has been supported by other studies (Bender, 1976; Ayres, 1979, 1982; Mitchell, 1985; Retief 1990).

Educational Kinesiology (EK)

Educational kinesiology is a combination of applied kinesiology and traditional learning theory, although some aspects of yoga and acupressure are also evident in the recommended programme.

Kinesiology is the study of muscles and their functions and particular attention is paid to the patterns of reflex activity that link effective integration between sensory and motor responses. It has been argued (Mathews, 1993) that often children develop inappropriate patterns of responses to particular situations and that these can lock the child into inappropriate habits.

Dennison and Hargrove (1986) has produced a series of exercises (Brain Gym) from which an individual programme can be devised for the child relating to the assessment. Many of these exercises include activities which involve crossing the mid line, such as writing a figure eight in the air or cross crawling and skip-a-cross, in which hands and legs sway from side to side. The aim is to achieve some form of body balance so that information can flow freely and be processed readily.

ASSISTED LEARNING

Assisted learning approaches are essentially teaching approaches which require considerable interaction between the learner and others. This interaction may take the form of some kind of participant modelling. There may be an element of repetition and even simplicity in these approaches but, based on the principles of modelling and of facilitating the learning process, they can be successfully utilised with reading, writing and spelling.

Paired reading, peer tutoring, cued spelling and the apprenticeship approach to reading will be discussed here in relation to the concept of assisted learning and consideration will be given to the degree of effectiveness these approaches may have in helping children with specific learning difficulties.

Paired Reading

Paired reading was originally devised to meet the need for a reading approach which could be both applied generally and utilised by non-professionals with a minimum of training (Morgan, 1976).

Studies have shown (Neville, 1975; Wilkinson, 1980; Bell, 1991) that releasing children from the burden of decoding can facilitate or enhance comprehension.

This is highlighted in a study examining the decoding processes of slow readers (Curtis, 1980) which found that the cognitive applications to decoding reduced the amount of attention available for other reading processes. This resulted in deficits in comprehension of text. Emphasis, therefore, can be placed on the use of context rather than the skill of decoding, but the question remains whether poor readers are able to utilise context as successfully as proficient readers.

Clark (1988) observed an inefficient use of context among dyslexic children, although she noted that dyslexic children utilised a wide variation of strategies and preferences in an attempt to use context to aid comprehension.

Lees (1986), however, in an examination of the data from four different studies concluded that poor readers had similar capabilities to good readers in the utilisation of context to aid word recognition. Evans (1984b) reported on two studies using paired reading for dyslexic children, both of which showed significant gains in reading comprehension and vocabulary.

Topping and Lindsey (1992), therefore, argue that the evidence suggests that poor readers have an over-dependence on decoding strategies at the expense of developing skills in comprehension, using contextual cues. This is a practice reinforced by many teaching programmes which over-emphasise analytical decoding approaches, resulting in sequential decoding processes which can inhibit full use of comprehension skills. This is indeed consistent with the literature on learning styles (Carbo, 1987) which suggests that young children tend to have a preference for processing information globally rather than analytically. Yet one must be cautious of fostering global processing methods such as whole-word, at the expense of analytical methods such as phonics, since the teaching approaches which combine both these approaches are arguably more effective (Vellutino and Scanlon, 1986; Reason et al., 1988).

Paired reading may be particularly useful for children with specific learning difficulties since it provides both visual and auditory input simultaneously. It is a simple technique which focuses on the following:

- parent and child reading together
- programme to be carried out consistently
- child selects reading material
- as few distractions as possible
- use of praise as re-inforcement
- discussion of the story and pictures (see Fig. 39).

The two principal stages of paired reading are: reading together and reading alone.

- **Reading together** is when the parent/teacher and child read all the words aloud, with the adult adjusting the speed so that the pair are reading in harmony. The adult does not allow the child to become stuck at a word and if this happens will simply say the word to the child. This process, together with discussion, can help the child obtain meaning from the text and therefore enjoy the experience of language and of reading.

Figure 39: Paired reading

- **Reading alone** occurs when the child becomes more confident at reading aloud. The adult can either read more softly, thus allowing the child to take the lead, or remain quiet. This can be done gradually to allow the child's confidence to build up (Topping, 1993). When the child stumbles at this stage, the adult immediately offers the word and then continues reading with the child again, until he/she gains enough confidence to read unaided.

Topping and Lindsey (1992) report on a number of other programmes, mostly from North America, which show similarities to paired reading. One such programme is the Neurological Impress Method (NIM). This method involves the student and the instructor reading aloud together in unison. The instructor sits a little behind the student and speaks directly into the right ear of the learner. No corrections are made during or after the reading session. The method is intended for use by professionals.

There are few evaluation studies of this particular technique but an interesting comment can be made on the strategy of speaking directly into the right ear. Presumably the purpose of this is to engage the left language hemisphere, yet a study looking at sensory deprivation, and particularly auditory perception (Johanson, 1992), suggests that children with reading problems have a better left ear than right in relation to auditory discrimination.

Evaluation of paired reading as a strategy

Although it is not yet clear why exactly paired reading is an effective method of teaching reading, it has been generally well evaluated (Topping and Lindsey, 1992).

Paired reading may well help children with specific learning difficulties develop a desire to read. Clearly an adult model, either parent or teacher, can act as a good reinforcer.

Other factors have also been attributed to the success of paired reading. These include the pacing of the text which helps to regulate the child's reading flow and may help to overcome the segmentation and syllabification problems outlined by many researchers (Bradley, 1990; Snowling, 1993a, b). The fact that it is multisensory, particularly utilising the combination of visual and auditory modalities may also be significant. It may also help to provide weaker readers with a global strategy through the practice of non-interruption of the reading flow. The value of paired reading in enhancing self-image should also not be ignored. The importance of this for children with reading problems (Lawrence, 1985, 1987) is well documented in the literature.

Some other advantages of paired reading are:

- failure is not an evident factor because if the child 'sticks' at a word the adult says the word almost immediately;
- the experience of gaining enjoyment from the language of the text helps reading become pleasurable and increases the desire to read;
- children are provided with an example of how to pronounce difficult words and can simultaneously relate the auditory sound of the word with the visual appearance of that word;
- children can derive understanding from the text because words are given expression and meaning by the adult and discussion about the text follows at periodic intervals.

Thus paired reading can be useful as:

- a strategy to develop motivation and confidence in reading;
- an aid to the development of fluency and expression in reading;
- a technique which could also enhance comprehension on the part of the reader.

Paired reading, however, is seen as complementary to other strategies such as structured language teaching and phonics skills and does not attempt to replicate or replace this dimension of learning to read. However, it utilises the participation of parents and this is clearly a great advantage, both for the child and the school.

Topping (1993) sees paired reading as a strategy which can reduce the anxieties of reading for dyslexic children, reduce their all-consuming fear of failure and encourage reading practice.

The approach is essentially one which can effectively combine the psycho-linguistic aspects of the use of context with the phonic skills associated with word attack. This coupled with parent or peer support and appraisal may well account for its success.

Cued Spelling

The cued spelling technique shares the same principles as paired reading and other peer tutoring developments (Croft and Topping, 1992).

The technique comprises ten steps for learning and spelling, four points to remember and two reviews (see Fig. 40). The points to remember help to consolidate the learning and the two reviews involve a daily and a weekly review. In the daily review the speller writes all the words for the day and checks them – the wrong words are then noted and the learner goes through the ten steps again for these words.

The speller adopts the same procedure for the weekly review and identifies the wrong words. Discussion would then take place on the best approach for the learner to tackle the wrongly spelt words.

If the learner writes a word inaccurately he/she is encouraged to delete the word from memory by erasing it or boldly scoring it out. This can be particularly useful if the learner has a strong visual memory and the image of the incorrect word may remain and be recalled at some future point.

The cued spelling technique is highly interactive but aims to encourage 'self-managed' learning. The technique attempts to eliminate the fear of failure through the use of prompt correction procedures. As in paired reading, modelling and praise are integral to the application of cued spelling. According to Topping and Watt (1993) seven year old children have been successfully trained in its use in about one hour, substantial progress can be made on norm-referenced spelling tests, and improvements have been found in error rate and qualitative indicators in continuous free writing.

A number of studies support Topping and Watt's assertion regarding the merits of the technique (Emerson, 1988; Scoble, 1989; Harrison, 1989).

Figure 40:   Cued spelling: the ten steps

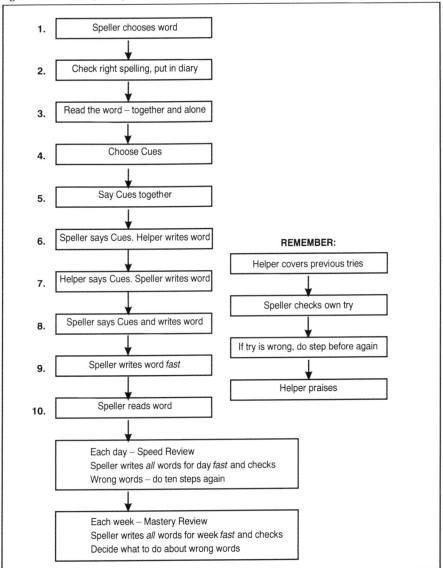

1. Speller chooses word

2. Check right spelling, put in diary

3. Read the word – together and alone

4. Choose Cues

5. Say Cues together

6. Speller says Cues. Helper writes word

7. Helper says Cues. Speller writes word

8. Speller says Cues and writes word

9. Speller writes word *fast*

10. Speller reads word

REMEMBER:

Helper covers previous tries

Speller checks own try

If try is wrong, do step before again

Helper praises

Each day – Speed Review
Speller writes *all* words for day *fast* and checks
Wrong words – do ten steps again

Each week – Mastery Review
Speller writes *all* words for week *fast* and checks
Decide what to do about wrong words

Reproduced by kind permission of Keith Topping, Centre for Paired Learning, University of Dundee
(Topping, 1992d)

Scoble (1988) describes how the technique is also used with adult literacy and provides some examples of the application of Cued Spelling in the home with spouses, parents and friends as tutors.

Oxley and Topping (1990) report on a peer-tutoring project using Cued Spelling in which eight seven and eight-year old pupils were tutored by eight nine-year-olds. The self concept as a speller of both tutees and tutors showed a significant positive shift compared to a control group.

France *et al.* (1993) demonstrate the effectiveness of Cued Spelling, particularly in the short-term, although they accept that further research on its longer-term effects is still required.

The Cued Spelling technique is relatively simple to apply and the pack includes a demonstration video.

Assisted learning implies that learning, quite rightly, is an interactive process and the role of peers and adults is of great importance. This form of learning in many ways minimises the adverse effects of failure, because if the child cannot respond to a particular text or situation then assistance is provided. The important point is, however, that assistance is not necessarily provided because the child is not succeeding, but because it is inbuilt into the reading or learning strategy. The learner, therefore, is not necessarily obtaining the sense of failing but rather of working cooperatively with another person.

This chapter has sought to describe the vast array of different types of teaching approaches which can be used with dyslexic children. It is fair to say that no one single approach holds the key to completely dealing with dyslexic difficulties and many of the programmes and strategies described in this chapter can be used together and can be complimentary to other teaching and curriculum approaches. Irrespective of the type of provision which is being used for dyslexic children, it is important that at all times every opportunity is taken to help access the full curriculum. This can present real difficulties with some dyslexic children, but this challenge can be met through careful planning, utilising the skills of teachers and being aware of the abundance of approaches and strategies available.

The next chapter will in fact focus on curriculum access and describe how many of the approaches described here can be effectively integrated within the school curriculum.

Chapter 6

Curriculum Access

Some important questions in relation to support for children with dyslexic difficulties are how can their specific needs be most effectively met within the school and the curriculum; and how can specialist teaching be most efficiently directed to help meet those needs?

The issue of specialist teaching interfacing with the mainstream curriculum is one which has been a source of concern and controversy for some time. Of particular concern is the question of the effectiveness of specialist teaching if it is divorced from the normal class curriculum, and the extent to which the gains that are made in any period of specialist teaching will be transferred to other areas of learning, thus enhancing the learner's performance in the mainstream curriculum.

Since the Warnock Report (DES, 1978), the focus has shifted from highlighting individual pupils' needs to attempting to view educational needs from the perspective of the 'community of learners'. The dilemma and the conflict arise if there is a mismatch between individual children's needs and those of the 'community of learners'. Not surprisingly with the focus on meeting the needs of all pupils, some traditional individual approaches have been difficult to implement. This, according to Bradshaw (1990), has led to a loss of the benefits of these approaches to pupils with specific learning difficulties.

This chapter will present some different approaches and initiatives which can be suitable for all children but may be particularly suitable for dyslexic children. These include initiatives such as Reading Projects and Thinking Skills programmes and approaches involving metacognitive aspects, circle time activities, differentiation and planned whole school policies and programmes.

READING PROJECTS

There have been a number of promising reading projects which have adopted a whole school, indeed whole community approach to literacy. Carefully planned these projects can ideally serve the needs of dyslexic children and their families. Some highly acclaimed projects are detailed below.

Reading in Partnership Project

This project commenced in 1992 in Sunderland and is still continuing in 1998. The principal aim of the project is to increase the level of reading competence of all children in year 3 at primary school. One of the important aspects of any major reading initiative is to ensure that it does not place an extra burden on the teaching staff. Careful planning therefore is necessary to prevent this. In Sunderland this was achieved through a funding programme to cover the replacement of teachers working on the project and a rolling programme was established of teachers within a school working on the project on a yearly basis. The teachers involved in the project benefited from intensive training and additional resources.

The intensive training for the teachers involved in the project included a course on assessing childrens reading difficulties, using information technology to support literacy; recording progress and meeting individual needs; language and communication difficulties; teaching strategies; raising self-esteem and specific learning difficulties in reading.

This programme alone provides a good example of how preparations can be made to meet dyslexic children's needs within a whole school literacy framework.

Throughout its existence the project has developed a number of exciting initiatives linked to the community. This has involved schemes to encourage parents and children to read together, one such scheme involved the active participation of the local newspaper and another the local libraries. Another of the successes of the project was the encouragement of local volunteers to become involved with the schools.

This project has successfully stimulated a community interest in reading and by doing so emphasised that literacy difficulties need to be dealt with at an early age. The overall ethos of the project helps all children achieve some degree of success in literacy. Dyslexic children in particular benefit from this in terms of enhanced training of teaching staff, additional resources, developed links between home and school and early intervention. This type of initiative can clearly help to minimise the effects of literacy difficulties.

Knowsley Reading Project – Using Trained Reading Helpers Effectively

This project Brooks *et al.* (1996) aimed to raise the overall standard of pupils reading in the borough by utilising a number of different strategies. In general the project resulted in a combined effort from parents, relatives and teachers. Increased individual support was given to pupils which meant supporting the development of reading throughout primary and secondary education, training teachers and other volunteers, providing the right sort of books for classroom libraries and home reading, helping pupils to choose books and assessing progress more effectively.

The project achieved considerable successes in increasing literacy standards of the children involved. In 1995 over 40 schools had joined the reading project and an evaluation of the impact of the project on 356 pupils from year 5 to year 6 was conducted (Brooks *et al.*, 1996). The results of the evaluation showed that the project was extremely effective with reading levels substantially improved with an accompanying rise in positive reading attitudes and habits. The evaluation cited an average of a 20-month improvement in reading age during a one-year period.

The project achieved its results through a carefully planned programme which involved setting up a training course on teaching techniques in reading, establishing a system for teachers, volunteers and pupils to record and monitor progress, and forming a support network of teachers, local councillors, school governors and members of the support services.

The project succeeded in substantially increasing the amount of individual attention pupils received with their reading – the key to improvement according to the evaluation report (NFER, 1996). Some of the reading strategies which helped pupils were older pupils reading to younger pupils, taking part in special reading activities, for example, special book collections, researching topics and providing a wider choice of books for class libraries and reading at home. One of the successes was also the interaction and mutual help offered between teachers and volunteers; indeed the evaluation report indicated but this was 'the main factor associated with the effectiveness of the Project' (p. 27). The continual monitoring of progress throughout the project also ensured that those pupils with considerable literacy difficulties would be identified and that their needs would be addressed within the project.

Newcastle Literacy Collaborative

The Newcastle literacy collaborative (Hunt, 1996) is essentially a community-based initiative. A joint collaboration between the Newcastle City Council and the Newcastle Library Trust it aims to raise standards and promote literacy for enjoyment and achievement in the Newcastle area. The collaborative have organised community reading and writing events for all ages including creative writing projects; additional support to schools to foster work with parents and in-service education for Newcastle education authority staff. There has also been liaison with youth and community workers to ensure that literacy is not just a school-based task, but one which can provide fun and enjoyment after school.

Whole-school policy

What is meant by whole-school dimensions or whole-school policies? Clearly they embrace an acceptance of the needs of all children within the school and furthermore an acceptance that the responsibility for certain pupils does not reside exclusively with some trained specialists, but rather that responsibility for all pupils rests with all staff under the direction of a school management team. These appear to be aims consistent with those of the leading projects described above.

The implications of these aims are two-fold. Firstly, identification and assessment procedures need to be established and monitored to ensure that children who may present specific learning difficulties, even in a mild form, are identified at an early stage. Secondly, the school needs to be resourced in terms of teaching materials and training of staff to ensure the educational needs of children with specific learning difficulties are effectively met. As these children progress through the school it is important that each new teacher they meet has at least some training and understanding of specific learning difficulties/dyslexia. Additionally, the school will need to possess a teacher with a high degree of specialist training to complement the class teacher input and to provide consultancy and training to staff and management.

THE CURRICULUM

Curricular aspects can promote whole-school involvement and interaction. There are a number of examples of teaching and learning programmes which involve every child in the school. Examples of this include self-esteem programmes, such as the Circle Time Programme (White, 1991) which can be undertaken by every teacher and every child in the school, at the same time. The content, aims and outcomes of this are, therefore, the same for all.

The White (1991) programme is essentially a resource pack which puts forward ideas and suggestions which can be used with whole classes or groups. The activities promote cooperation and communication between children and encourage sensitivity and awareness of others. Mosley (1996) has also produced a highly acclaimed circle time programme with a whole school perspective. This contains a range of activities which can be integrated into the school day following a short teacher training course. It is essential that the emotional needs and self-esteem of dyslexic children are not forgotten and programmes such as these are ideal for ensuring this within a whole-class activity.

Thinking skills programmes provide another example of a piece of work which can be undertaken by all, irrespective of a child's particular skills or abilities (De Bono, 1986; Blagg et al., 1988). These involve children in decision making and problem solving activities without having to read long instructions. Essentially the programme has a minimal amount of reading thus the dyslexic child can participate virtually on the same terms as other children in the class. Indeed dyslexic children can often show skills in problem solving and creativity (West, 1991).

There are also some good examples of differentiation (Barthorpe and Visser, 1991; Dodds, 1996) which in fact lend themselves to an assessment of the individual child as a learner and the most appropriate learning styles and strategies for that particular child.

SECONDARY SCHOOL DIMENSIONS

Consultancy

The secondary school is usually considerably larger than the primary school, and pupils are seen by many different teachers throughout the school day. In some cases because of the sheer numbers of pupils, teachers may take some time to become familiar with the abilities and difficulties presented by their pupils. Learning support staff, however, are usually in a better position to identify and recognise the pupils' strengths and weaknesses and it is, therefore, of considerable importance that sufficient time is allocated to consultation, not only between learning support staff and subject teachers, but between teachers in different subjects. In this way teachers can obtain a more complete picture of the pupil.

A good account of this which highlights the whole school approach of a team of specialist teachers is given by Blair *et al.* (1996). The principle features of the approach described by Blair and colleagues are featured in the aims of the team which include the need to be seen as a whole school resource, provision of individual specialist help to pupils; the development of a whole school policy for approprite learning and to act as a source of information on pupils, the curriculum, teaching styles and methodology and to circulate that information to subject departments and teachers.

Preparation for Examinations

Examinations and the examination system do not naturally favour the dyslexic student. Factors such as writing within a time limit, reading under pressure and recalling information almost instantly, are usually those the dyslexic child finds difficult. The help which can be provided, such as a 'reader' to read the script, or a scribe, can be useful, but requires considerable preparation and practice. Such forms of aid should not be provided only at examination time. The student would need to become familiar with this form of help if it were to be seriously considered. This emphasises that preparation for examinations and special concessions should begin virtually as soon as the pupil enters secondary school.

It is important, therefore, that dyslexic students are known, not only to specialist teachers but to all subject teachers, since the type of examination help required will vary from subject to subject. Identifying students for examination concessions, and helping to maximise the benefits of these concessions should, therefore, be seen as a whole-school issue. Administrative structures, therefore, need to be in place to monitor these arrangements. This may include a school sub-group, preferably involving the school psychologist, guidance teacher, management, support and some subject teachers. The function of such a group would be to discuss students who may need special arrangements, and how these could be effectively implemented within the school system. It is important that dyslexic students are not unduly restricted because of the nature of the school examination system, and that *all* their abilities are assessed *equally* and not only their performances in the area of literacy.

Primary/Secondary Liaison

This is an extremely important aspect. Primary–secondary transfer is by its very nature a period which can affect pupil's self-esteem and general confidence (Reid, 1986). Dyslexic pupils can be extremely vulnerable at this point. It is, therefore, extremely important that early and effective liaison between primary and secondary schools takes place.

It is acknowledged that there are some practical constraints in relation to this, but time-tabling and school policy should recognise the need to allow key members of staff sufficient flexibility to allow for effective liaison. Such liaison should commence as early as possible during the school year prior to transfer. This would allow, for example, some key staff from the secondary school an opportunity to monitor the progress of the dyslexic pupil throughout the final year at primary. This is clearly preferable to being handed a report, even a comprehensive one, just before transfer takes place. Early liaison allows the secondary staff to build up a picture of the pupil; begin to plan and prepare subject teachers in the secondary school to deal with the kinds of difficulties presented; and to report on the progress and strategies employed during the final year at primary school.

METACOGNITIVE ASPECTS

Metacognition, which essentially means thinking about thinking, has an important role in how children learn and can be a vital tool to help dyslexic children make reading more meaningful and help in the transfer of learning from one situation to another. Flavell (1979) greatly influenced the field of metacognition and its applications to the classroom. Since then many studies have been conducted in metacognition and various models developed. Brown *et al.* (1986) provide a model containing four main variables which are found in the learning situation. These include:

- **Text** – i.e. the material to be learnt
- **Task** – the purpose of reading
- **Strategies** – how the learner understands and remembers information
- **Characteristics of the learner** – prior experience, background knowledge, interests, motivation

It is important that each of these factors is considered in the teaching of reading. Clearly the text needs to be meaningful and motivating to the reader. The top ten books children like to read from an evaluation of the Knowsley Project (described earlier in this chapter) are shown in Fig. 41.

Figure 41:   1995 top ten books children like to read (N=356 9–10 year olds)

	%
Ghost/horror/supernatural	45
Magazines	40
Joke books	32
Sport	28
Adventure stories	27
Animal stories	21
Comics	21
School stories	16
Mystery	16
Fairy tales	16

Reproduced from NFER (1996) with permission

The task, the purpose of reading, is extremely important and needs to relate to the interest level of the text. Strategies, particularly for dyslexic children, can be of extreme importance as these can make the difference between the text being meaningful or not. Strategies will be discussed more fully in the section on learning styles and study skills and the importance of prior experience, previous knowledge and other characteristics of the learner are highlighted in Chapter 2, 'The Acquisition of Literacy'. These show how background knowledge and pre-reading discussion are vital prerequisites for a meaningful reading experience.

In relation to direct instruction in metacognition Rowe (1988) sees three aspects of importance. These are:

- Children's knowledge of their metacognitive activity, which can be achieved through thinking aloud as they perform particular tasks.
- The encouragement of conscious awareness of cognitive activity such as self-questioning, e.g. Have I done this before? How did I do it? Is this the best way to tackle this problem?
- The encouragement of control over learning. To develop particular strategies for dealing with a task, whether it be reading, spelling or creative writing.

Wray (1994) reports on an interesting study by Ekwall and Ekwall (1989) which defines differences between good and poor readers. The researchers suggest that the main difference is in fact related to comprehension monitoring behaviour. For example, good readers generate questions while they read; are able to transfer what they read into mental images; re-read if necessary and actively comprehend while they read.

Poor readers on the other hand lack a clear purpose of reading; view reading as essentially a decoding task and seldom re-read or actively comprehend while they read. Tregaskes and Daines (1989) report on some metacognitive strategies such as visual imagery, obtaining the main ideas from text, developing concepts through strategies such as mind maps or webbing and self-questioning which attempts to relate previous knowledge with the new material to be learned. It is important that dyslexic students are encouraged to use these metacognitive strategies, otherwise they may become too entrenched in the actual process of reading rather than in the meaning and purpose of the activity.

Wray (1994) suggests that teachers should teach metacognitive strategies directly, and always within the context of meaningful experiences, for example, within children's project work. Cue cards which contain ideas for thinking aloud are also suggested as being useful to stimulate self-questioning during creative writing.

Metacognition therefore should be an integral part of the learning process and, to be an effective component, it should be embedded within the curriculum and within curricular activities.

LEARNING STYLES

The acquisition of a successful learning style and of appropriate processes for learning is an important determinant of how successfully the curriculum can be accessed by students.

It is, therefore, rather surprising that the actual processes involved in learning have not been afforded a higher profile within the curriculum and in the education system in general. Certainly, educational thinking has moved considerably away from advocating a content-driven curriculum with its aim of filling the student with knowledge, and from the presupposition that if the student had the ability the content would be retained, and if not it would need to be recycled into a simpler 'watered down' form. Although educational reforms have helped to steer a course away from such a dilution of the curriculum, there arguably and unfortunately remains a tendency, or at least a risk, that this may still be offered to dyslexic learners.

The reasons for this are twofold. Firstly, the difficulties of dyslexic learners may be undiagnosed or mis-diagnosed and consequently their skills and abilities may be overlooked. Secondly, the pressures inherent in teaching children with severe literacy problems may prevent teachers from focusing on the learning process as, perhaps understandably, they will harbour a preoccupation with improving attainments. As a result it is more likely that teachers will look for a solution to a severe literacy difficulty through curriculum and resources approaches rather than a detailed analysis of the learning processes and learning style of the child. That is not to say that these points are overlooked entirely – they are most certainly not, and may in some cases determine the teacher's decision to use a particular programme or approach.

The Process of Learning

What does one mean when using the term 'process of learning'? There are three principal elements to learning: the input, the cognition and the output (see Fig. 42). The input can be absorbed in various forms, for example: by hearing or speaking; seeing events, print or illustrations; writing or experiencing through whole-body activities. The cognition is when the material is undergoing some

Figure 42

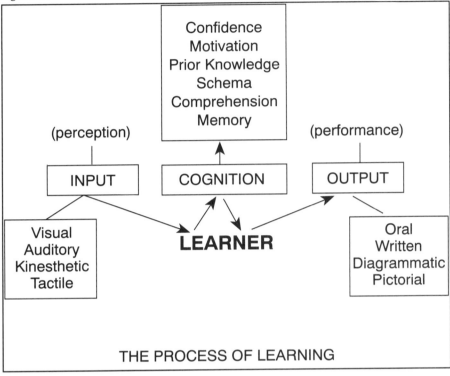

THE PROCESS OF LEARNING

form of change as the learner attempts to make sense of it; and the output indicates the level of understanding which the learner has achieved with the new material. Consideration needs to be given to the learner and the learning style at all stages of these processes. This is particularly important for dyslexic learners as they can display particular difficulty in the input and output stages and this can influence the 'cognition' process, thus preventing the learner from obtaining a full understanding of the learning task.

In order that the dyslexic child can effectively access the curriculum it is important that these three dimensions are matched to the learner – a mismatch would obviously result in increased stress being placed on the learner with an accompanying degree of demotivation and possible task failure. There is no one single recipe for success. All of the modes of input of information are important in learning, although very young children are inclined to respond best to input of a tactile or kinaesthetic nature, and not necessarily of a visual or auditory nature, indeed very few students prefer learning by listening. It is necessary, therefore, to consider each child individually in relation to the components of the learning process; individual preferences may be evident and these will influence the success or otherwise of both teaching and learning.

Figure 43

Learning Styles Model
Designed by Dr Rita Dunn and Dr Kenneth Dunn

Reproduced with permission (Dunn and Dunn, 1993)

The Concept of Learning Style

Learning style is a broad term to describe those factors which influence all aspects of learning. This is summarised in the extract below:

> Learning styles are characteristic, cognitive, affective and physiological behaviours that serve as relatively stable indicators of how learners perceive, interact with, and respond to the learning environment.   (NASSP (1979) quoted in Keefe (1987))

According to this definition, learning style encompasses a broad perspective incorporating cognitive style as well as the physiological/environmental factors and affective/emotional considerations of learning. Thus the three elements considered in Fig. 42 are all incorporated into the learning styles framework. It is therefore crucial that in dealing with dyslexic learners, both in assessment and in teaching, factors associated with learning style are taken into consideration.

Keefe (1987) proposes a three-dimensional view of learning styles incorporating cognitive, affective and physiological aspects. The cognitive dimension includes modality preferences, attention, automisation, memory processes and concept development; the affective dimension includes personality variables which can influence learning such as persistence and perseverance, frustration and tolerance, curiosity, locus of control, achievement motivation, risk taking, cautiousness, competition, cooperation, reaction to reinforcement and personal interests; the physiological dimension includes sex related behaviour, health-related behaviour, time of day rhythms, need for mobility and environmental elements. These dimensions and elements have been the focus of considerable research and applied models have been developed. One of the most widely used and well researched models, developed by Rita and Kenneth Dunn, is illustrated in Fig. 43. This model is one of the most popular and widely accepted models of learning styles. It has been the subject of extensive research (Dunn and Dunn, 1992).

Given (1996) skilfully merged several approaches to personality and learning styles into one comprehensive model for teaching and learning. Her model used Dunn and Dunn's (1993) five learning style domains for the structural framework. Within this structure she includes personality types as first articulated by Carl Jung and later organised by David Kolb (1984) and Susan Dellinger (1989). The five major personality types Given developed (Fig. 44) define the predominant ways individuals react to the world – by intuition, empathy, analysis, ambition, or inquiry. Intuition falls in the emotional domain, empathy in the sociological domain, analysis is representative of the psychological domain, ambition which suggests movement and action falls in the physiological domain, and enquiry, because it is conducted within an environment, represents the environmental domain.

Given calls the merged styles 'areas of influence' because each area is interdependent with and influences all other areas. When individual personality types and learning styles are accepted, habit formation for life-long learning is nurtured such as the habits of self-determined learning, collaborative learning, intentional learning, self-managed learning and reflective learning. When they are

Figure 44

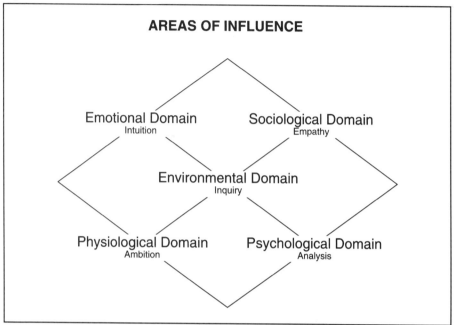

Reproduced by kind permission of Barbara Given (Personal Correspondence, 1995)

Figure 45

| |
| Planning learning style-based instruction involves several steps: |
| 1. Diagnosing individual learning styles |
| 2. Profiling class or group tendencies and preferences |
| 3. Determining significant group strengths and weaknesses |
| 4. Examining subject content for areas that may create problems for learners with weak skills. |
| 5. Analysing student prior achievement scores and other products (curriculum-referenced tests, skill tests, portfolios, etc.) for patterns of weakness that may reflect cognitive skill deficiencies |
| 6. Augmenting (remediating weak cognitive skills) |
| 7. Assessing current instructional methods to determine whether they are adequate or require more flexibility |
| 8. Modifying the learning environment and developing personalized learning experiences. |

From Keefe J. (1991) *Learning Style: Cognitive and Thinking Skills*

ignored or left to chance, individuals learn in a trial and error, hit and miss fashion which tends to result in low self-esteem, intolerance and negativism, limited achievement, lethargy and depressed interest in learning. Given states that a learning environment that honours individual personality and learning styles and one that fosters corresponding learning habits allows each person to reach his or her fullest potential in all five interconnected areas.

The learning styles research suggests that consideration of learning styles within teaching programmes and the curriculum can help students 'learn how to learn' and that 'at risk' students such as those weak in analytic and discrimination skills can learn to control their learning and thus process information more efficiently and effectively.

Keefe (1991) suggests that teachers planning learning styles based on instruction should follow the steps outlined in Fig. 45.

Learning Styles and Dyslexia

Multisensory strategies are used widely in the teaching of dyslexic children. The evidence suggests that the effectiveness of these strategies is based largely on the provision of at least one mode of learning with which the learner feels comfortable. Thus, if the learner has a difficulty dealing with information by way of the auditory channel, this could perhaps be compensated for through the use of the visual channel. The use of such compensatory strategies is well documented in the literature and is a feature of teaching programmes for dyslexic children. It is logical therefore that consideration of the learner as an individual should be extended to a holistic appreciation of the learner's individual style. Factors such as affective and physiological characteristics will have some bearing on how the dyslexic child responds to the learning situation, and a holistic perspective should therefore be applied both in assessment and teaching of dyslexic children.

Looking at, for example, the Dunn and Dunn learning styles model, one can recognise how the elements identified can influence the performances of dyslexic learners. It must be appreciated that dyslexic learners are first and foremost learners, and like any other learners will be influenced by different conditions. Some dyslexic students therefore, will prefer a 'silent' environment for concentration while others may need some auditory stimuli, perhaps even music, in order to maximise concentration and performance. Similarly, with 'light' – individual preferences such as dim light and bright light should be recognised.

In relation to emotional variables, two of the elements, responsibility and structure, should certainly be addressed. It has been well documented that dyslexic learners benefit from imposed structure – most of the teaching programmes recognise this and follow a highly structured formula. At the same time, however, taking responsibility for one's own learning can be highly motivating and generate success – dyslexic learners therefore should not be deprived of the opportunity to take responsibility as some may possess a natural preference for responsibility and structure.

In relation to global and analytic preferences dyslexic students, like other learners, will display differences. Carbo et al., (1986) showed how most primary aged children are more global than analytic, but much of the teaching, including reading programmes, has a tendency to be analytic. It is thus important that if an analytic reading scheme such as a phonic, structured and sequential approach is used it must be balanced by global activities such as creative work, language experience and visual imagery.

Dunn and Dunn's model identifies five principal characteristics and twenty-one elements, all of which affect student learning (see Fig. 43). It is hypothesised that all these elements have to be considered during the assessment process and in subsequent planning of teaching.

Deschler and Schumaker (1987) discuss the creation of a 'strategic environment' in the classroom. This involves the teacher performing classroom tasks such as giving directions, reviewing assignments, giving feedback, classroom organisation and classroom management in a 'strategic' fashion. The creation of such an environment is helped by, for example, the teacher thinking aloud when discussing problems, so that students can understand some of the processes and strategies which a good learner uses in solving problems.

For example, Deschler and Schumaker describe how the use of such metacognitive strategies may be achieved. They suggest the teacher may start by analysing the problem, then a specific cognitive strategy might be selected to deal with the problem; perhaps referring to previous knowledge, but this may then be rejected when the teacher realises that it is inadequate to solve the problem, another strategy would then be selected; its effectiveness would be monitored and finally a self-coping statement would be generated regarding the teacher's ability to deal with the problem. This complete process would be a public one with the teacher thinking aloud. This would enable students to cue in to the teacher's strategies and encourage, not necessarily the replication of the teacher's strategies, but the student's own metacognitive thinking.

This example helps to highlight the link between metacognition (learning how to learn) and (learning styles) one's learning preferences. Clearly, it begs the question of whether one should be manipulating students' learning preferences to suit an appropriate learning situation. Nevertheless the teacher has a responsibility to help identify both preferred and appropriate learning styles and encourage and develop these in students. This is particularly the case for dyslexic learners who may become so 'hooked' into the learning aspects which cause them to fail, such as the difficulty with decoding, that they fail to develop or utilise other avenues of learning. The decoding difficulty effectively blocks the development and awareness of their learning skills and this requires recognition and consideration by the teacher so that s/he can help the student recognise and develop a learning style and learning skill. This is particularly important as it should be recognised that it is just as appropriate to learn to read by **decoding**, as it is by **recognising** words that have become familiar, as it is to learn new words through a **kinaesthetic** floor game, as it is to learn through **tactile** resources.

The important point is that all children can learn to read *initially* through their learning style which can subsequently be reinforced by the deployment of other strategies, thus allowing other skills to be developed. Competence in decoding, therefore, may be one of the *additional* skills rather than the *initial* one, since it would be difficult for dyslexic children to acquire this skill in the beginning stages of reading. In support of this viewpoint Dunn (1992) contends that the strategy of decoding appears to be the best for analytic auditory learners; linguistics is most successful with analytic visuals, and whole language is most successful with global auditory and visual learners. It is important to match the method and the child's strong preferences (Sullivan, 1993).

Learning Styles Assessment

Students' learning styles can be assessed using questionnaires (Dunn, Dunn and Price, 1975–1989) and through observational strategies (Reid, 1992). In relation to the former, several instruments have been developed to identify individual students' learning styles (Canfield and Lafferty, 1970; Dunn, Dunn and Price, 1975; Gregorc, 1985; Hill, 1964; Keefe *et al.*, 1986). Most of these measure one or two elements on a bipolar continuum. Three instruments – the Learning Style Profile (Keefe *et al.*, 1986), Cognitive Style Mapping (Hill, 1964), the Learning Style Inventory (LSI) (Dunn, Dunn and Price, 1975, 1979, 1985, 1987, 1989), and its Primary Version (Perrin, 1983) are considered comprehensive in nature; that is, they assess multiple elements in combination with each other. The LSI (Dunn, Dunn and Price, 1977–1989) is a comprehensive and widely used assessment instrument in elementary and secondary schools.

The Learning Styles Inventory directs students to 'answer the questions as if you are describing how you concentrate when you are studying difficult academic material'. The instrument can be completed in approximately 30 to 40 minutes by elementary and secondary students. After answering all the questions on the LSI answer form (the test itself), each student's answer sheet is optically read and processed individually. Each student then receives his/her own LSI individual printout – a graphic representation of the conditions in which each learns most efficiently.

STUDY SKILLS

Study skills are an essential component of any programme which aims to access the curriculum for dyslexic children. There is some evidence that dyslexic children require particular help in this area principally, due to their organisational problems. A well-constructed study skills programme therefore is essential and can do much to enhance concept development, metacognitive awareness, transfer of learning and success in the classroom.

Such programmes will vary with the age and stage of the learner. A study skills programme for primary children would be different from that which may help students cope with examinations at secondary level. Well developed study skills habits at the primary stage can provide a sound foundation for tackling new material in secondary school and help equip the student for examinations. Some of the principal factors in a study skills programme which will be discussed in this section include the following:

- communication skills
- transfer of knowledge and skills
- mapping and visual skills
- memory skills.

Communication Skills

Communication skills is a fairly general term and relates to those aspects of study skills governing oral and written communication. Some of the factors which influence such skills include:

- organisation
- sequencing
- context
- schemata development
- confidence and motivation

Organisation

Children with specific learning difficulties/dyslexia may require help to organise their thoughts. A structure should therefore be developed to help encourage this. It may not be enough to ask children, for example, on completion of a story, 'What was the story about?' They need to be provided with a structure in order to elicit correct responses. This helps with the organisation of responses (output) which in turn can help to organise learning through comprehension (input). A structure which the teacher might use to elicit organised responses may include:

- What was the title?
- Who were the main characters?
- Describe the main characters.
- What did the main characters try to do?
- Who were the other characters in the story?
- What was the story about?
- What was the main part of the story?
- How did the story end?

In this way a structure is provided for the learner to retell the story. Moreover, the learner will be organising the information into a number of components such as 'characters', 'story', 'conclusion'. This will not only make it easier for the learner to retell orally, but will help to give him/her an organisational framework which will facilitate the retention of detail. The learner will also be using a strategy which can be used in other contexts. This will help with the new learning and the retention of new material.

Sequencing

Dyslexic children may have some difficulty in re-telling a story or giving information orally in the correct sequence. It is important that sequencing of information should be encouraged and exercises which help facilitate this skill can be developed. Thus, in the re-telling of a story, children should be provided with a framework which can take account of sequence of events. Such a framework could include:

- How did the story start?
- What happened after that?
- What was the main part?
- How did it end?

Various exercises, such as the use of games, can be developed to help facilitate sequencing skills.

Contextual aspects are also important elements in acquiring study skills techniques. Context can be used to help the learner in both the sequencing and organisation of materials as well as in providing an aid to comprehension.

Context can be in the form of syntactic and semantic context. In study skills, semantic context can be particularly valuable as a learning and memory aid. If the learner is using or relying on semantic context, this provides some indication that the material is being read and learnt with some understanding. The context can therefore help to:

- retain information and aid recall;
- enhance comprehension;
- transfer learning to other situations.

Schemata Development

The development of schemata helps the learner organise and categorise information. It also ensures the utilisation of background knowledge. This can aid comprehension and recall.

When children read a story or a passage, they need to relate this to their existing framework of knowledge – i.e. their own schema. So when coming across new knowledge, learners try to fit it into their existing framework of knowledge based on previous learning, which is the schema they possess for that topic or piece of information. It is important for the teacher to find out how developed a child's schema is on a particular topic, before providing more and new information. Being aware of this will help the teacher ensure the child develops appropriate understanding of the new information. Thus some key points about the passage could help the reader understand the information more readily and provide a framework into which the reader can slot ideas and meaning from the passage. Schemata, therefore, can help the learner:

- attend to the incoming information;

- provide a scaffolding for memory;
- make inferences from the passage which also aid comprehension and recall;
- utilise his/her previous knowledge.

There are a number of strategies which can help in the development of schemata. An example of this can be seen in an examination of a framework for a story. In such a framework two principal aspects can be discerned.

- The structure of the story.
- The details related to the components of the structure.

The **structure** of a story can be seen in the following components:

- background
- context
- characters
- beginning
- main part
- events
- conclusion

The **details** which may relate to these components can be recalled by asking appropriate questions. Taking the background as an example, one can see how appropriate questioning can help the learner build up a schema to facilitate understanding of the rest of the story.

- What was the weather like?
- Where did the story take place?
- Describe the scene.
- What were the main colours?

Previous Learning

Schemata depend to a great extent on the learner's previous knowledge. It can, therefore, be useful to provide the learner with cues or information relating to the story, before it has been read. In this way the learner is able to select and modify schemata of his own which will help to predict the material to be read and so help it become meaningful. The example of Fig. 46 illustrates this point. The passage can be read with the existing schemata one may possess in relation to 'lunch', 'school' and 'holiday camp'. The words servers and board would refer to the people serving the food and the menu board.

Figure 46

LUNCH AT THE SCHOOL HOLIDAY CAMP

Everyone was rushing around. Time was running out fast. The servers were looking around but most people were looking at the board. It seemed to be a repeat of yesterday and naturally Tom and Jane were disappointed.

If, however, the title was different and read 'Rain stops play again in mixed doubles' the meaning would be entirely different because the reader would use a different set of schemata (see Fig. 47). In this case the servers would be the tennis players whose turn it was to serve and the board would refer to the scoreboard.

Figure 47

RAIN STOPS PLAY AGAIN IN MIXED DOUBLES
Everyone was rushing around. Time was running out fast. The servers were looking around but most people were looking at the board. It seemed to be a repeat of yesterday and naturally Tom and Jane were disappointed.

If the passage was given *without* a title this could lead to confusion and misconception regarding the text. It is important therefore to provide the learner with a set of cues, such as the title and some key ideas about the text *before* the reading is tackled.

Background Knowledge

Background knowledge is an important aid to comprehension. It is postulated that background knowledge in itself is insufficient to facilitate new learning, but must be skilfully interwoven with the new material which is being learnt. It is important that the learner is able to use the new information in different and unfamiliar situations. Hence the connections between the reader's background knowledge and the new information must be highlighted in order for the learner to incorporate the new knowledge in a meaningful manner.

The ideas contained in a text therefore must be linked in some way to the reader's background knowledge and that the ideas need to be presented in a coherent and sequential manner. Such coherence and sequencing of ideas at the learning stage not only allows the material to be retained and recalled, but also facilitates effective comprehension. Being aware of the learner's prior knowledge therefore of a lesson is of fundamental importance. Before embarking on new material prior knowledge can be linked with the new ideas, in order to pave the way for effective study techniques and strategies to enhance comprehension and recall.

Confidence and Motivation

Confidence and motivation are important for effective studying. Study skills programmes can help achieve this by:

- Enabling the student to succeed.

  It is important that the learner meets with some initial success – success builds on success and early and significant success is an important factor when new material is being learnt.

- Provision of tasks unrelated to the learning which is taking place.

    Through the provision of tasks, even simple ones such as 'fetching a ruler', the learner can feel more at ease and prepared to tackle the new material with more confidence and motivation.

- Encouraging independent thinking.

    It is important to help promote independent thinking. Being able to make decisions and come to conclusions without too much direction from the teacher can instil confidence in a learner, and help to motivate the learner to tackle new material.

Some thinking skills programmes such as Somerset Thinking Skills and the CORT programme devised by Edward De Bono can not only help to achieve enhancement in thinking skills, but can also help students to use these skills by helping them to structure their own studying. This can help to develop appropriate study habits and maximise retention and transfer.

Transfer of Knowledge and Skills

A key aspect of effective study skills training is the transfer of skills to other curriculum areas. A number of studies support the view that to achieve this great importance must be given to the context in which learning takes place (Nisbet and Shucksmith, 1986). Study skills, therefore, should be integrated into day-to-day teaching in a meaningful context, and not as a separate area of the curriculum. Nisbet and Shucksmith criticise the study skills movement for being too general, too removed from context, and in many cases merely consisting of a collection of 'tips' for coping with specific difficulties. To overcome these pitfalls it is necessary to teach study skills within some theoretical or thematic perspective such as schemata theory or reciprocal teaching, in order that applicability to the wider curriculum and transfer of skills can be achieved (Brown, 1993).

Reciprocal teaching refers to a procedure which both monitors and enhances comprehension by focusing on processes relating to questioning, clarifying, summarising and predicting (Palincsar and Brown, 1984). It is an interactive process. Brown (1993) describes the procedure for reciprocal teaching in the following way:

> The teacher leads discussion by asking questions . . . this generates additional questions from participants, the questions are then clarified by teacher and participants together. The discussion is then summarised by teacher or participants, then a new 'teacher' is selected by the participants to lead the discussion on the next section of the text.

This procedure can be referred to as scaffolding, in which a 'scaffold' or supports are built to develop the understanding of text. This may be in the form of the teacher either providing the information or generating appropriate responses through questioning and clarifying. The supports are then withdrawn

gradually, when the learner has achieved the necessary understanding to continue with less support.

Cudd and Roberts (1994) observed that poor readers were not automatically
making the transfer from book language to their own writing. As a result the
students' writing lacked the precise vocabulary and varied syntax which was
evident during reading. To overcome this difficulty Cudd and Roberts introduced a scaffolding technique to develop both sentence sense and vocabulary.
They focused on sentence expansion by using vocabulary from the children's
readers, and using these as sentence stems encouraged sentence expansion. Thus
the procedure used involved:

- selection of vocabulary from basal reader;
- embedding this vocabulary into sentence stems;
- selecting particular syntactic structures to introduce the stem;
- embedding the targeted vocabulary into sentence stems to produce complex
  sentences;
- discussing the sentence stems, including the concepts involved;
- completing a sentence using the stems;
- repeating the completed sentence providing oral reinforcement of both the
  vocabulary and the sentence structure;
- encouraging the illustration of some of their sentences, helping to give the
  sentence a specific meaning.

Cudd and Roberts have found that this sentence expansion technique
provides a 'scaffold' for children to help develop their sentence structure and
vocabulary. Preliminary examination of writing samples of the students has
revealed growth in vocabulary choice and sentence variety. The children,
including those with reading and writing difficulties, were seen to gain better
control over the writing process and gained confidence from using their own
ideas and personal experiences.

Transfer of skills can best be achieved when emphasis is firmly placed on the
process of learning and not the product. This encourages children to reflect on
learning and encourages the learner to interact with other learners and with the
teacher. In this way effective study skills can help to activate learning and provide the student with a structured framework for effective learning.

Nisbet and Shucksmith describe one example of such a framework which
focuses on preparation, planning and reflection.

Preparation looks at the goals of the current work and how these goals relate
to previous work. Planning looks at the skills and information necessary in order
to achieve these goals, and the reflection aspect assesses the quality of the final
piece of work, asking such questions as, 'What did the children learn from the
exercise and to what extent could the skills gained be transferred to other areas?'

This example displays a structure from which it is possible to plan and
implement a studies skills programme, and at the same time evaluate its
effectiveness in relation to the extent of transfer of knowledge and skills to
other curricular areas.

Mapping and Visual Skills

Learners with specific difficulties usually have orientation problems which can be evident in directional confusion (Miles and Miles, 1991). This aspect, even though it may not directly affect every aspect of the curriculum, can lead to loss of confidence which *can* permeate work in other areas.

To what extent can the teacher help to promote and enhance visual and orientation skills in children with specific difficulties?

According to the principles of skill transfer (Nisbet and Shucksmith, 1986) it is important that such enhancement takes place within the curriculum and is contextualised within a meaningful task. Games or specific exercises in mapping and orientation can help to build up confidence in the learner but there is some uncertainty as to whether such exercises, in isolation, would have a significant skill enhancement effect, and so it is important to use directional and visual cues as much as possible within the context of the curriculum. It may be advantageous therefore to develop specific exercises from materials the learner is using and to focus particularly on visual cues and directional aspects.

For example, if the student is working on a thematic study of the Romans, exercises and questions can emphasise particular directional aspects such as:

- direction of travelling armies;
- location of walls, forts and camps;
- planning of towns, forts and camps.

These aspects are likely to be central to most studies on the Romans, but students with dyslexic difficulties would benefit from the additional focus on directional aspects of the study. The use, and indeed the construction, of maps utilising the principles of multisensory learning (see Chapter 5) would also be helpful.

Memory Skills

Children with dyslexic difficulties may have difficulties in remembering, retaining and recalling information. This may be due to short term memory problems or naming difficulty, i.e. difficulty in recalling the name or description of something without cues. It is important therefore to encourage the use of strategies which may facilitate remembering and recall. Such strategies can include repetition and over-learning, simple mnemonics and mind mapping.

Repetition and Over-learning

Short-term memory difficulties can be overcome by repetition and rehearsal of materials. This form of over-learning can be achieved in a variety of ways and not necessarily through conventional, and often tedious, rote learning.

In order to maximise the effect of repetition of learning it is important that a multisensory mode of learning is utilised. Repetition of the material to be learned can be accomplished through oral, visual, auditory and kinaesthetic modes. The learner should be able to see, hear, say and touch the materials to be learned. This reinforces the input stimuli and helps to consolidate the information for use, meaning and transfer to other areas. There are implications here for multi-mode teaching, including the use of movement, perhaps drama, to enhance the kinaesthetic mode of learning.

Simple Mnemonics

Mnemonics can be auditory or visual, or both auditory and visual. Auditory mnemonics may take the form of rhyming or alliteration while visual mnemonics can be used by relating the material to be remembered to a familiar scene, such as the classroom.

MNEMONICS – MONTHS OF YEAR

Jason D was a famous pop star

His song *JANUARY* was number 1 in the charts

He had a row with his girlfriend as he didn't get any Valentine Cards on *FEBRUARY 14th.*

He MARCHed straight over to *APRIL'S* HOUSE

'*MAY* I come in?' he said

'I'm on the phone, you have to wait till I'm finished talking to JUNE'

So he waited:	*J*	*A*	*S*	*O*	*N*	*D*
	U	U	E	C	O	E
	L	G	P	T	V	C
	Y	U	T	O	E	E
		S	E	B	M	M
		T	M	E	B	B
			B	R	E	E
			E		R	R
			R			

Maxwell (1997) Personal correspondence.

Mind Mapping

Mind mapping is now widely used (Buzan, 1993). It can be a simple or a sophisticated strategy depending on how it is developed. It is used to help the learner to remember a considerable amount of information and encourages students to think of, and develop, the main ideas of a passage or material to be learned. It adopts in many ways some of the principles already discussed in relation to schemata theory.

Essentially mind maps are individual learning tools and someone else's mind map may not be meaningful to you. It is important, therefore, that children should create their own, in order to help with both understanding of key concepts and in the retention and recall of associated facts.

Mind mapping can help not only to remember information, but also to help organise that information and this exercise in itself can aid understanding. Elaborate versions of mind maps can be constructed using pictorial images, symbols and different colours.

Summary

Study skills undoubtedly are important, and it is essential that the development of these skills is given a high priority for children with dyslexic difficulties. The main aspects which have been discussed here (communication skills, which can be aided by organisation, sequencing, context, schema, confidence and motivation; the transfer of these skills to other areas of the curriculum; mapping and visual skills; and strategies in remembering and retention) are all important. These aspects can be developed with and by the learner. Although the teacher can help to facilitate these strategies and skills in the learner, it is still important that any skill or strategy which is developed must be personalised by the learner. This means that different learners will adopt different ways of learning and remembering materials, but the responsibility to allow the learner to do this and to understand the principles associated with study skills rests with the teacher.

Curriculum access therefore for children with dyslexic difficulties can be achieved if:

- the needs of the pupils are accurately assessed;
- effective liaison exists within school, between schools and with outside agencies;
- specialist teaching and programmes are available when necessary
- differentiation of the curriculum is in terms of mode of delivery so that it is essentially access to the curriculum which is being differentiated;
- sufficient supports are available for all professionals within the school to help deal with the demands of teaching pupils with specific learning difficulties within a system-orientated approach.

Chapter 7

Dyslexia in Further and Higher Education

IS DISABILITY RELATED TO CONTEXT?

There is an increasing awareness in further and higher education of the need to identify and understand the difficulties experienced by dyslexic students (Singleton, 1996c).

While it is appreciated that dyslexic students by the very nature of their difficulty, will encounter some problems in relation to note-taking, written assignments, and completion of reading tasks, and in general organisation of course work, it is suggested here that institutions, by increasing their understanding and empathy towards dyslexic students, can provide the necessary support structure which could minimise some difficulties which may be experienced by the dyslexic student. This chapter will, therefore, deal with some of the issues in relation to the accessibility of further and higher education for dyslexic students, the support which can be provided to help ensure the successful completion of the course of study and some suggestions which may be useful for students themselves, particularly in relation to essay-writing.

EXPERIENCING FURTHER AND HIGHER EDUCATION

Waterfield (1996) provides some suggestions of supports which institutions can provide to help dyslexic students prior to actual commencement of the course. These include access open days, informal information days for potential students, an 'action line' available to dyslexic applicants and an information handbook for students with disabilities such as dyslexia. In Scotland there are also Access Centres and a national network of disability coordinators.

While these institutional pre-entry supports can be of great benefit to the dyslexic applicant, quite often the completion of the application form, which is usually completed without support from the institution, can present some difficulties. In addition to application completion the difficulty of course selection which often necessitates a considerable amount of reading of course information, can also be a problem (McLoughlin, *et al.*, 1994).

The actual application form, therefore, can present a difficulty and in particular the less structured parts of the application. For example, the sections in the form relating to 'additional information which may support the application'. This is usually an open-ended section and dyslexic applicants may have difficulty in providing the most relevant information to support their application, unless some structure or detailed guidance is provided. If no structure or sub-headings are provided the dyslexic student should attempt to draft some sub-headings before completing this section. An example of how this may be done is shown in Fig. 48. The exercise should also be helpful in preparing the dyslexic student for an eventual interview.

Figure 48

Additional information to support application

Before completing this section the dyslexic student should consider the following.
• What skills do you think are necessary for the course?
• In what way has your previous experiences helped you develop these skills?
• Why do you think these skills would help you in your course ?
• What would you wish to achieve through your experiences gained from this course?
• In what way do you think the course would help you achieve this?
• Make two lists on your page – on the left-hand side the skills/experiences you have already acquired and on the right-hand side the skills/experience you think would be helpful for the course for which you have applied. Compare the two lists. Look at what you still need and write down how you can eventually acquire these skills/experiences.

The Interview

The actual interview itself can often be seen as an ordeal for most applicants, but perhaps more so for dyslexic applicants. Many factors are important during interviews such as being able to identify key points in questions and respond appropriately. These may present some difficulty for dyslexic students. Gilroy (1995) offers very clear guidance to dyslexic students applying to higher education and suggests some interview questions which may be asked of the dyslexic student applying for a university course of study. These include:

• Why have you chosen to study this subject?
• Why have you chosen this department?
• What do you see yourself doing when you graduate?
• What do you do in your spare time?

- Can you explain to us what dyslexia is?
- How does it affect your work?
- How did you find out that you were dyslexic?
- What kind of support do you need?

INSTITUTIONAL SUPPORTS

Herrington (1996) suggests that institutional supports should be enabling, not compensatory; students should essentially manage their own learning and should determine their own model of support. The overriding principle therefore is essentially facilitating rather than compensatory.

Practical guidance based on this principle has been developed by Closs *et al.* (1996) who suggest that supports may involve some or all of the following:

- additional lecture notes;
- guidance on appropriate and accessible texts;
- advice on the best use of microtechnology to aid study and to produce assignments and the negotiation of special arrangements for examinations or other forms of assessments.

Cottrell (1996) suggests that a number of considerations need to be made before making recommendations. She argues that there is a common misconception that 'dyslexia' equals 'computer' and that is all that is necessary to support dyslexic students. It is important to appreciate that there are a range of supports which can be available and that these supports should be suggested in relation to the difficulties the student experiences or may encounter throughout the course. Cottrell suggests that disability **is** related to context and that institutional settings may reduce the effects of dyslexia.

SUCCEEDING IN FURTHER AND HIGHER EDUCATION

There are a number of factors which can contribute to the dyslexic student succeeding in further and higher education. The key areas include preparation for examinations, successfully completing essays, preparation for tutorials, being able to access resources, effective note-taking in lectures and learning from others such as course tutors and other course members. In addition to the above factors dyslexic students need to be familiar with the means and process for accessing additional support and resources should these be required. Sutherland and Smith (1997), in a large-scale research study involving secondary schools, show how the use of laptop computers can improve the quality of written work and the general confidence of the dyslexic student. It is important therefore that this facility be provided and encouraged in further and higher education.

ESSAY WRITING

McLoughlin *et al.* (1994) highlight some of the difficulties dyslexic students can encounter in a course of study and suggest some strategies for dealing with these. Some problems include lack of confidence and feelings of inferiority, verbal and written communication problems, difficulties in time-keeping, poor memory, lack of organisational skills, coping with large volumes of reading, poor concentration and being unaware of spelling errors. Most of these aspects could also have some bearing on perhaps one of the most important aspects of a course of study – essay writing.

Quite often students receive little guidance on choosing an appropriate essay from a list of alternatives, or on organising their time effectively to research the essay title and plan the written response to include the key points and develop arguments around each of the points. Dyslexic students may have particular difficulty in identifying key points and often lack confidence in presenting a written answer. This can contribute to an abbreviated argument which does not reflect the dyslexic student's background reading, effort or abilities. How should the dyslexic student therefore tackle an essay question?

Choosing a Topic

It is important not to waste too much time selecting an actual question and once a decision has been made on the actual question to be tackled, it is important to adhere to that and not change to another question midway through researching the question. This can be tempting if confronted by a 'tough' article or complex concepts but effective use of time is important and changing can prove wasteful of time.

When examining the various alternatives it is a good idea to write down a few points on each of the questions you think you are in a position to tackle. This should just take a few minutes, but give you experience in interpreting and understanding essay questions. This in itself is a useful skill which needs to be practised. It also allows you to make an actual decision, perhaps based on your current knowledge of the topic, your interest and your understanding of what is actually being asked.

Researching the Question

Initial Stage

Before actually reading and researching the question you will need to identify the key areas which should be examined in your reading. These may change or be modified in the light of your reading, but such a list will provide you with a starting point to guide you with your reading. For example if the question is along the lines of 'Examine the assertion that "care in the community" is politically motivated', even without any real in-depth knowledge of the above area, one could suggest some questions and aspects which need to be addressed. These may include:

- what is care in the community?
- what are the political implications of it?
- what other factors/theories relate to the concept of care in the community?

These will provide you with an overview of the question and some specific pointers for subsequent discussion.

Reading Stage

The reading stage is probably the stage which will be most time-consuming. It will provide you with the content for your answer but it is important that you select your reading carefully otherwise valuable time may be lost through irrelevant reading.

It is probably useful to identify a core text, perhaps a general one, but one which will provide you with much of the information you may need. Throughout your reading of the main texts you should write down the main points and issues from your reading which relate to the question. It is important to note therefore that the organising of your information starts during the initial stages of your reading and not after you find yourself with pages and pages of scrambled notes. The actual amount of notes you take varies from individual to individual, but the key point is their relevance in terms of the question. If the notes are organised into relevant aspects relating to the question this will help considerably when you are writing the essay.

Having a framework for your reading also helps in the selection of additional material from perhaps research articles or specialist books. You will have a fairly good idea of what you are looking for so time wasted on irrelevant reading will be minimized.

At this stage it is also important to make a note of all specific references you use rather than attempt to locate them on completion of the written essay.

Writing Stage

Quite often dyslexic students are reluctant to put 'pen to paper' and may unnecessarily delay the writing stage. This in fact should take place as you progress with the reading. After each part of the reading it is a good idea to write some implications or arguments which can be readily integrated into the finished essay. So the writing up, at least in the initial draft, should take place at the same time as your reading. The stages involved in writing an essay are shown below.

Introduction

For the dyslexic student the introduction may be the most important part of the essay. The introduction should therefore

- identify the key points in relation to the topic
- very briefly provide an answer to the actual question
- provide a plan on how the question will be answered

The introduction should, therefore provide a framework for your answer and a good introduction will help considerably in providing the detail of your answer in the main part of your essay.

The Main Part

The main part of your essay should essentially follow the key points outlined in your introduction. You should, therefore, continually refer back to your introduction to ensure that your argument is relevant to the points made in the introduction and the actual essay question. The main part should consist of argument and evidence on each of the points and always in relation to the actual question. It is important to support each point you make with well-referenced evidence.

Conclusion

A good conclusion is an essential part of your essay. It should be a re-interpretation of your introduction but adding some of the points you made in your main part of the essay. The conclusion should also leave the reader in no doubt as to your answer to the essay question.

References

It is important to write down references throughout the reading stage of your essay. You may also wish to write down page numbers for your own benefit in case you need to refer back to the original source.

Your course tutor would very likely provide you with an acceptable referencing format, but if in any doubt you could refer to some of the standard books in your subject and use the referencing style of these books.

Coles (1995), in a particularly helpful book, describes some stages of essay writing for students in general. These include:

- choosing the question
- initial planning
- understanding what is being asked
- the essay plan
- reading and note-taking

- additional material
- organise the main stages of the argument
- break the subject down into its main topic areas
- organise each main section
- add the detail
- divide each main stage of the arguments into separate paragraphs
- write the introduction
- first final draft
- write the conclusion
- final draft
- edit it at least twice

This can provide a useful framework for the dyslexic student. The drafting and editing is of course extremely important.

TUTOR'S ROLE

It is important for the tutor to appreciate that dyslexic students will often take longer than other students to plan and complete a written piece of work. A pre-assignment discussion to help the student talk through some of the main issues would be helpful, as would an interim discussion on progress. The student may need some precise guidance on reading as it is important that the dyslexic student does not waste time in reading aspects of a book which are not totally relevant.

Feedback

It is extremely important that the dyslexic student receives adequate feedback. One-to-one feedback is essential in order to highlight the strengths and the weaknesses of the written assignment.

Some aspects of the written assignment which may need to be commented on are:

- spelling
- grammar
- organisation
- introduction
- relevance of argument
- use of evidence
- the extent to which the question has been answered
- examples of how the arguments could be developed.

Throughout the feedback an opportunity should also be provided for dyslexic students to develop the essay and the arguments orally. This can boost their confidence for subsequent essays.

INSTITUTIONAL GUIDANCE

Some colleges of further education and universities now provide dyslexic students with clear guidelines on how they can seek help and access resources. This kind of support clearly varies from institution to institution but the student nevertheless should enquire at the earliest possible stage what sort of help is available for dyslexic students.

In 1995 the Higher Education Funding Council in both Scotland and England and Wales commissioned a Working Party of experts in the field of dyslexia in Higher Education to investigate the present provision and suggest available strategies for the future in relation to identification, assessment and support for dyslexic students (Singleton, 1996c). This type of initiative, although it may take some time to impact on all institutions, provides considerable hope for the future. In particular it is hoped that the good practices identified in the report in terms of institutional support for dyslexic students will be replicated elsewhere. In this way the context for accessing higher education courses will become more favourable and more supportive to all students with disabilities.

Chapter 8

Review of Resources

This chapter will give consideration to a number of the resource materials which are currently available for use with students with specific learning difficulties (dyslexia).

GENERAL TEXTS

Specific Learning Difficulties (Dyslexia)
Challenges and Responses
Peter D. Pumfrey and Rea Reason
Routledge (1992).

This is an extremely useful text book for anyone wishing to further their knowledge within the field of specific learning difficulties.

The authors provide the reader with a sound, well researched background relating to concepts and definitions, cognitive, emotional and social factors, intervention and evaluation. There are also interesting sections on psychological issues and the responses from a national survey involving local education authorities, education psychologists, organisations and examination boards.

Dimensions of Dyslexia
Vol. 1: *Assessment, Teaching and the Curriculum*
Edited by Gavin Reid
Moray House Publication (1996)

This comprehensive text consists of thirty one chapters from the field of research, psychology and teaching from within the UK and the United States.

There are twelve chapters on assessment providing examples of the most up-to-date research and practice. This includes phonological assessment, listening comprehension, computer assisted assessment, metacognitive and psychological assessment and a framework for assessment which should be helpful to teachers is also included.

The teaching section contains chapters on approaches on reading, spelling, mathematics and music. The curriculum section looks at differentiation, provision in mainstream schools and reading units and whole school approaches to meeting the needs of dyslexic learners. The concluding section is on continuing education. This section consists of chapters which look at the needs of adults and students in further and higher education.

Dimensions of Dyslexia
Vol. 2: Literacy, Language and Learning
Edited by Gavin Reid
Moray House Publication (1996)

This text consists of thirty-two chapters with contributions from practitioners within the UK and United States.

There are sections on reading and writing, speech and language, motor development, learning styles and strategies, social and emotional aspects and a final section provides perspectives on dyslexia from different perspectives.

The reading and writing section deals with phonological difficulties, compensatory strategies, metacognition, paired reading and assessing and promoting handwriting skills. The speech and language section provides explanations and implications for language difficulties, its relationship with dyslexia and specific factors affecting bilingual learners. The other sections include dyspraxic and motor problems, learning styles, attention deficit disorder, empowering students, policy issues, role of parents and models of assessment and intervention.

Dyslexia – Integrating Theory and Practice
Edited by Margaret Snowling and Michael Thomson
Whurr Publishers (1991).

The book presents a selection of the papers prepared for the Second International Conference on Specific Learning Difficulties held in 1991, and consists of twenty-eight chapters representing different aspects of specific learning difficulties. There is a chapter on 'biological bases' which focuses on neurological research; one on literacy which looks at recent research on phonological processing; and the other chapters provide some practical help in areas such as mathematics, study skills, communication, reading and writing.

A worthwhile reference book, useful for both researcher and teacher.

Dyslexia in Children – Multidisciplinary Perspectives
Edited by Angela Fawcett and Rod Nicolson
Harvester Wheatsheaf (1994).

This book, useful for those undertaking research in dyslexia or wishing to obtain a deeper understanding of the underlying causes and different facets within dyslexia contains three distinct sections. These are phonological skills, reading and dyslexia, visual skills, motor skills and speed of processing and views on the underlying causes of dyslexia.

Topics such as the phonological deficit hypothesis, automaticity, and visual and motor difficulties are dealt with in some detail. Can be a useful source book.

The Dyslexia Handbook
Edited by Jane Jacobson
British Dyslexia Association (1997).

This useful book contains information on dyslexia, schools and associations which can be beneficial to parents and teachers. The Handbook is updated and revised each year. It contains: information about the British Dyslexia Association and other organisations helping dyslexic people; some information about dyslexia such as indicators of dyslexia and formal and informal assessment; a directory providing contacts of local associations and schools; and a section on managing dyslexia in primary, secondary and further education with some guidance on the use of information technology.

Dyslexia – An International Journal of Research and Practice
Edited by T. R. Miles
John Wiley & Sons.

This excellent journal provides reviews and reports of research, assessment and intervention practice. It reports on theoretical and practical developments in the field of dyslexia with contributions from many different countries. Published four times a year, this official journal of the British Dyslexia Association is essential reading for those involved in the field of dyslexia.

The Many Faces of Dyslexia
Margaret Byrd Rawson
Orton Dyslexia Society, Maryland (1988).
Renamed International Dyslexia Association (IDA) in 1997.

As the title suggests this excellent text examines the different dimensions of dyslexia. In many ways the book epitomises the IDA's four-way analysis of dyslexia:

- the differences are personal;
- the diagnosis is clinical;
- the treatment is educational;
- the understanding is scientific.

Like the Orton Society, the book portrays the 'united whole'. It looks at education, neurophysiological and social aspects of the dyslexic learner, the history and developments of the Orton Society, the 'interfaces and reflections' and the different facets of dyslexia.

A very useful book.

Dyslexia – Theory and Practice of Remedial Instruction
Diana Brewster Clark
York Press Inc., Maryland (1988).

This excellent text provides an understanding both of the nature of dyslexia and of the reading process as well as evaluative comment on a wide range of teaching programmes for dyslexic children.

It provides a superb overview of teaching for dyslexics including aspects such as phonological awareness training, reading comprehension, instruction, handwriting and composition instruction, spelling and the reading–writing relationship.

A very useful book.

Annals of Dyslexia. An Interdisciplinary Journal of the Orton Dyslexia Society (now the International Dyslexia Association – IDA)

This comprehensive journal is published annually by the IDA, Baltimore, USA. It represents the most current issues, debates and practices from researchers, clinicians and teachers involved in the field of dyslexia. An invaluable source book for those engaged in study of dyslexia.

Dyslexia Matters
Edited by Gerald Hales
Whurr Publications (1994).

This text contains fifteen chapters examining the theoretical constructs of dyslexia, the specific nature of dyslexia, the identification of dyslexia, education management of the dyslexic child and diverse routes to a wider understanding of dyslexia. The book can be a good resource for the researcher, there are also three useful chapters on education management and a chapter on the importance of self-esteem and the emotional needs of dyslexic individuals The contributors are all experienced practitioners and researchers from the UK and the United States, Canada and Australia.

Policy, Practice and Provision for Children with Specific Learning Difficulties
Jill Duffield, Sheila Riddell and Sally Brown
Avebury Publishing, England (1995).

This text provides a detailed analysis of a major research project funded by the Scottish Office Education Department conducted by the University of Stirling. It deals with the background to the research, an analysis of provision, the role of the examination system and teacher education, the perceptions of parents, learning support and voluntary organisations and provision within the health service. It concludes with a summary of the debate concerning policy, practice and provision in dyslexia, highlights issues such as competing policies reflecting different ideological stances, economic considerations, the nature of specific learning difficulties and controversy concerning recognition and what constitutes effective provision.

How to Detect and Manage Dyslexia – A Reference and Resource Manual
Philomena Ott
Heinemann (1997).

This manual provides a wealth of information which can be useful to professional, parents and dyslexic students and adults. It provides an interesting historical context detailing the growing awareness and impact of dyslexia in education, legislation and society. There are useful chapters on early identification, reading, writing, spelling and mathematics which provide information on approaches for tackling dyslexia. This book also contains informative chapters on music, looking at the implications of dyslexia for the musician and comprehensive chapters on the adolescent and adult dyslexic.

Dyslexia – A Hundred Years On
T. R. Miles and Elaine Miles
Open University Press (1991).

An extremely useful and informative text which provides an excellent overview of causes and sub-types. It also provides an informative summary of teaching methods and programmes as well as some commentary on the debate regarding the concept of dyslexia.

The important area of brain research and genetics which is revealing much useful information to help explain the basis of dyslexic difficulties is discussed. The debate on the concept of dyslexia is commented on by way of thesis and anti-thesis, such as 'dyslexia is a medical matter – dyslexia is an educational matter' and 'dyslexia is a unity – dyslexia is a diversity'! The authors point out that these debates reflect a difference in emphasis rather than total disagreement.

Specific Learning Difficulties (Dyslexia): A Teacher's Guide
Margaret Crombie
Ann Arbor Publishers, Northumberland (1997).

This guide aims to meet the needs of teachers who must deal with the problems but who have not necessarily an in-depth knowledge of specific learning difficulties (dyslexia). The book considers various aspects of a child's difficulties, including the incidence and the nature of the problems. The assessment process is discussed and guidance is offered on how to interpret the results.

An eclectic approach is adopted in discussing the practicalities of teaching the dyslexic child in the classroom situation. Various areas of the curriculum are considered in relation to the child's learning. Ideas to help the teacher cope and meet the needs of dyslexic children in a mixed-ability classroom are of a practical nature. Further suggestions are offered in areas of curriculum support such as memory and motivation.

The book concentrates mainly on the primary school age-group of children, adopting the view that if needs are met at this stage, then later difficulties will be minimised.

The appendices at the end contain details of useful assessment and teaching materials as well as addresses for obtaining these.

Dyslexia and Other Learning Difficulties – The Facts
Mark Selikowitz
Oxford University Press (1994)

This short text, which presents an Australian perspective, discusses a wide variety of aspects such as theories of causation, reading, spelling, writing, arithmetic, language, attention difficulties, coordination and clumsiness and social and emotional difficulties. Contains some useful ideas.

Understanding Learning Difficulties: A Guide for Teachers and Parents
James Chapman
ERDC Press, Massey University, New Zealand (1988).

This book is one of the products of the author's long engagement in researching and teaching in the area of learning disabilities. Essentially it is written for teachers and parents and the jargon-free style of the book is suitable for this dual readership. The book provides a broader understanding of the problems children with learning difficulties experience in schools.

Your Child's Growing Mind
Jane M. Healy
A Main Street Book, Doubleday, New York (1994).

This updated book provides a comprehensive insight which helps the teacher and the parent understand the development of children and their learning potential. It examines the foundations of intelligence, and neurological development and provides guidelines for 'brain-building play'.

Jane Healy successfully combines brain development, learning style and educational, social and cultural aspects to illustrate how the potential of learning-disabled children may remain unfulfilled. She discusses how educators need to get to the heart of learning and appreciate how children learn, and hence discusses factors which can seriously discourage and undermine learning.

She provides numerous examples of how to motivate children to learn. For example to encourage children to write she suggests 'Read aloud on a regular basis, even with older children. Delve into poetry, literature, essays and good journalism. Don't be afraid to broaden your own tastes . . . Do not waste time on watered-down versions of classics with 'pop' language. You'll be surprised how much children can understand and enjoy (even Shakespeare!) if it is read to them dramatically in a pleasurable atmosphere.'

The author's closing paragraph epitomises the essence and flavour of the book when she asserts that 'learning is something that children do, not something that is done to them. You have the wisdom to guide the process but not the power to control it'.

A very useful and informative book.

Endangered Minds
Jane M. Healy
Touchstone, Simon & Schuster (1991).

In this useful, interesting and insightful text Jane Healy explains, complemented by research from several disciplines, how changing lifestyles may be altering children's brains in critical ways. She questions many aspects and assumptions about current educational trends through analysing children's performances and attainments. She also discusses how 'technological and social changes' have propelled us into an uncertain world – of video, computers, the 'global village'. She does not criticise parents or teachers, but rather describes the helplessness of the adult to keep in touch with children and their developmental needs, in the face of 'contemporary pressures'.

She describes how some dyslexic children who have been provided with language and literacy stimulation can compensate for their difficulties in reading with such success that they may altogether escape detection, often by displaying talents in predominantly right-hemisphere skills such as visual arts, mathematical reasoning, music and mechanical aptitude. She explains how neuro-scientists are finding out more about the dyslexic brain, particularly in relation to pre-natal cell migration which, if it goes wrong, can affect literacy development, but also discusses Galaburda's studies (1988) as showing the enormous capacity of the human brain to compensate for innate difficulties, given the right kind of support.

This book, therefore, discusses how society is coping with children's development and the changing brain and how support which children need should be provided by adults. The author argues that the quality of curiosity is one which needs to be preserved. Neglect of this and of the associated factors such as language, thought and imagination can truly endanger children's minds.

About Dyslexia – Unravelling the Myth
Priscilla L. Vail
Programs for Education/Modern Learning Press, USA (1990).

Throughout this book Priscilla Vail helps the reader become aware of dyslexic people's abilities and needs. She highlights the need to acknowledge and foster a positive self-concept among dyslexic students and illustrates the teacher's role in helping to foster this especially in the area of creativity – 'they need chances to pretend, to invent their own personal imagery and to keep imagination alive'. This short, well written book can be a useful motivator to both teacher and student.

Children's Learning Difficulties – A Cognitive Approach
Julie Dockrell and John McShane
Blackwell (1993).

This excellent reference book provides a thorough and well researched understanding of cognitive dimensions and of cognitive approaches to assessment in reading, language and number work. The authors classify learning difficulties, analyse tasks and discuss the interaction of the task, child and the environment. In relation to reading difficulties the publication examines reading components, word recognition, causes of decoding difficulties, perceptual deficits, phonological processing, memory deficits, sentence processing and metacognitive knowledge.

Perspectives on Dyslexia Vol. 1
Neurology, Neuro-psychology and Genetics
Edited by George Th. Pavlidis
John Wiley & Sons (1990).

This is an extremely well-researched and useful reference book for students and teachers. This volume includes sections and chapters looking at sub-types of dyslexia, the role of genetics, cerebral asymmetries and different correlates of reading disability. Additionally there is an extensive section on the significance of eye movements in diagnosing dyslexia.

Pavlidis presents many fascinating insights into the importance of eye movements in reading and presents predictive evidence relating eye movements at the beginning of schooling to subsequent school performance. The issue of abnormal eye movements among dyslexic students also receives considerable attention.

This volume consists of contributions from international researchers.

Perspectives on Dyslexia Vol. 2
Cognition, Language and Treatment
Edited by George Th. Pavlidis
John Wiley & Sons (1990).

This second volume in the series examines issues relating to diagnostic criteria for dyslexia, cognitive deficits, phonological deficiencies, meta-linguistic aspects and perspectives on spelling.

There are also sections looking at dyslexia in adulthood, social factors and some alternative treatments. This latter aspect provides an interesting insight into hemispheric functions. Dirk Bakker discusses the 'balance model of reading acquisition' which describes initial reading as requiring visual-spatial skills while advanced reading requires semantic-syntactic analysis. Thus since visuo-spatial skills are primarily a right hemispheric function and semantic-syntactic analysis is a left hemispheric function, Bakker asserts that beginning readers would predominantly use the right hemisphere in reading while advanced readers use the left. This is followed up by a summary in the final chapter looking at the retraining of basic neurological functions.

The Neurological Impress Method (NIM) is discussed. This is a direct reprogramming of the brain not unlike the 'look and listen' method in the Netherlands and treatment methods based on 'Living Language' such as 'look and say' and whole word methods. The assumption here is that training focusing on the strong functions is preferable and more effective as compared with training the weak function with the objective of strengthening it. This, however, is still a controversial issue. The authors of this chapter (Dumont, Oud, Van Mameren-Schoehuizen, Jacobs, Van Herpen and Van den Bekerom) discuss their own study of a treatment programme and highlight the importance of starting such a programme as early as possible and of sustaining it. They describe their treatment programme as meeting the principles for teaching dyslexics: structured, sequential, cumulative and separate learning tasks. Their programme included phonological training, preparatory reading to illustrate phoneme-grapheme correspondences, initial reading – grapheme by grapheme, the recognition and reading of polysyllabic words, sentence reading, texts and reading for memory. One can note from this the cumulative and sequential flow of the programme.

In general this volume contains interesting well researched chapters which can provide the basis for further study.

Neuro-psychological Correlates and Treatment, Vol. 1 and Vol. 2
Edited by Dirk J. Bakker and Harry Van der Vlugt
Swets and Zeitlinger, Amsterdam (1989).

This is an excellent publication for those engaged in research. It contains discussion on a range of research studies on initial reading performance, motor precursors of learning disabilities, dyslexia sub-types, the neuro-anatomy of dyslexia and EEG studies. The second volume looks at cognitive processes, in particular auditory information processing and top down attention deficit; social aspects such as personality, adjustment problems and integration. There is also a section on remediation focusing on mathematics, audio support, strategies and verbal practice.

Understanding Specific Learning Difficulties
Margot Prior
Psychology Press (1996).

This book presents an Australian perspective of some important aspects of specific learning difficulties. It examines neuropsychology and its use in understanding learning difficulties, diagnosis and assessment, reading, spelling and mathematics, 'remedial' techniques and resources and the relationship between behaviour problems and learning difficulties.

There is a clear psychology bias throughout the book which can be seen particularly in the assessment chapter which begins by providing aims of clinical, psychological and educational assessment. Most of the chapters are accompanied by case studies. An informative and extremely readable book.

Dyslexia – A Multidisciplinary Approach
Edited by Patience Thomson and Peter Gilchrist
Chapman & Hall (1997).

This book presents multidisciplinary perspectives on dyslexia. These include views from an education psychologist, speech and language therapist, occupational therapist, orthoptist, pediatrician, school counsellor, remedial teacher and head teacher. The general perspective of the book is one which emphasises the need for a holistic approach in dealing with dyslexic children. The insights provided by the contributors of this book are highlighted through the use of case studies.

Other General Texts Include the Following:

Augur J. (1992) *This Book Doesn't Make Sense.* Bath Educational Publishers.

Blight J. (1986) *A Practical Guide to Dyslexia.* Egon.

Chasty H. and Friel J. (1991) Children with special needs: *Assessment, Law and Practice. Caught in the Act.* London, Jessica Kingsley Publishers.

Ellis A. (1991) *Reading, Writing and Dyslexia: A cognitive analysis.* Open University.

Hales G. (ed.) (1990) *Meeting Points in Dyslexia.* British Dyslexia Association, London.

Hales G. (ed.) (1994) *Dyslexia Matters.* Whurr Publishers.

Heaton P. and Winterson P. (1986) *Dealing with Dyslexia.* Better Books.

Miles T. R. (1983) *Dyslexia: The Pattern of Difficulties.* Collins.

Miles T. R. and Miles E. (eds) (1992) *Dyslexia and Mathematics.* Routledge.

Miles T. R. and Gilroy D. (1986) *Dyslexia at College.* Methuen.

Miller R. and Klein C. (1986) *Making Sense of Spelling.* DCLD London.

Naidoo S. (ed.) (1988) *Assessment and Teaching of Dyslexic Children.* ICAN London.

Pinsent, P. (ed.) (1990) *Children with Literacy Difficulties.* David Fulton – published in association with the Roehampton Institute.

Pumfrey, P. D. and Elliott, C. D. (1990) *Children's Difficulties in Reading, Spelling and Writing.* Falmer Press.

Sharon H. (1987) *Changing Children's Minds.* Condor Press.

Snowling M. (1991) *Children's Written Language Difficulties.* NFER Nelson.

Snowling M. (1990) *Dyslexia: A Cognitive Developmental Perspective.* Blackwell.

Stoel Van Der S. (ed.) (1990) *Parents on Dyslexia.* Multilingual Matters, Clevedon.

Thomson M. (1989) *Developmental Dyslexia.* Whurr, London.

Tyre C. and Young P. (1994) *Specific Learning Difficulties: a staff development handbook.* QED, Staffordshire.

Webster A. and McConnell C. (1987) *Children with Speech and Language Difficulties.* Cassell.

Welchman M. (1981) *Suggestions for Dyslexic Child at Home.* Better Books.

Welchman M. (1983) *Dyslexia – Your Questions Answered.* Better Books.

Young, P. and Tyre, C. (1983) *Dyslexia or Illiteracy? Realising the Right to Read.* Open University Press.

READING

How to Teach your Dyslexic Child to Read – A Proven Method for Parents and Teachers
Bernice A. Baumer
Birch Lane Press, Carol Publishing Group (1996).

This book describes an intensive one-to-one teaching programme which includes charts, graphs and lesson plans. The programme is aimed for the child from kindergarten through to third grade in a step-by-step procedure. It provides detailed instructions on teaching phonics, spelling and syllables. There are also examples of word lists and other exercises focusing on initial consonants, vowels, blends and dipthongs.

The Art of Reading
Edited by Morag Hunter-Carsch
Blackwell Education, Oxford (1989).

This volume represents a collection of thirty-two contributions from a wide range of experts focusing on pre-reading aspects, reading policy and practice, classroom communication and literacy difficulties, and complemented by contributions from the international arena.

The book contains a wealth of interesting ideas on reading, including enhancing reading comprehension through creating visual images, whole school language policy, linguistics, word processing, and adult basic literacy.

A useful reference book.

Beginning to Read: The New Phonics in Context
Marilyn Jager Adams
Heinemann (1990)

This is a précis of the classic text on reading, 'Beginning to Read. Thinking and learning about print'. The précis maintains the scholarly presentation of the main text but, because it is shorter and more direct, it provides a ready means of acquiring information on principles and practices involved in reading and the reading debate.

The work provides perspectives on reading and describes the development of reading skills in young readers. The last chapter 'concerns and conclusions' provides useful pointers in 'predictors of reading acquisition'. An excellent text for researchers and practitioners.

Reading Problems – Consultation and Remediation
P. G. Aaron and R. Malatesha Joshi
Guilford Press (1992).

This is a superb text on reading, particularly for those engaged in extended study. In addition to looking at the psychology of reading, including sensory encoding, word recognition, sentence and text comprehension and metacognition, the authors discuss differential diagnosis of reading disabilities and intervention strategies.

The book is an extremely well researched piece of work and with its emphasis on 'consultative approaches to educational intervention' should prove to be extremely useful to educational psychologists as well as teachers involved in further study.

Reading Development and Dyslexia
Edited by C. Hulme and M. Snowling
Whurr Publishers (1994).

The chapters in this book present a selection of the papers presented to the Third International Conference of the British Dyslexia Association. The book is divided into three sections – the normal development of reading skills, the nature and causes of reading difficulties, and the remediation of reading difficulties. All the contributors, well known in their field, represent an international perspective on issues relating to reading and dyslexia.

Reading by the Colours:
Overcoming Dyslexia and other Reading Disabilities through the Irlen Method
Helen Irlen
Avery Publishing Group, New York (1991).

This extremely interesting and informative book discusses and describes Helen Irlen's work relating to Scotopic Sensitivity Syndrome and the use of colour filters to help students with reading problems.

The book provides an explanation of Scotopic Sensitivity Syndrome and how it affects reading. There is a chapter discussing how it particularly relates to dyslexia. The author acknowledges that if the dyslexic student has a phonological difficulty or a language problem then coloured filters will not totally remediate the difficulty. If, however, the difficulty is diagnosed as visual/perceptual then coloured filters can improve reading.

The book also contains an extremely useful section on screening and the importance of colour selection.

Phonological Skills and Learning to Read
Usha Goswami and Peter Bryant
Lawrence Erlbaum Associates (1990).

This book examines issues relating to phonological knowledge and analyses the role of phonological skills in early reading. A range of aspects such as the relationship between phonological awareness and reading, the development of phonological awareness in childhood, the role of rhyming and the use of onset and rhyme strategies in reading are discussed.

The authors refer to considerable research and provide an interesting argument that children, in learning to read, do not rely on letter-sound relationships but instead learn to read using a global strategy, thus recognising words as a pattern. This is contrasted in writing and spelling where children do depend heavily on letter-sound relationships. The authors, however, also argue that the relationship between phonological processing and early reading may be based on onset and rhyme strategies which form phonological units and strings of letters and not on grapheme-phoneme correspondence. This extremely well researched book provides a sound basic coverage of all aspects of phonological processing and literacy.

Games to Improve Reading Levels
Jim McNicholas and Joe McEntree
A NASEN Publication, NARE Publications, Stafford (1991).

This short text consists of seventy-four interesting games which can bring pleasure and motivation in helping the development of reading skills. The authors justify the use of games as an approach by asserting that children learn most of their concepts of self, orientation, size and number by playing games. They also argue that children will respond more readily without instructions and can be observed more naturally in a game playing 'mode'. The authors, however, do stress that there should be some check to ensure that learning is, in fact, taking place.

The vast number of games included in this slim volume are neatly categorised into those relating to body image, directional orientation, auditory factors, visual aspects, vocabulary, word attack and word building, reading for meaning and paper and pencil games to improve reading and writing. There is also a section on the use of games to develop phonic skills.

A very useful publication.

Phonics and Phonic Resources
Edited by Mike Hinson and Pete Smith
Nasen Publication (1993).

This useful volume examines the field of phonics teaching. It discusses the concept of phonics teaching, referring to reading schemes, other published materials and computer software and games.

The book provides some useful suggestions such as teaching phonics as a small group activity, particularly when sounds are being taught for the first time, to ensure that 'fine' pronunciation is acquired by the child.

A useful chapter discusses the direct teaching of phonics in terms of organisation, teaching initial letters, blending, recording and monitoring progress.

In relation to assessment the book discusses a number of strategies such as miscue analysis, running record (Clay, 1985) and individual and group phonic tests.

A large part of the book comprises a list and some details of available resources appropriate to help with:

- visual discrimination
- auditory discrimination
- initial letter sounds
- final letter sounds
- short 'a', 'e', 'i', 'o' 'u' (vowel sounds)
- short vowel revision
- 'b', 'd', 'p' confusion
- double consonants at end
- final consonant blend revision
- consonant digraphs
- magic 'e'
- consonant blends
- vowel digraphs
- prefixes, suffixes
- silent and soft letter sounds
- compound words

This should prove to be a useful reference book on phonics for the class teacher.

Recipe for Reading
Nina Traub with Frances Bloom
Educators Publishing Service Inc., Cambridge MA (1993).

This revised and expanded edition provides a sequentially organised and well evaluated programme for teaching reading. The authors believe the technique to be effective for children with specific learning difficulties, and assert that a 'recipe for reading, like all good recipes, requires that you (i) know what ingredients are needed, (ii) understand how they are to be combined and (iii) are able to adapt the recipe to individual needs'.

The programme is based on exposure to a structured phonic base to help beginning readers develop an awareness of sounds and eventually word attack skills.

The sequence of introducing sounds is determined by auditory, visual and kinaesthetic factors rather than alphabetic order. For example, of the first nine letters to be taught 'c', 'o', 'a', 'd' and 'g' have similar kinaesthetic factors and these are highlighted. The other four letters which make up the first nine are 'm', 'l', 'h' and 't'.

The programme is clearly highly structured and utilises a range of phonic materials such as phonetic sound cards, phonetic word cards, phonetic phrase cards, phonetic storybooks, word games and sequence charts.

The teacher's manual provides an easy-to-follow guide to lesson procedure including how the letters and sounds are introduced, introduction of two syllable words, vowel digraphs and spelling rules. There is also a useful section on prefixes and suffixes.

Reading Recovery in New Zealand
A Report from the Office of Her Majesty's Chief Inspector of Schools
HMSO London (1993).

This booklet provides an extremely interesting and informative account of an HMI's visit to New Zealand to study the application of the Reading Recovery Programme.

It provides a summary of a Reading Recovery Programme and highlights a lesson which the report suggests 'aims to make pupils into independent and autonomous readers'.

In relation to the effectiveness of the programme the report suggests that evidence of short- and long-term benefit is available although clearly because of other 'contaminating' factors it is more difficult to distinguish the effects of the Reading Recovery Programme from other intervening factors.

The report compares the New Zealand system of teaching reading in the early stages with that of the UK and notes many similarities in relation to philosophies and classroom organisation of materials. It is also noted, however, that New Zealand primary schools appear to give more time to language activity and early reading than is the case in the UK.

Although the report accepts that the limitations of the visit in terms of time and scale meant that a fully comprehensive and reliable survey was not possible, it did acknowledge some key issues such as the importance of literacy in the New Zealand education system, supported by the free distribution of the national reading scheme (Ready to Read series), school journals containing collections of reading materials, and widely shared professional procedures in diagnosis.

The report concludes that although the Reading Recovery Programme is particularly well suited to the New Zealand context, 'there is no reason to suppose that it is not transferable to other education systems'.

All Language and the Creation of Literacy
Orton Dyslexia Society Inc., Baltimore (1991).

This useful publication includes the presentations at two separate symposia – 'Whole Language and Phonics' and 'Language and Literacy'.

The whole language and phonics section is represented by five expert contributors – Sylvia Richardson, Joanna Williams, Jeanne Chall, Diane de Ford and Marilyn Jager Adams.

Sylvia Richardson provides an historical perspective describing the evolution of approaches – looking at visual, auditory and kinaesthetic approaches and the attempts to provide combined approaches. She also comments on the need to acknowledge diversity in education in order to help meet the needs of every child.

This is developed by Adams who asks the question – 'Why not phonics and whole language?' She provides an excellent exposition of the whole language approach, citing the lack of precise definition but agreeing that this should not prevent educators from enlisting some of the benefits of this approach such as child-centred instruction and integration of reading and writing. She argues that whole language should be a core component of 'a long overdue and highly constructive educational revolution'.

The section on Language and Literacy sees Sylvia Richardson discussing the roots of literacy and Margaret Snowling looking at speech processing and spelling. Snowling shows that dyslexic children's spelling is generally more impaired than their reading and that the phonological spelling system is an extension of the speech processing system.

A section on organising decoding instruction is presented by Marcia Henry in which she argues that the education system should be equipping students with strategies to understand and deal with the structure of words. Robert Calfee, Marlyn Chambliss and Melissa Beretz look at the aspect of comprehension and discuss a four component core model – connect, organise, reflect and extend. They also discuss the importance of prior experience in reading comprehension. They argue that teachers need to recognise that every student possesses some background knowledge relevant to any classroom topic and should attempt to help students share that knowledge. This can be done by developing a collective, coherent framework during the early stages of engaging in the topic. They argue that learning is more effective and efficient for every person 'when it connects with prior experience'.

A very useful and stimulating publication.

Other Useful Books on Reading Include:

Augur J. (1990) *This Book Doesn't Make Sense.* Bath Educational Pub.
Aaron P. G. (1988) *Dyslexia and Hyperlexia.* Kluwer Press.
Beard R. (1990) *Developing Reading 3–13.* Hodder & Stoughton.
Bryant P. and Bradley L. (1990) *Children's Reading Problems.* Blackwell.
Brady S. and Shankweiler D. (1992) *Phonological Processes in Literacy.* York Pub.
Clay M. (1992) *Reading – The Patterning of Complex Behaviour.* Heinemann Educational.
Conlan J. and Henley M. (1992) *Word Mastery.* Oxford University Press.
Harris C. (1993) *Fuzzbuzz Books/Spell/Words/Letters.* Oxford University Press.
Hunt R. and Franks T. (1993) *Oxford Reading Tree Pack.* Oxford University Press.
Kratoville B. L. (1989) *Word Tracking: Proverbs: High Frequency Words.* Ann Arbor Pub.
Lunzer E. and Gardner K. (1984) *Learning from the Written Word.* Oliver & Boyd.
Jones-Elgar R. (1989) *The Cloze Line.* Ann Arbor Pub.
Smith J. and Bloom M. (1985) *Simple Phonetics for Teachers.* Methuen.
Snowling M. and Hulme C. (1993) *Reading Development and Dyslexia.* Whurr Publishers.
Stevens M. (1992) *Into Print.* Scottish Consultative Council on the Curriculum, Edinburgh.
Stirling E. G. (1990) *Which is Witch,* checklist of homopohones. St David's College, Llandudno, North Wales.
Topping K. (1986) *Paired Reading Training Pack.* Centre for Paired Learning, Psychology Department, University of Dundee.
Topping K. J. (1987) *Peer Tutored Paired Reading: Outcome Data from Ten Projects.* Educational Psychology 7,2, pp. 133–145.
Tyre C. and Young P. (1994) *Specific Learning Difficulties,* a staff development handbook. Q.E.D. Pub.
Wade B. and Moore M. (1993) *The Promise of Reading Recovery.* Educational Review Publications–Headline Series No. 1. University of Birmingham.
Wade B. and Moore M. (1994) *The Promise of Reading Recovery.* Educational Review Publications–Headline Series No. 1. University of Birmingham.
Waterland L. (1986) *Read with Me.* Thimble Press.
Wolfendale S. (1990) *Word Play.* NARE Pub.
Young P. and Tyre C. (1990) *Dyslexia or Illiteracy: Realising the Right to Read.* Open University.

TEACHING PROGRAMMES

Helping Children with Reading and Spelling: A Special Needs Manual
R. Reason and R. Boote
Routledge (1994).

This excellent manual consists of teaching plans incorporating a range of strategies intended for use with children who have difficulty learning to read, write and spell. The main themes of the book are encapsulated in the model of literacy learning outlined by the authors – that is one which incorporates and distinguishes between meaning, phonics and fluency. The authors rightly suggest that these three areas interact with each other at all stages from beginning reading to achieving competency.

Part one of the book develops this theme followed by part two which looks at reading, part three spelling and part four applications to the classroom.

The reading sections look at assessment, and the development of reading skills through four stages, each stage incorporating aspects of meaning, phonics and fluency. There are plentiful examples with clearly presented case studies.

The spelling section contains: descriptions of stages in learning to spell; developing strategies for spelling; a personalised spelling programme and games and activities. The handwriting section follows the spelling chapter from the viewpoint that handwriting is a skill which supports the development of spelling. This chapter provides good examples relating to concepts about handwriting, materials and resources, models and teaching methods.

The last two chapters provide informative examples of how teachers have utilised the information, strategies and models described in the preceding pages. This section can be extremely useful for teachers.

An excellent, comprehensive, well-presented manual.

Phonological Awareness Training: A New Approach to Phonics
Jo Wilson
Educational Psychology Publishing, University College London (1993).

This is a specific programme on a particular aspect of literacy development–phonological awareness. The programme complements other types of activities such as stories, poems and rhymes which are beneficial to the development of phonological awareness. The essential component of PAT is the use of analogies to help children read and spell.

It is suggested that research shows that familiarity with onsets and rimes is a necessary prerequisite to competence in phonics, and programmes utilising the principle of onsets and rimes can help children learn to read.

The programme consists of 25 worksheets, reading lists, dictation sheets and 'rime' display sheets. The programme can be used with an individual child or with a group and is suitable for children of seven years and upwards.

Sound Linkage – An Integrated Programme for Overcoming Reading Difficulties
Peter Hatcher
Whurr Publications (1994).

This extremely useful book contains ten sections on developing phonological awareness. Each section deals with a different aspect, for example, section three deals with phoneme blending and section six with phoneme segmentation.

Each section includes a series of activities relating to the skills being addressed in that particular section.

The book opens with a test of phonological awareness and the complete package is essentially a self-contained programme on phonological awareness. A detailed, practical and well-researched book.

Maths and Dyslexics
Anne Henderson
St David's College, Llandudno (1989).

This publication is an extremely readable short reference for teachers faced with helping dyslexics with mathematical difficulties. The author identifies some major difficulties such as fear, poor short-term memory and difficulties identifying symbols and directions, and discusses these with examples. The book also refers to some other problems with mathematics such as language, the use of equipment, decimals, percentages, proportions and time.

Each section has a 'how to help' section, which provides handy hints on aspects which need particular attention and the book is well equipped with examples.

Dyslexia Basic Numeracy
Vicki Burge
Helen Arkell Dyslexia Centre (1986).

A very easy to follow short publication on basic numeracy. It provides advice on spatial awareness, number formation, language and terminology in mathematics, error analyses and gives special consideration to aspects of maths such as multiplication tables, fractions, decimals and percentages.

Specific Learning Difficulties in Mathematics – A Classroom Approach
Olwen El-Naggar
Nasen (1996).

This book offers a comprehensive view of the difficulties which can be experienced by children with specific learning difficulties in mathematics. There are excellent chapters on assessment, developing an individualised programme and implications for classroom teachers.

The assessment chapter looks at the use of mathematical language and the use of symbols. It also suggests that one should be looking at the pupils' compensatory strategies and attention span. There is an excellent checklist of characteristics (pp. 24–25) which can provide some guidance on assessment such as memory difficulties, visual perceptual problems, sequencing problems, spatial awareness and the use of problem-solving strategies.

In the section on instruction there is an example of an individualised programme which is extremely detailed, followed up by a brief section on implications for classroom practice.

What to Do When You Can't Learn the Times Tables
Steve Chinn
Marko Publishing (1996).

This is a very practical book aimed at providing strategies to help dyslexic students learn tables. It is not intended to be a quick-fix book and each of the methods suggested require practice and perseverance. It suggests that the use of a table square is a more efficient method than learning the tables than through a linear collection of facts. The book is full of interesting and useful ideas to minimise the memory load on the dyslexic student and to provide strategies which with practice can help the dyslexic student become a more efficient and successful learner in mathematics.

Teaching Talking – Teaching Resources Handbook
Ann Locke and Maggie Beech
NFER-Nelson (1991).

This kit is an excellent reference set for teaching talking. Three packs are available: nursery pack; infant pack; junior pack.

The set contains a teaching procedures workbook, teaching resources handbook and comprehensive assessment record forms. The teaching talking programme is in three stages which are usually implemented over a period of a year. This first stage is based on classroom observations, the second on 'low key' instruction with a group of children and the third involves working with a small group who are not progressing well and need more intensive help.

Assessment

The pack includes detailed profile checklists from ages 0–1; 1–2 and 2–5, and further checklists for those children identified as having significant language learning difficulties. The assessment pack also contains specific charts on speaking and listening, listening and understanding, play and social development and record sheets on pre-language, emerging language and maturing language.

Resources

The resources handbook provides ideas on promoting listening skills, developing vocabulary, enquiring, planning and developing talking, reading and writing and encouraging independence in talking.

The suggestions include a variety of games, use of songs, poems and stories, encouraging the development of phonic skills and rhyming with clapping rhymes, music and movement as well as games such as 'I Spy', odd word out and construction of riddles.

Teaching Procedures

The teaching procedures handbook provides an overview of the teaching process for children with significant language learning difficulties and outlines how to use the record sheets and screening procedures most effectively. It also provides some case studies.

A very useful and comprehensive resource pack

Mathematics for Dyslexics – A Teaching Handbook
S. J. Chinn and J. R. Ashcroft
Whurr Publishers, London (1993).

This comprehensive text examines a broad range of aspects relating to mathematics and outlines strategies which can effectively be used by dyslexic students. The central message of the book is the need to understand the way each child learns as an individual and this is particularly underlined in the chapter on cognitive styles in mathematics. This very useful text also includes chapters on testing and diagnosis of number concepts and of computational procedures for addition, subtraction, multiplication and division. A very useful teaching handbook.

Phonic Rhyme Time
Mary Nash-Wortham
The Robinswood Press (1993).

The book contains a collection of phonic rhymes which the author suggests will help with speech and reading. It provides an excellent understanding of speech sounds and their creation, helped by charts showing categories of phonic sounds and a phonic rhyme chart. After the first section the book provides a collection of rhymes and an analysis of the key phonic aspects of the rhymes.

Attention without Tension: A Teacher's Handbook on Attention Disorders
Edna D. Copeland and Valerie L. Love
3 C's of Childhood Inc. Atlanta, GA (1992).

This comprehensive volume provides the reader with a useful guide and understanding of the field of attention deficit disorders (ADD) and attention deficit disorders with hyperactivity (ADHD).

The book begins with some key facts which indicate that about 30–40% of all referrals to child psychologists, psychiatrists and mental health agencies are related to children with some form of attention disorder.

The chapter on causes of attention disorders provides the reader with a fairly clear focus for the suggestions which follow. The authors acknowledge five major factors as contributory causes of ADHD and ADD including heredity, organic factors, diet and allergies, environmental toxins and other medical problems. They also acknowledge that social, cultural, educational and stress factors can cause, or exacerbate, attentional problems in many children.

Interestingly, the authors also assert that while it is not always the case that ADD/ADHD children have a coexisting learning difficulty in a significant proportion, in 20–40% a co-existent learning disability is evident. In those cases such difficulties tend to be a combination of auditory/visual perception and processing; sequencing; fine motor; visual motor integration; eye/hand coordination, reading/spelling/maths disorders and written language problems. The whole field of ADD requires considerable attention because of the range of difficulties which can be exhibited.

The authors also describe in a very clear manner some of the characteristics of ADD in relation to distractibility – short attention span, difficulty completing tasks, day-dreaming, easily distracted, much activity but little accomplished, enthusiastic beginnings but poor endings. They also describe the characteristics of other factors associated with ADD/ADHD stemming from impulsiveness, overactivity and hyperactivity, immaturity and emotional difficulties.

The comprehensive section on treating attention disorders should be of considerable value to teachers. This section focuses on goal setting, classroom management and organisation and various forms of assessment schedules such as the Copeland Symptom Checklist for Attention Deficit Disorders. In general this volume can provide the teacher with many ideas which can be adapted to help dyslexic children who may also exhibit signs of attention disorders.

Alphabet Soup – A Recipe for Understanding and Treating Attention Deficit Hyperactivity Disorder
A Handbook for Parents and Teachers
James Javorsky
Minerva Press Inc., Clarkston, MI (1993).

This handbook provides a comprehensive and informative guide to both parents and teachers who are involved with children with ADD. It provides an outline of the characteristics of ADD as well as of some of the causes of diagnostic procedures.

It provides suggestions for dealing with ADD by altering the classroom environment, developing individual learning plans and giving medical treatment.

A useful appendix contains a parents' guide to test results and outlines of individual learning plans.

Action Rhymes and Games
Max de Boo
Scholastic Publications (1992).

This book for early years provides a wealth of ideas and activities to help young children develop language, motor skills, social skills and creativity. There are also activities relating to music, mathematics and science.

The book comprises short, easy-to-follow activities together with objectives and further follow-up activities. For example some of the activities contained in the section 'Language Skills and Understanding' include the encouragement of recall and summarising, developing listening skills, providing experience of action verbs, sounds and prepositions, encouraging pronunciation skills and rhyming and reinforcing the concept of 'in' and 'out'.

A very useful resource work.

Words – Integrated Decoding and Spelling Instruction based on Word Origin and Word Structure
Marcia K. Henry
Lex Press, CA, USA (second edition 1993).

This approach to reading and spelling is intended to supplement mainstream classroom activities. The approach emphasises decoding and spelling instruction based on word origin and word structure. The programme follows the principles outlined in the Orton–Gillingham programme (Gillingham and Stillman, 1956) and Project Read (Calfee and Henry, 1985). The lessons focus on spelling patterns and rules and word features, and students learn about Latin root words, their orthographic features and how they generate additional words. There are follow-up activities which reinforce these patterns. A framework matrix is provided which illustrates word origins and structure as guides for decoding and spelling. Thus Anglo-Saxon, Latin and Greek word origins are categorised into letter-sound correspondences, syllable patterns and morpheme patterns.

Each lesson has a purpose and an objective with follow-up activities. The lessons contained in Unit 1 'Organising Letter-Sound Correspondences' include consonant blends, consonant digraphs, long and short vowels and vowel digraphs. There are reviews and a unit test at the end.

Other lesson units include 'Syllable Patterns', 'Layers of Language', 'Morpheme Patterns', 'Strategies for Decoding Long Words' and 'Strategies for Spelling Long Words'.

Tutor 1 – Structured, Sequential, Multi-sensory Lessons based on the Orton–Gillingham Approach
Marcia K. Henry and Nancy C. Redding
Lex Press, CA, USA (1990).

This book of forty-two lessons is intended for primary aged children who are having difficulty in reading, writing or spelling.

The techniques and the presentation are based on the Orton–Gillingham approach and utilises a multisensory approach in a structured and sequential manner. The lessons provide a framework which teachers will need to supplement with their own materials. The initial lessons present new consonants or vowels, blending and dictation and copying, tracing and writing on paper while saying letter names. There are also activities focusing on auditory, sequential memory and story reading. Some lessons highlight linguistic awareness such as asking students to say some words beginning with specific blends which the tutor provides.

The book contains a useful section on spelling rules based on silent 'e', plurals, soft 'c' and 'g', double letter rule, suffixes and polysyllabic words.

Reasoning and Reading – Level 1
Joanne Carlisle
Educators Publishers, Cambridge, MA, USA (1993).

This is essentially a training programme focusing on reasoning, language and reading comprehension – areas which the author believes are intrinsically intertwined in the process of learning and understanding. Thus the programme ensures that word recognition is an important aspect in reading comprehension, that reading comprehension is related to general language comprehension and that reasoning is a crucial ability not only to develop ideas but as an approach to reading and comprehension.

It can readily fit into existing schemes and can be used as support material for a mainstream class. The programme is divided into four units – Word Meaning, Sentence Meaning, Paragraph Structure and Meaning, and Reasoning.

The section word meaning looks at word relationships, e.g. categorising and identifying words which have common characteristics but have quite different meanings. This unit also looks at similarities and differences, related words, analogies and using words in context.

The unit sentence meaning looks at what a sentence is, jumbled sentences and word order.

The paragraph structure and meaning unit looks at main ideas, writing structure and key words.

The reasoning unit looks at aspects such as fact or opinion, judging opinions, relevant information, use of inference and solving problems.

An excellent book with an accompanying teachers' guide which highlights some of the important aspects of reading in context to gain some real understanding from text.

Differentiation: Your Responsibility: An In-Service Training Pack for Staff Development
T. Barthorpe and J. Visser
Nasen Publication (1991).

This in-service training pack perceives differentiation in the same manner as envisaged in the Warnock Report (DES, 1978).

> The purpose of education for all children is the same; the goals are the same. But the help that individual children need in progressing towards them will be different.

The authors of this pack therefore anticipate that teachers will require a clear understanding of the learning processes of children, a knowledge of task analysis, to collaborate with colleagues, and knowledge of curriculum design and implementation in order to successfully achieve effective differentiation.

The pack aims to help schools formulate policies and practices for themselves and to give all children access to the full curriculum. The pack contains a number of master overhead transparencies and practical hints for using the materials. The materials are arranged in three sections – 'Understanding of the

Term Differentiation', 'Pupils and Learning' and 'Differentiation in the Class-room'. There are also suggestions for delivery of the in-service sessions with examples.

A very useful resource.

Dyslexia and Mathematics
Edited by T. R. Miles and E. Miles
Routledge (1992).

This book contains a collection of very useful chapters on different aspects of mathematics. It provides a theoretical perspective to provide a platform for the chapters on diagnosis and cognitive styles, language, reading and writing aspects of mathematics and the needs of, and strategies for, secondary pupils.

IT Support for Specific Learning Difficulties
Edited by Sally McKeown
NCET (1992).

This booklet provides the teacher with a useful catalogue of hardware and software which can be useful with children with specific learning difficulties. It discusses the nature of the problem, illustrates how word processing can help with literacy skills and exemplifies this by using case studies. Information on software packages is provided, in particular predictive word processing packages such as Mindreader and PAL (Predictive Adaptive Lexicon). The former is an American package (Brown Bay software) while the latter was produced by a team at the University of Dundee. The booklet has a useful appendix with addresses for software and useful contacts.

Computers and Dyslexia – Educational Applications of New Technology
Edited by C. Singleton
Dyslexia Computer Resource Centre, University of Hull (1994).

This text is the product of a conference organised by the Dyslexia Computer Resource Centre held at the University of Coventry. It contains informative chapters on reading and writing, keyboard skills, the Somerset Talking Com-puter Project, memory and mathematics, and assessment and screening. An excellent source book on this increasingly important area and its application in the classroom.

ACCELEREAD, ACCELEWRITE: A guide to using talking computers to help children learn to read and write
Vivienne Clifford and Martin Miles
iansyst Ltd, 72 Fen Road, Cambridge, England (1994).

This guide helps the teacher access talking systems for the microcomputer. The emphasis is on developing the practical skills, but the guide also provides a theoretical understanding of the system.

The guide provides suggestions for using the applications for creative and curriculum-based work. The first two sections examine the hardware which can be utilised and the theory behind the approach.

Essentially it provides the basis for a structural approach to developing phonological skills in a multisensory way. Thus the pupil reads the story, then types it into the computer, the computer then repeats each word of the sentence to the child as the space bar is pressed. The whole sentence is also spoken once the sentence has been completed.

The guide emphasises self-monitoring, auditory and visual feedback. An excellent resource.

Using Computers with Dyslexics
Ted Pottage
Dyslexia Computer Resource Centre, University of Hull, (third edition, 1994).

This is an extremely useful booklet containing a wealth of information on points to consider when choosing hardware and software. There is also a useful section on the use of computers for dyslexics looking at keyboarding skills, building language skills and programmes for maths skills.

British Dyslexia Association
Computer Booklets
BDA in Conjunction with Dyslexia Computer Resource Centre (1997).

The BDA have produced a set of low-priced computer booklets with introductory leaflets. The introductory leaflets look at portable computers, keyboard skills and computer management, software, talking computers and information for dyslexic adults.

There are also more detailed booklets on exams, maths, early literacy and numeracy skills and dyslexic adults and computers. Information technology is an important area for dyslexic students and these booklets offer a clear account of how this continually developing area can be effectively accessed by dyslexic students and teachers.

The Gift of Dyslexia. Why Some of the Smartest People Can't Read and How They Can Learn
Ronald D. Davies with Eldon M. Braun
Souvenir Press (1997).

This book describes a specific approach on tackling dyslexia devised and indeed experienced by the author. The author describes dyslexia as a type of disorientation, similar to the type of disorientation one experiences sitting in a motionless car, when a car moves alongside. The author therefore sees dyslexia as a perceptual factor and the programme described in the book emphasises the role of perception. The exercises which are part of the programme – Davis Orientation Mastery – describe perceptual ability assessment, basic symbol mastery and symbol mastery for words.

Other Useful Teaching Programmes Include:

Augur J. and Briggs S. (1992) *Hickey Multi-Sensory Language Course* (2nd ed.). Whurr Publishers.

Bell N. (1991) *Visualizing and Verbalizing for Language Comprehension and Thinking.* Academy of Reading Publishers. CA, USA.

Cooke A. (1993) *Tackling Dyslexia: The Bangor Way.* Whurr Publishers.

Cowdery L., McMahon J., Montgomery D., Morse P. and Prince M. (1984–8) *Kingston Programme-Teaching Reading through Spelling.* Frondeg Hall Publishers.

Cox A. R. (1993) *Foundations for Literacy.* Educ. Pub. Service, USA.

Davies A. (1996) *Handwriting, Reading and Spelling System* (THRASS) Collins Educational.

Henry M. K. and Redding N. C. (1993) *Word Lists: Structured, Sequential, Multi-sensory.* Lex Press, USA.

Hornsby B. and Pool J. (1989 and 1993) *Alpha to Omega Activity Packs. Stage 1, 2 and 3.* Heinemann Educational Publishers.

Kimmell G. M. (1989) *Sound Out.* Academic Therapy Publishers.

Kratoville B. L. (1989) *Word Tracking: Proverbs /High Frequency Verbs.* Ann Arbor.

McNicholas J. and McEntree J. (1991) *Games to Develop and Improve Reading Levels.* NASEN Pub.

Miles E. (1992) *Bangor Dyslexia Teaching System* (2nd ed). Whurr Publishers, London.

Reason R. and Boote R. (1991) *Learning Difficulties in Reading and Writing.* NFER Nelson.

Russell S. (1993) *Phonic Code Cracker.* Jordanhill Publications.

Russell J. P. (1989) *Graded Activities for Children with Motor Difficulties.* Cambridge University.

Selman M. R. (1989) *Infant Teacher's Handbook.* Oliver & Boyd.

Singleton C. (1991) *Computers and Literacy Skills.* BDA University of Hull.

Slingerland B. H. (1993) *Specific Language Disability Children.* Educ. Pub. Service, USA.

Smith J. and Bloom M. (1985) *Simple Phonetics for Teachers.* Methuen.

Thomson M. and Watkins W. (1990) *Dyslexia: A Teaching Handbook.* Whurr Publishers

Topping K. (1992) *Promoting Cooperative Learning.* Kirklees Metropolitan Council.

Wendon L. (1992) *Letterland Teaching Programs.* Letterland, Cambs.

Wilkins A. (1993) *Intuitive Overlays.* IOO Marketing Ltd, 56–62 Newington Causeway, London.

LEARNING SKILLS/SELF-ESTEEM

Take Time
Mary Nash-Wortham and Jean Hunt
The Robinswood Press, Stourbridge, England (second combined editions revised 1993).

There is a growing awareness of the link between language and movement, and this book highlights the connection with a series of movement exercises to help children with difficulties in speech and literacy.

It provides a useful section on pointers to areas of difficulty which include timing and rhythm, directional problems, spatial orientation and movement, fine motor centrality and laterality. This is followed by exercise sheets to help promote development in these areas. All the exercises are clearly set out and appropriately illustrated. The five motor control exercises for speech, writing and reading would be particularly useful for dyslexic children.

Analogical Reasoning in Children
Usha Goswami
Lawrence Erlbaum Associates (1992).

This interesting and useful book discusses the view that analogies are important in learning, problem solving and discovery. Piaget's theory of analogical reasoning is initially examined and information processing models of analogical reasoning are discussed.

There are also chapters looking at analogies in babies and toddlers and in the real world of the classroom.

The book argues strongly for the importance of analogies in learning and development and relates this to classroom situations and classroom learning.

Word Play
Sheila Wolfendale and Trevor Bryans
NARE Publications, Stafford (1990).

This very useful booklet contains language activities for young children and their parents. It also provides a theoretical explanation for the programme, based on cooperation and partnership between parents and teachers. The introduction to the language activities section describes the procedure and the stages in implementing the programme: preparation; implementation; and measuring progress.

The activities are easy to follow and sure to be enjoyed by all involved in the programme. They provide some good ideas for conversational time with young children, story telling and story making as well as drama and games. The games and activities involve all the senses and provide a useful 'ideas' booklet for teachers and parents of young children.

Mapping Inner Space – Learning and Teaching Mind Mapping
Nancy Margulies
Zephyr Press (1991).

The use of mind mapping is becoming a valuable study tool and thinking skill for many students. In this text Nancy Margulies identifies mind mapping as a 'flexible, evolving system with unlimited potential'. The evolution of the practice of mind mapping is highlighted by the examples contained in this volume. Virtually every point made in the text is illustrated with a mind map and the easy-to-follow chapter headings make this a useful teacher manual in mind mapping. Essentially the text helps to prepare teachers to teach the skill of mind mapping to students.

The author suggests that to become a mind mapper it is initially useful to record your own ideas selected from topics such as plans for the day, the week, memories of a specific event, strategies for a new project, interests and hobbies, or a recent book. It may be essential to start with these meaningful and manageable topics since otherwise there is a risk of becoming daunted by the sophistication, elaboration and creativity of the ideas for mind maps illustrated later in this volume.

The author makes a useful distinction between the generation of ideas and the organisation of ideas, the two processes which together form the basis of a mind map. For those who are not naturally visually inclined a step-by-step symbol making guide is included. Following this manual, which is essentially an experiential volume, most readers should be able to develop and understand the concept and uses of mind maps.

Get Better Grades
Margie Agnew, Steve Barlow, Lee Pascal and Steve Skidmore
Piccadilly Press, London (1995).

This short text on study skills looks at attitude, organisation, listening and note taking, reading and writing skills and revision for exams. The information is presented in an eye catching manner and there is a vast amount of useful study strategies more suitable for older children and even some adults. Study skills is important for maximising the skills of dyslexic students, this book will certainly help in that process.

Learning Styles
Priscilla L. Vail
Modern Learning Press, Rosemont, New Jersey (1992).

This volume explores various aspects of learning styles from kindergarten through to fourth grade and provides over 130 practical tips for teachers.

Priscilla Vail analyses how children process information – three dimensionally or two dimensionally, simultaneously or sequentially, visually, auditorily, kin-aesthetically or tactilely. Additionally, she focuses on how children make connections in relation to retrieving information already learned and consolidating that new information. She also addresses other types of personality and learning preferences such as utilising imagery, factual information and aesthetic stimuli.

The many suggested activities which follow on from this analysis provide the reader with easy-to-follow ideas on respecting and enhancing the individual learning styles of children. One of the suggested tips is for utilising kinaesthetic and tactile learning skills.

> Teach sound/symbol correspondence and letter formation by using the large muscles of the arm to 'sky write' The letters formed in the air should be as large as the arc of the child's swing. Teach a little verbal accompaniment such as 'd' starts the way 'b' starts, fills the 'house space', closes the circle, goes all the way up through the attic and back down through the house!
>
> (from *Learning Styles*, Priscilla Vail).

A very useful book.

The Mind Map Book – Radiant Thinking
Tony Buzan
BBC Books (1993).

This book by Tony Buzan, the originator of mind maps, provides an excellent detailed description of the concept and uses of the mind mapping strategy. The book illustrates how mind maps can be developed from, for example, brainstorming with words. There are plentiful exercises to help the reader practice the strategy at different levels. The text also highlights the versatility of mind mapping by describing its uses in personal, educational, business and professional areas.

Learn Playful Techniques to Accelerate Learning
Regina G. Richards
Zephyr Press (1993).

This comprehensive, easy-to-follow volume of interesting activities provides useful strategies for learning for students of all ages. It is based on the set of strategies which the author calls 'Learning – Learning Efficiently and Remembering Mnemonics'. The foreword highlights important points which provide a scenario and context for the chapters which follow, by reminding the reader that 'teachers do not cause learning' but they can create conditions for enhancement of learning where it is 'safe to try, possible to succeed and worth the effort'.

The book focuses on learning styles and highlights hemispheric specialisation indicating how the left brain codes and processes messages in language, operating in a linear, sequential and logical fashion while the right deals with non-verbal material operating in a holistic, inventive, informal and symbolic mode. Reference is made to Healy's use of the terms 'lumpers and splitters' in relation to learning styles – the 'splitter' organises information and plans tasks precisely, whereas the 'lumper' uses predominantly right brain skills, processes information holistically and simultaneously. Richards acknowledges that the brain prefers cooperation rather than conflict and that most activities utilise both hemispheres.

The book provides an interesting chapter on the concept of visualisation in learning. It looks initially at simple visual skills and proceeds to visualisation skills. There is a useful chapter on memory foundations for multiplication which provides a step by step method for developing the strategy.

Spelling is also considered and suggestions are provided for creating mnemonic links in spelling. The author encourages the identification of patterns in words such as canoe and shoe and the use of this link mnemonically to facilitate remembering the pattern. Similar mnemonic techniques are encouraged for reading and this chapter provides exercises and visual help on the strategy known as 'COPS', i.e. categorisation, organisation, punctuation and spelling in relation to re-reading a piece of work.

There are also chapters on mind mapping, the use of music and rhythm in the classroom, and a development of the earlier theme of visual skills and visualisation.

Unicorns are Real: A Right-Brained Approach to Learning
Barbara Meister Vitale
Jalman Press (1982).

This book begins with a clear introduction to hemispheric specialisation. It describes different modes of processing information such as linear and holistic, symbolic and concrete, sequential and random, logical and intuitive, verbal and non-verbal, and abstract and analogic.

This is followed by a useful section on modality and dominance screening looking at the characteristics of hemispheric dominance in relation to general factors, eye, hand and body.

The major part of the book is occupied by interesting and useful activities in relation to students' learning strategies. These include exercises on phonics, sequencing, mathematics, writing, organisation, and aspects of reading such as visual tracking. The exercises are easy to follow and can be particularly useful in enhancing right-brain skills and self-esteem in younger children.

In the Mind's Eye: Visual Thinkers, Gifted People with Learning Difficulties, Computer Images and the Ironies of Creativity
Thomas G. West
Prometheus Books (1991, second edition 1997).

This text highlights the positive side of dyslexia. It provides extensive profiles of gifted people such as Faraday, Einstein and da Vinci who were all dyslexic and examines patterns in creativity and relates these patterns to computers and visual images and the implications of these for dyslexic students and adults. There are some excellent insights into the potential of the dyslexic learner, perhaps encapsulated in the statement, 'We ought to begin to pay less attention to getting everyone over the same hill using the same path. We may wish to encourage some to take different routes to the same end. Then we might see good reasons for paying careful attention to their descriptions of what they have found. We may wish to follow them some day.'

Study Skills
Charles Cuff
Cambridge Educational (1989).

Study skills are extremely important to help provide dyslexic children with the opportunity of developing independent study habits.

This study skills programme for children aged 8 to 12 contains four volumes. The slim books consist of a range of varied activities in which the child has to complete a task. The exercises help to provide key skills such as organisation, selecting of main points, abbreviations, dictionary speed search and categorisation of information.

Useful activity books for this age group.

Somerset Thinking Skills Course
Nigel Blagg, Marj Ballinger, Richard Gardner, Mel Petty and Gareth Williams
Basil Blackwell in association with Somerset County Council (1988).

This series of books contains seven modules and a handbook designed to facilitate the development of learning skills. The modules include Foundations for Problem Solving, Analysing and Synthesising, Comparative Thinking, Positions in Time and Space, Understanding Analogies, Patterns in Time and Space, and Organising and Memorising.

Each module contains teacher guidelines and pupil materials and consists of illustrated materials which present the basis of the problem, including the background, strategies for proceeding with the task, resources and key vocabulary. Ideas on how the teacher may proceed to involve students in the task and how their responses can be transferred and generalised to other contexts are also highlighted in each exercise.

A very useful series of activities which cut across traditional subject boundaries and encourage the development of metacognitive and thinking skills.

Teaching Elementary Students through Their Individual Learning Styles
Rita Dunn and Kenneth Dunn
Allyn & Bacon (1992).

The Dunn and Dunn learning styles model has been extensively researched. This book translates this accepted research into practical techniques and provides varied and relevant activities and instructional guidelines for teachers.

The authors discuss skills, styles and the learning context. They discuss the concept of learning styles, illustrate how to identify individual learning styles and discuss different approaches to teaching and classroom design based on the learning styles model developed by the authors.

This volume contains a wealth of information and resources on helping teachers develop an awareness of, and skills and provision to acknowledge and respond to, the individual needs and learning styles of children. Volumes for kindergarten and secondary students are also available in the same series.

Learning and Teaching Style – In Theory and Practice
Kathleen A. Butler
Learners Dimension, PO Box 6, Columbia, CT (1987).

This useful volume is largely influenced by the 'Mindstyle' model of learning style developed by Anthony F. Gregorc. Butler provides an understanding of the model which highlights the qualitative differences among individuals and the 'four mind channels' of 'concrete sequential, abstract sequential, concrete random and abstract random'. Each channel has its own particular behaviour and characteristics, e.g. concrete sequential individuals display the practical, predictable, organised and structured aspects of behaviour while concrete random individuals show the original experimental, investigative and risk taking aspects of behaviour.

The abstract sequential individual displays intellectual, logical, conceptual, rational and studious characteristics while the abstract random person shows emotional, sensitive, holistic, interpretative and thematic preferences.

The volume describes this model in relation to teaching styles with many good examples; profiles children's learning styles showing criteria for identification; and discusses style application. The chapter on style application, teaching approaches and lesson design makes this useful for teachers, but the main purpose of the book is to help teachers to become aware of the importance of style and to use this awareness and understanding in the classroom.

Doing Your Research Project: A Guide for First-Time Researchers in Education and Social Science
Judith Bell
Open University Press (second edition, 1993).

This publication can help the student plan and implement a research project. There are chapters on planning, recording, negotiating access, interviews and questionnaire design. Chapters on reviewing the literature, interpreting and presenting the evidence and writing the report make this a useful reference book for students embarking on research projects.

Learning to Learn – A Study Skills Course Book
Pat Heaton and Gina Mitchell
Better Books Publishing (1987).

This study skills manual aimed at the older student should prove an excellent resource for both teacher and student.

It is divided into twenty-one units, each unit focusing on a different aspect of study skills. The units include 'notetaking', 'essay preparation and planning', 'references and bibliographies', 'interview techniques' and 'dealing with examinations'.

The units are clearly written and expressed in an experiential manner, actively involving the student throughout.

Dyslexia and Stress
Edited by T. R. Miles and Ved Varma
Whurr Publications (1995)

This book describes the different types of stress experienced by dyslexic people. The importance of this area is highlighted by the range of chapters presented in this book. These include stress in early education, in the adolescent, at college, in the workplace, among gifted dyslexics and within the family.

There is also a chapter in which dyslexics speak for themselves, providing personal perspectives of how the disability affected their lives. It is important in a book which looks at the psychological and emotional aspects of the dyslexic individual to include these personal perspectives. It is also important for all involved in the field of dyslexia to appreciate the emotional effect of the difficulty as experienced by the dyslexic person.

Quality Circle Time in the Primary Classroom
Jenny Mosley
LDA (1996)

This book is a guide to enhancing self-esteem, self-discipline and positive relationships. It focuses on quality circle time in the classroom following on from the authors previous book, *Turn your School Around.*

The book is divided into five parts – one on establishing positive relationships in the classroom, part two on creating a calm and positive classroom ethos, part three on exploring the use of circle time activities, part four on circle meetings and part five provides further information on circle time, for example, how it can relate to the national curriculum.

This book is a very comprehensive guide to circle time activities and how the activities can be integrated and utilised within the school setting. It contains plentiful ideas and suggestions for further activity related to circle time and the programmes and activities are all underpinned by a circular model developed by the author showing how circle time can be implemented within the school system. An excellent resource.

Other Texts Which May be Useful Include:

Baddeley A. (1987) *Working Memory.* Clarendon, Oxford.
Berry R. (1986) *How to Write a Research Paper* (2nd edition). Pergamon Press, Oxford.
Buzan T. (1988) *Make the Most of Your Mind.* Pan Books.

Caine R. N. and Caine G. (1991) *Making Connections.* Banta.

de Bono E. (1992) *CORT Thinking.* Pergamon Press.

Gardner H. (1985) *Frames of Mind.* Basic Books, USA.

Keefe J. W. (1993) *Learning Style: Theory: Practice: Cognitive Skills.* NASSP Pub. USA.

Levine M. D. (1993) *All Kinds of Minds.* Educ. Publisher.

Levine M. D. (1992) *Keeping A Head in School.* Educ. Publisher.

Lewis I. and Munn P. (1993) *So You Want to do Research.* SCRE, Edinburgh.

Macintyre C (1993) *Let's Find Why.* Moray House Publications.

McCarthy B. (1987) *The 4-Mat System.* Excel Inc.

Munn P. and Drever E. (1993) *Using Questionnaires in Small Scale Research.* SCRE, Edinburgh.

Nisbet J. and Shucksmith J. (1986) *Learning Strategies.* Routledge.

Pollock J. and Waller E. (1994) *Day to Day Dyslexia in the Classroom.* Routledge.

Selmes I. (1987) *Improving Study Skills.* Hodder & Stoughton.

Sharron H. (1987) *Changing Children's Minds.* Condor Press.

Springer S. P. (1989) *Left Brain, Right Brain.* Freeman.

Stirling E. G. (1991) *Help for the Dyslexic Adolescent.* Better Books.

Williams L. V. (1983) *Teaching for the Two-Sided Mind.* Simon & Schuster.

ASSESSMENT

Psychological Assessment of Dyslexia
Martin Turner
Whurr Publishers (1997).

This book provides a comprehensive analysis of psychological assessment. The book contains chapters on abilities, individual variation, cognitive anomalies and structures for charting individual attainment and reporting. There is also a chapter on recommendations for specialist teaching with an analysis of a casework sample.

The important area of testing for teachers is not forgotten and there are also sections on the younger child, the adult and a discussion on some of the issues relating to resources.

As the title suggests the book is essentially concerned with psychological assessment and the detailed analysis it provides should prove extremely beneficial to educational psychologists in particular.

Reading Assessment for Teachers (RAT Pack)
M. Cooper, R. Parker and S. Toombs
Wiltshire County Council (1991).

This is a very comprehensive and useful pack. Essentially a training course of six sessions, it provides a detailed analysis of reading errors and reading performance. The authors acknowledge the work of Marie Clay (1985) and Helen Arnold (1984) which has clearly influenced the development of the pack.

In addition to providing a clear guide to miscue analysis, the guide also offers some practical guidance on setting clear targets, avoiding unnecessary assessment, monitoring of progress and providing effective feedback. Indeed Session 2 'Further Assessment and Setting Aims' provides a very useful special needs file which allows the teacher to record detailed information on the pupil's progress on print concepts, text reading, word recognition, reading strategies and comprehension, and allows for a summary of diagnostic assessment, short-term aims and suggested changes to curriculum management of teaching arrangements.

Sessions 4 and 5 follow up the assessment by focusing on teaching. These sessions offer a summary of a range of strategies including paired reading, 'praise, prompt and praise', ideas for reading without the teacher, and a technique known as the Coventry technique which is a systematic approach to acquiring a basic sight vocabulary based on the child's own language. There are also suggestions for teaching print skills including grapho-phonemic skills, letter-sound correspondence, sounding out, principles of phonics, teaching and the multi-sensory approach.

A well balanced approach to assessment and teaching which has been positively evaluated (Cooper, Toombs and Parker, 1992).

Phonological Assessment of Specific Learning Difficulties
Edited by Norah Frederickson and Rea Reason
Educational and Child Psychology, Vol. 12, No. 1 (1995).

This booklet (88 pages) discusses the role of phonological assessment in specific learning difficulties and explains the development of the Phonological Assessment Battery. The booklet begins with Frith providing an excellent theoretical model which highlights the role of phonological skills and justifies the nature of the tests selected for the Phonological Assessment Battery. The following chapters provide some insights into the rationale and composition of the specific subtests which comprise the Assessment Battery.

Learning Inventory Manual – Tests and Remediation
Barbara Meister Vitale and Waneta B. Bullock
Ann Arbor Publishers, Northumberland (1989).

This set of materials helps the teacher determine the student's level of competence in a range of tasks and the student's difficulties and the reasons for those difficulties. The Level C materials aim to evaluate the students' skills in visual dissemination skills, visual motor coordination skills, sequential memory skills, aural skills, and comprehension skills.

The tests are aimed at students in the 10–14 age range. Each of the above dimensions of assessment has an accompanying explanation describing the classroom implications and some guidelines for remediation. It also provides some ideas for which of this publisher's other materials are most suited to help deal with the difficulty. For example, for visual discrimination difficulties the book suggests exercises in visual tracking, recognising visual cues and visual discrimination.

The materials are also available in different skill levels and include a student work book.

Assessment – A Framework for Teachers
Ruth Sutton
Routledge (1992).

This very readable book on assessment provides a useful overview of the field. It contains an informative glossary identifying key phrases (mainly in relation to the English National Curriculum) such as attainment targets and records of achievement. The author also discusses different types of assessment and the criteria for effective assessment, looking at validity, reliability, manageability, moderation and standardisation.

Other aspects of assessment such as planning assessment, objectives, record keeping and providing feedback to learners and parents are also discussed, as is the aspect of whole-school issues. Issues relating to the development of a whole-school policy, the use of performance indicators, cross-curricular assessment and progression are examined.

Diagnosing Dyslexia – A Guide to the Assessment of Adults with Specific Learning Difficulties
Cynthia Klein
Adult Literacy and Basic Skills Unit, Kingsbourne House, London (1993).

This useful and well presented book provides a clear methodology for assessing adults, including the diagnostic interview, reading, writing and spelling assessment, and providing oral and written feedback.

The essence of the book centres round the need to provide a qualitative analysis of the students' or adults' difficulties and Klein suggests this can be achieved through an in-depth interview, a miscue analysis of reading, a reading comprehension test, spelling error analyses and an analysis of a piece of free writing.

This book provides a checklist to assist with the diagnostic interview, a marking system for miscue analysis with an indication of different types of errors such as visual or phonic, and some examples from passages highlighting error analysis.

There is also a summary of visual processing problems, auditory processing problems and motor processing problems, a section on the reading process, and an appendix containing examples of reading and spelling tests.

Bury Infant Check
L. E. A. Pearson and J. Quinn
NFER Nelson (1986).

This check is designed to identify those children who may display difficulties in language skills, number skills and perceptual motor skills such as copying shapes and visual discrimination. There is also a quick check procedure based on observation and responses from selected items.

Suffolk Reading Scale
Frank Hagley
NFER Nelson (1987).

This standardised test can be administered as a group test or on an individual basis. The results provide normative data on the reading level of an individual or a group and assist in selecting reading materials at appropriate levels for children. There is also an age equivalent and book titles page which is useful for the teacher.

The scale, although initially standardised in Suffolk, has now been standardised to match a nationally representative sample. It has three levels, each consisting of sentences or phrases with words missing and the pupil has to select the appropriate word from a multiple choice list. There are both computer and hand scoring sheets.

Test of Initial Literacy (TOIL)
Anne Kispal, Alison Tate, Tom Groman and Chris Whetton
NFER Nelson (1989).

This test is designed to provide information relating to the strengths and weaknesses of children in reading and writing.

It consists of nine separate scores based on tests of letter matching, word matching, copying, grammatical punctuation, orthographic punctuation, spelling of homophones, spelling, writing style and free writing. The tests are suitable for children aged between 7 and 12 years and the results provide acceptable score ranges for each of the tests.

Keele Pre-School Assessment Guide
Stephen Tyler
NFER Nelson (1980).

There are two sections to this assessment guide. In the first section the teacher records aspects of the child's behaviour and in the second section cognitive, social, physical and linguistic skills are itemised and arranged in ascending order of difficulty.

The cognition section includes items relating to space and time, properties of objects, sorting and classification skills, memory, number and problem solving. The language section includes language use, speech, vocabulary and comprehension.

This guide forms a useful short booklet for the pre-school or early years teacher.

Diagnostic Reading Record
Helen Arnold
Hodder & Stoughton (1992).

This assessment consists of a teacher's handbook and pupil profile sheets which aim to provide a means of assessing reading development through both observations using miscue analysis, and examination of oral reading through discussion, focusing on the level of understanding which the child has of the passage.

The author has also geared the assessment to the strands of the English National Curriculum which can help teachers make judgments about pupils' levels of achievement in relation to the National Curriculum. The teacher's manual contains informative case studies highlighting key aspects of the diagnostic reading record profile and examples of scoring the passage using miscue analysis.

The reading passages are in the form of photo-copiable masters.

An excellent assessment resource for the teacher.

Practitioner's Guide to Dynamic Assessment
Carol S. Lidz
Guilford Press (1991).

This publication represents a highly accomplished piece of work on dynamic Assessment. This form of assessment is described by the author as one which involves active participation by the learner, facilitates learning by focusing on the process not the product of learning, and provides information to help determine how change is best accomplished.

The book examines different dynamic assessment models, examines research, and looks at pre-school learning and curriculum based adaptation. There are also some case studies with sample reports and a useful appendix with examples of record forms.

Opening the Door – Guidance on Recognising and Helping the Dyslexic Child
Edited by A. Brereton and P. Cann
British Dyslexia Association, Reading (1993).

A very informative text on the crucial area of early recognition. The chapters reflect the perspectives of different professionals such as the teacher, doctor, speech therapist, psychologist and a physical education consultant. There is also an interesting chapter on hyperactivity and attention deficit, as well as an early recognition checklist which can be completed by both parents and teachers.

An Observational Survey of Early Literacy Achievement
Marie M. Clay
Heinemann Education (1993).

A text containing detailed descriptions of observation surveys in reading and writing. The class teacher will find this an extremely useful book – clearly presented, it provides examples and descriptions of observational strategies including how to take a running record of reading texts and other observation tasks such as letter identification, concepts about print, word tests, writing and dictation.

There is also a useful chapter on strategies to help with text, words and letters with examples of survey summaries.

Non-Reading Intelligence Tests
D. Young
Hodder & Stoughton (1989).

The Non-Reading Intelligence Test is primarily orally administered and can help the test administrator obtain an intelligence score for poor readers which may be a more accurate reflection of their ability.

There are three levels corresponding to chronological age, which ranges from six years four months to thirteen years eleven months. Each level contains a number of sub-tests and the author indicates that this test has been used to assist in the diagnosis of children with specific learning difficulties.

Other Assessment Materials Include:

Ames E. (1991) *Teach Yourself to Diagnose Reading Problems.* Macmillan Educational.

Arnold H. (1992) *Diagnostic Reading Record.* Hodder & Stoughton.

Arnold H. (1984) *Making Sense of It: Miscue Analysis.* Hodder & Stoughton.

Aubrey C., Eaves J., Hicks C. and Newton M. (1982) *Aston Portfolio.* LDA.

Boder E. and Jarrico S. (1982) *Boder Test of Reading-Spelling Patterns.* Harcourt Brace Jovanovich.

Bradley L. (1980) *Assessing Reading Difficulties: Diagnostic, Remedial.* NFER Nelson.

Burt C. (1975) *Burt Word Reading Test.* Hodder & Stoughton for SCRE.

Clay M. (1985) *The Early Detection of Reading Difficulties.* Heinemann Educational.

Edwards P. (1992) *Edwards Reading Test.* Heinemann Educational.

Hagley F. (1987) *Suffolk Reading Scale.* NFER Nelson.

Jones-Elgar R. (1989) *The Cloze Line.* Ann Arbor Pub.

Kaufman A. A. (1992) *Intelligent Testing with WISC-R.* Psychological Corporation.

Klein C. (1993) *Diagnosing Dyslexia.* Albsu.

McCleod J. (1994) *GAP Reading Comprehension Test.* Heinemann Educational.

Miles T. R. (1983) *Bangor Dyslexia Test.* LDA Cambs.

Neale, M. (1989) *Neale Analysis* NFER Nelson.

Newton M. and Thompson M. (1982) *The Aston Index.* LDA Cambs.

Raven J. C. (1988) *Mill Hill Manual and Vocabulary Scale.* NFER Nelson.

Raven J. C. (1992:1993) *Standard Progressive Matrices.* Oxford Psychologists Press, Oxford.

Robertson A. H., Henderson A., Robertson A., Fisher J. and Gibson M. (1983, second edition 1995) *Quest Reading and Number Screening Tests.* Nelson.

Slingerland B. H. (1985) *Screening Tests for Identifying Children with Specific Learning Disabilities.* Educators Pub.

Sutton R. (1992) *Assessment-Framework for Teachers.* Routledge.

Tyler S. (1980) *Keele Pre-school Assessment Guide.* NFER Nelson.

Vincent E. and de la Mare M. (1987) *New Macmillan Reading Analysis.* Macmillan Educational.

Vincent D. and Claydon J. (1982) *Diagnostic Spelling Test.* NFER Nelson.

WRITING/MOTOR SKILLS

Dysgraphia – Why Johnny Can't Write: A Handbook for Teachers and Parents
Diane Walton Cavey
Pro-Ed Inc. Austin, TX (second edition, 1993).

This book focuses on dysgraphia by looking at explanations of dysgraphia, presenting this from the parents' and teachers' perspective with suggestions for developing a teaching programme. It also looks at vocational training and a useful glossary is included.

For parents the book provides some early warning signs and some tasks which may be helpful. Examples of dysgraphic characteristics and ideas for teaching provide the teacher with useful guidelines for assessment and teaching. A very useful book.

Putting Pen to Paper: A New Approach to Handwriting
Melvyn Ramsden
Southgate, Devon (1992).

A very comprehensive and useful book on handwriting. The materials are well presented with plentiful examples. The book examines some misconceptions about handwriting, and some principles in relating handwriting to language, reading and spelling. The stages of teaching handwriting are addressed, supported by numerous graphics. There is also a separate chapter on the initial stages of handwriting.

Inspirations for Writing
Sue Ellis and Gill Friel
Scholastic Publications (1992).

This book provides the teacher with a vast collection of superb ideas to motivate children in joined writing tasks. The consistent relation of tasks to the curriculum context with the book is especially useful. It is well illustrated with chapters including functional, imaginative and collaborative writing. Each chapter has an activities section with indications of the age range most suited to the task. The ranges tend to be from five to nine years although there are some for children of up to twelve years.

The book also includes 30 pages of photo-copiable material related to some of the activities.

Joining the ABC
Charles Cripps and Robin Cox
LDA, Cambridge (1991).

This book focuses on why handwriting and spelling should be taught together. It provides both a theoretical and practical perspective on handwriting and spelling, and answers questions such as 'what kind of perceptual activities will help children differentiate between letters and joins in writing?' and 'do five year olds have the motor control for joining letters?'

The book discusses some issues relating to the teacher, such as the level of writing teachers should expect from each age group, implications for classroom organisation and the role of parents. There is also a simple guide for developing children's writing looking at handwriting, spelling and composing skills.

The chapter on resources and teaching techniques provide ideas for developing motor control and hand/eye coordination. An extremely useful reference book for teachers.

Graded Activities for Children with Motor Difficulties
James Russell
Cambridge Educational (1988).

Although motor skills and literacy are two distinct strands of development there is a growing awareness of the link between the two, and hence this programme of activities may be extremely useful in helping the teacher tackle the difficulties associated with dyslexia. The programme is aimed at both primary and secondary sectors and can be used by teachers with little or no specialist training. It provides a comprehensive and easy to follow series of lessons each aimed at different aspects of motor development. These include gross motor control; balancing, catching, throwing and jumping; body and spatial awareness, visual tracking and handwriting activities.

Each of the fourteen programmes has a clear set of objectives, illustrations and a number of complementary activities.

Praxis Makes Perfect
Dyspraxia Trust, PO Box 30, Hitchin, Herts SG5 1UU (1991).

This is an excellent publication which should be beneficial to teachers and parents. It contains nine chapters all on areas concerning dyspraxia. Dyspraxia is defined an an 'impairment or immaturity in the organisation of movement which leads to associated problems with language, perception and thought'.

There are, therefore, chapters on understanding dyspraxia and views from teachers, psychotherapists and occupational therapists. The book contains excellent guidance on dealing with handwriting problems, advice on activities for dyspraxic children and general considerations at school, including social integration in the classroom.

Developmental Dyspraxia: A Practical Manual for Parents and Professionals
Madeleine Portwood
Durham County Council, Educational Psychology Service, County Hall, Durham.

This excellent manual provides a thorough insight into dyspraxia. It is extremely readable, well illustrated and appropriate for both parents and teachers.

The first two chapters provide a neurological orientated background but without the learning terminology which usually accompanies such explanations. These chapters are followed by a chapter entitled 'What is dyspraxia'. This provides an excellent summary from 6–12 months through to 7 years describing some observable behaviours found in dyspraxic children.

The definition which the author uses to describe dyspraxia is located in this chapter: 'motor difficulties caused by perceptual problems, especially visual-motor and kinaesthetic motor difficulties' (p. 15).

The following chapters look at assessment of the junior age child, attainment tests, cognitive assessment, screening. The rest of the manual focuses on re-mediation programmes for different age groups – these contain a wealth of ideas. The book concludes with useful addresses and contacts for parents and teachers.

Some Other Useful Publications in Writing Include:

Alston J. (1991) *Assessing and Promoting Writing Skills.* NASEN Pub.
Alston J. and Taylor J. (1992a) *Handwriting Helpline.* Dextral Books.
Alston J. and Taylor J. (1992b) *Writing Lefthanded.* Dextral Books.
Handwriting Reviews, published annually by *The Handwriting Interest Group,* provide useful guidance for teachers.
Harrison P. and Harrison S. (1989) *Writing for Different Purposes.* Folens.
Ramsden M. (1992) *Putting Pen to Paper.* Southgate Pub.
Sassoon R. (1995) *The Acquisition of a Second Writing System* Intellect Ltd.
Smith P. (1994) *Teaching Handwriting.* UK Reading Association.
Topping K. (1992) *Paired Writing Information.* Kirklees Metropolitan Council.

SPELLING

Spelling: Caught or Taught – A New Look
Margaret L. Peters
Routledge (revised edition, 1985).

This book highlights the generally agreed notion that reading is taught but spelling is caught – that it occurs incidentally. But as Margaret Peters points out – not all children catch it. This book therefore attempts to display how spelling can in fact be taught to those who for some reason do not 'catch it'.

The book looks at predictors of spelling ability such as verbal ability, visual perception of word form and perceptuo-motor ability. She discusses the skills used in spelling such as recall, learned behaviour, and letter relationships and sequences. She argues that spelling is different from reading, which is a more 'flexible' skill with performance variation depending on the purpose for which the child taps into his syntactic and semantic linguistic resources. There is also a more predictive element in reading than in spelling.

In relation to teaching children spelling Margaret Peters discusses the importance of attention and perception, visual skills, associative learning techniques (for example words within words and letter string), developing imagery and developing within children a firm strategy for learning new words.

There is also a chapter on the assessment of spelling, looking at normative spelling tests and positive assessment of spelling strategies.

A very useful book for the teacher.

Spelling in Context – Strategies for Teachers and Learners
Margaret L. Peters and Brigid Smith
NFER Nelson (1993).

This book includes a revision of Margaret Peter's well known *Diagnostic and Remedial Spelling Manual*. Divided into eight chapters, it discusses the role of spelling and writing within both the composing process and the secretarial process. Aided by an abundance of samples of children's work, the authors illustrate the process of writing and the teacher's role in guiding, monitoring and correcting.

There are also chapters on spelling development and classroom management. They include a suggested layout of a writing corner, a list of resources for the writing area, supporting the pupil, the use of the computer, presentation and display as well as aspects of spelling development such as phonological awareness. The assessment section, called 'Diagnosing Specific Spelling Difficulties', provides a very useful diagnostic grid of mis-spellings. It also contains detailed analysis of mis-spellings and strategies for spelling instruction and spelling recovery. The chapter which describes the diagnostic grid is well illustrated with examples supporting the look, cover, write, check routine. This is followed by a chapter containing ten case studies highlighting the diagnostic criteria for intervention, and support strategies from children aged from five to thirteen.

An extremely useful and very teacher-friendly volume.

Spelling Made Easy – Multi-sensory Structured Spelling
Violet Brand
Egon Publishers (1989).

This comprehensive spelling programme consists of four levels of work for different stages. Each stage comprises a teacher's book and copymaster worksheets. Level 1 aims to help the learner become familiar with the recognition and uses of word families within the context of a text. This is extended in Level 2, and Level 3 provides children with the opportunity to use their English skills in a variety of ways.

A very successful spelling programme which can be applied at both primary and secondary stages.

Remedial Spelling
Violet Brand
Egon Publishers (1985).

Part of the Spelling Made Easy series, this publication consists of a teacher's text and sixty proof-reading passages. The author contends that the teaching of spelling should be diagnostic and structured in such a way as to meet the needs of the student.

The text contains test passages and teaching points with extensive revision and reinforcement exercises. The proof-reading masters should prove to be a useful resource for the teacher with proof passages and teaching points.

Structures in Spelling
Tim Brown and Deborah F. Knight
New Readers Press (1992).

An excellent text very suitable for the secondary and adult student which examines basic word structures looking at prefixes, roots and suffixes. The book consists of thirty four lessons, with plentiful exercises divided into eight units each focusing on elements of spelling structures.

Patterns in Spelling
Tim Brown and Deborah F. Knight
New Readers Press (1990)

This is a series of four books, each book focusing on a different element of spelling. These elements are short vowels, long vowels, consonant blends and digraphs and other vowel sounds and spellings. The series' approach encourages students to look for common patterns in words and the essence of this is that the students discover these patterns themselves. This excellent series is well presented in a series of lessons each with many examples and exercises aimed to achieve the objectives set out at the beginning of each lesson. An extremely useful set of books for use with secondary and adult students.

Unscrambling Spelling
Cynthia Klein and Robin R. Miller
Hodder & Stoughton (1990).

This book examines the teaching of spelling by looking at a range of strategies and methods including analysis of errors, strategies for remembering spellings, look, cover, write and check method, the use of individualised spelling programmes within the classroom and programmes combining spelling and handwriting.

There are also useful resource sheets relating to a range of aspects such as identifying learning style, analysing errors, word building, editing and proof-reading.

A very useful resource containing a range of materials which are easy for the class teacher to use.

The Following May Also Be Useful:

Brown G. D. and Ellis N. C. (1994) *Handbook of Normal and Disturbed Spelling Development: Theory, Processes and Interventions.* John Wiley & Sons.
Childs S. and Childs R. (1992) *The Childs' Spelling System – The Rules.* Better Books.
Cripps C. (1992) *A Hand for Spelling.* Cambridge Institute of Education.
Dykes B. and Thomas C. (1989) *Spelling Made Easy.* Hale & Iremonger, Sydney.
Miller R. and Klein C. (1986) *Making Sense of Spelling.* DCLD, London.
Sillars S. (1991) *Spelling Rules OK!* Chalkface Project, Milton Keynes.
Pollock J. (1990) *Signposts to Spelling.* Heinemann Educational.
Pratley R. (1988) *Spelling it Out.* BBC Books.
Rudginsky L. T. and Haskell E. C. (1990) *How to Spell.* Educators Publishing Service.
Seymour P. H. K. (1986) *Cognitive Analysis of Dyslexia.* Routledge & Kegan Paul.
Topping K. (1992) *Cued Spelling Training Tape.* Kirklees Metropolitan Council.
Vincent D. and Claydon J. (1982) *Diagnostic Spelling Test.* NFER Nelson.

PARENTS/ADULTS

Living with Dyslexia
Barbara Riddock
Routledge (1996).

This book provides an overview of dyslexia from a range of perspectives including educational, emotional, social, parent, teacher and children. There is a chapter dedicated to case studies.

The book is essentially the product of a research project conducted by the author and one of the aims of the book is to examine how information on living with dyslexia can be collected in a systematic manner, and integrated with other forms of research to increase ones understanding of dyslexia.

Another aim of the book is to raise constructive debate on the advantages and disadvantages of using the label 'dyslexia'. Essentially, the author provides a broader perspective of dyslexia indicating that it is more than just a reading disability. This in fact is borne out by children's own views, which is the focus of one of the chapters.

An informative and interesting book, useful for parents, teachers and researchers.

Dyslexia – Parents in Need
Pat Heaton
Whurr Publishers (1996).

This book describes some of the responses from parents in answer to some very important research questions affecting parents of dyslexic children. It deals with aspects such as early signs, language difficulties, parents' feelings and perceptions, practical aspects and factors influencing effective liaison with the school.

Section two of the book contains activities including over twenty pages of word searches and other game-type activities for identifying vowels and consonants. Since the book is based on first-hand accounts it should prove useful to parents.

Parents on Dyslexia
Editor: Saskia Van der Stoel
Multilingual Matters, Clevedon (1990).

This book provides readable information in relation to a number of questions parents may raise relating to dyslexia. These include how the difficulties can be manifested at home and school, post-school and career aspects, social consider- ations, assessment, identification and provision. The book represents a com- prehensive survey of the field, illustrated by a number of case studies with comments from specialists. Although the context for parents differs from area to area this text could still prove a valuable aid to parents requiring an account of dyslexia which is more advanced and detailed than simplistic pamphlets, but which is free from the academic and professional jargon often found in general texts.

Dyslexia – A Parents Survival Guide
Christine Ostler
Ammonite Books, Godalming (1991).

This well organised and comprehensive volume will be helpful to parents and professionals. It examines the problem of dyslexia and suggests how parents may deal with any anxieties, placing liaising with school as an essential step.

Christine Ostler also examines the difficulty from the child's perspective, highlighting her experiences as a parent of a dyslexic son, and as a trained teacher of dyslexic children.

The book contains particularly useful sections on study skills and looks at reading, spelling and maths from the perspective of helping the dyslexic child develop coping strategies through effective study habits.

This well-written, easy-to-read book will provide parents with useful factual information in relation to support groups, and useful resources and addresses. The range of appropriate coping strategies interspersed throughout the book provides pointers for both parents and teachers and encourages effective liaison to help minimise the damaging effects of dyslexia.

Breaking Down the Barriers
Aspects of the First 25 Years of SPELD in New Zealand.
Peggy Buchanan
SPELD, Box 27–112, Wellington, New Zealand (1996)

The New Zealand Federation of Specific Learning Disabilities Associations (SPELD) celebrated their 25th anniversary with this informative and inspiring publication. It describes how the Association began, its development with its extensive network of branches and how it works in relation to the education system. There is also a chapter on conferences and keynote speakers which SPELD have invited to New Zealand over the last 25 years.

It also provides an account of SPELD's drive for dyslexia to be recognised through legislation and initiatives in the field of teacher training. This book should be an inspiration to parents and parents' associations.

Adult Dyslexia – Assessment, Counselling and Training
David McLoughlin, Gary Fitzgibbon and Vivienne Young
Whurr Publishers (1994).

This very useful publication focuses on the needs of adult dyslexics. A fairly detailed introduction sets the tone of the book by examining some of the characteristics of dyslexia, particularly memory difficulties. This is followed by two chapters, one on screening and the other on formal assessment. The remainder of the book discusses methods of dealing with dyslexic difficulties in the work-place, through career counselling and through teaching strategies. Though a short book (100 pages) it contains some useful information in the important area of adult dyslexia which has been somewhat neglected until recently.

Specific Learning Difficulties (Dyslexia) – A Resource Book for Parents and Teachers
Colin Lannen, Sionah Lannen and Gavin Reid
Red Rose Publications (1997)

This book presents some key strategies, in a clear, user-friendly fashion, for dealing with dyslexia. The book will be particularly useful to parents and class teachers. There are chapters on reading, creative writing, spelling, mathematics, dyspraxia and handwriting. There are also over twenty pages detailing resources and materials suitable for dyslexic students. The text is supported by clear and humorous illustrations in a book which contains many suggestions for parents and teachers of dyslexic children.

The Following May Also Be Useful:

Cicci R. (1987) *Dyslexia: Especially for Parents.* Orton Dyslexia Society, USA.
Crisfield J. (ed.) (1996) *The Dyslexia Handbook.* British Dyslexia Association, Reading.
Crisfield J. and Smythe I. (eds) (1993, 1994) *The Dyslexia Handbook.* British Dyslexia Association, Reading.
Hornsby B. (1992) *Overcoming Dyslexia.* Optima.
Osmond J. (1993) *The Reality of Dyslexia.* Cassell.
Selikowitz M. (1993) *Dyslexia and Other Learning Difficulties.* Oxford University Press.

References

Aaron, P. G. (1989) *Dyslexia and Hyperlexia*. Boston, MA, Kluwer.

Aaron, P. G. (1994) Differential diagnosis of reading disabilities. In Hales, G. (Ed.), *Dyslexia Matters*. London, Whurr.

Aaron, P. G. and Joshi, R.M. (1992) *Reading Problems – Consultation and Remediation*. New York, Guilford Press.

Ackerman, T., Gillet, D., Kenward, P., Leadbetter, P., Mason, I., Mathews, C., Tweddle, D. and Winteringham, D. (1983) Daily teaching and assessment – primary aged children. In *Post Experience Courses for Educational Psychologists*. 1983–84, pp. 33–52. University of Birmingham, Department of Educational Psychology.

Adamik-Jászó, A. (1995) Phonemic awareness and balanced reading instructions. In P. Owen and P. Pumfrey (Eds), *Emergent and Developing Reading: Messages for Teachers*. London, Falmer Press.

Adams, M. (1990) *Beginning to Read: Thinking and Learning About Print*. Cambridge, MA, MIT Press.

Adams, M. J. (1990) *Beginning to Read: The New Phonics in Context*. Oxford, Heinemann.

Ainscow, M. and Tweddle, D. (1984) *Preventing Classroom Failure: An Objectives Approach*. Chichester, John Wiley.

Allen, J., Brown, S., and Munn, P. (1991) *Off the Record: Mainstream Provision for Non-Recorded Pupils*. Scottish Centre for Research in Education Report, Edinburgh.

Alston, J. (1993) *Assessing and Promoting Writing Skills*. NASEN Publishers.

Alston, J. and Taylor, J. (1992a), *Handwriting Helpline*. Dextral Books.

Alston, J. and Taylor, J. (1992b), *Writing Lefthanded*. Dextral Books.

Ames, E. (1991) *Teach Yourself to Diagnose Reading Problems*. Macmillan Educational.

Aram, D. M. and Healy, J. M. (1988) Hyperlexia: A review of extraordinary word recognition. In Obler, L. K. and Fein, D. (Eds), *Exceptional Brain*. New York, Guilford Press.

Arnold H. (1984) *Making Sense of It*. London, Hodder & Stoughton.

Arnold, H. (1992) *Diagnostic Reading Record*. London, Hodder & Stoughton.

Aubrey, C., Eaves, J., Hicks, C. and Newton, M. (1981) *Aston Portfolio*. LDA.

Augur, J. (1992) *This Book Doesn't Make Sense*. Bath, Educational Publishers.

Augur, J. and Briggs, S. (1992) *The Hickey Multisensory Language Course*. London, Whurr.

Ayres, A. J. (1979/92) *Sensory Integration and the Child*. Los Angeles, CA, Western Psychological Services.

Ayres, D. B. (1994) Assessment of intelligence, cognition and metacognition: reflections, issues and recommendations. Thesis presented in partial fulfilment of PhD. George Mason University, Virginia, USA.

Baddeley A. (1987) *Working Memory*. Oxford, Clarendon.

Bakker, D. J. (1990) *Neuropsychological Treatment of Dyslexia*. New York, Oxford University Press.

Bakker, D. J. and Van der Vlugt (1989) *Neuro-psychological Correlates and Treatment.* Amsterdam, Swets & Zeitlinger.

Bakker, D. J., Licht, R. and Kappers, E. J. (1994) Hemispheric stimulation techniques in children with dyslexia. In M. G. Tramontana, M. G. and S. R. Hooper (Eds), *Advances in Child Neuropsychology,* Vol. 3. New York, Springer Verlag.

Banks, J. (1996) Towards a policy of allocating resources. *Paper presented at National Seminar Policy and Provision for Dyslexia,* 3 December 1996. Scottish Dyslexia Forum, Scotland.

Bannatyne, A. (1974) Diagnosis: a note on the re-categorisation of the WISC scaled scores. *Journal of Learning Disabilities,* **7**, 272–3.

Bar-Tal, D. (1984) The effects of teachers' behaviour on pupils' attributions: a review. In Barnes, P., Oates, J., Chapman, J., Lee, V. and Czerniewska, P. (Eds), *Personality, Development and Learning.* Sevenoaks, Hodder & Stoughton.

Barthorpe, T. and Visser, J. (1991) *Differentiation: Your Responsibility and In-service Training Pack for Staff Development.* Nasen Publications.

Baumer, B. A. (1996) *How to Teach Your Dyslexic Child to Read – A Proven Method for Parents and Teachers.* Birch Lane Press.

Beard, R. (1990) *Developing Reading 3–13.* London, Hodder & Stoughton.

Becker, W. C. (1977) Teaching reading and language to the disadvantaged – what we have learned from field research. *Harvard Educational Review,* **47**, 518–43.

Bedford-Feull, C., Geiger, S., Moyse, S., and Turner, M. (1995). Use of listening comprehension in the identification and assessment of specific learning difficulties. *Educational Psychology in Practice,* **10**(4) 207–14.

Bell, J. (1993) *Doing Your Research Project.* Open University Press.

Bell, N. (1991a) Gestalt imagery: a critical factor in language comprehension. Reprint from *Annals of Dyslexia,* Vol. 41. Baltimore, MD, Orton Dyslexia Society.

Bell, N. (1991b) *Visualizing and Verbalizing for Language Comprehension and Thinking.* Paso Robles, CA, Academy of Reading Publications.

Bender, M. L. (1976) *The Bender-Purdue Reflex Test.* San Rafael, CA, Academic Therapy Publication.

Bergeron, B. (1990) What does the term 'whole-language' mean? Constructing a definition from the literature. *Journal of Reading Behaviour,* **22**: 301–29.

Berry, R. (1986) *How to Write a Research Paper.* Oxford, Pergamon Press.

Biggar, S. and Barr, J. (1993) The emotional world of specific learning difficulties. In Reid, G. (Ed.), *Specific Learning Difficulties (Dyslexia) Perspectives on Practice.* Edinburgh, Moray House Publications.

Biggar, S. and Barr, J. (1996) The emotional world of specific learning difficulties. In G. Reid (Ed.) *Dimensions of Dyslexia,* Vol. 2, *Literacy, Language and Learning.* Edinburgh, Moray House Publications.

Bishop, D. V. M. (1989) Unstable vergence control and dyslexia – A critique. *British Journal of Ophthalmology,* **73**, 223–45.

Blachman, B. A., Ball, E. L., Black, R. S. and Tangel, D M. (1994) Kindergarten teachers develop phoneme awareness in low-income, inner city classrooms: does it make a difference? *Reading and Writing,* **7**, 1–18.

Blagg, N., Ballinger, M., Gardner, R., Petty, M. and Williams, G. (1988) *Somerset Thinking Skills Course.* Oxford, Blackwell/Somerset County Council.

Blair, D., Milne, A., Fenton, M., Gibson, M., Masterton, J., Triay, I. and Morton, A. (1996) Learning support provision within a mainstream secondary school. In G. Reid (Ed.) *Dimensions of Dyslexia.* Vol. 1: *Assessment, Teaching and the Curriculum.* Edinburgh, Moray House Publications.

Blau, H. and Loveless, E. J. (1982) Specific hemispheric routing – TAKV to teach spelling to dyslexics: VAK and VAKT challenged. *Journal of Learning Disabilities,* **15**, 8, 461–6.

Blight, J. (1986) *A Practical Guide to Dyslexia.* Egon Publishers.

Bloom, B. S. (1976) *Human Characteristics and School Learning.* New York, McGraw-Hill.

Blyth, P. (1992) *A Physical Approach to Resolving Specific Learning Difficulties*. Chester, Institute for Neuro-Physiological Psychology.

Boder, E. and Jarrico, S. (1982) *Boder Test of Reading-Spelling Patterns*. New York, Grune & Stratton.

Bonar, B. and Lowe, D. (1995) *The screening initiative. A project for early invervention*. Strathclyde Regional Council Psychological Service, Renfrew Division, Scotland.

Bradley L. (1980) *Assessing Reading Difficulties: Diagnostic Remedial*. NFER Nelson.

Bradley, L. (1989a) Predicting learning disabilities. In Dumant, J. J. and Nakken, H. (Eds), *Learning Disabilities. Cognitive, Social and Remedial Aspects*. Vol. 2. London, Academic Press.

Bradley L. (1989b) Specific learning disability: Prediction–intervention–progress. Paper presented to the Rodin Remediation Academy International Conference on Dyslexia, University College of North Wales.

Bradley, L. (1990) Rhyming connections in learning to read and spell. In Pumfrey, P. D. and Elliott, C. D. (Eds), *Children's Difficulties in Reading, Spelling and Writing*. London, Falmer Press.

Bradley, L. and Bryant, P. (1991) Phonological skills before and after learning to read. In Brady, S. A. and Shankweiler, D. P. (Eds), *Phonological Processes in Literacy*. London, Lawrence Erlbaum.

Bradley, L. and Huxford, L. M. (1994) Organising sound and letter patterns for spelling. In Brown, G. D. and Ellis, N. C. (Eds), *Handbook of Normal and Disturbed Spelling Development, Theory, Processes and Interventions*. Chichester, John Wiley.

Bradshaw, J. R. (1990) A service to ourselves or our clients? *Support for Learning* **5**,(4), 205–210.

Brady, S. and Shankweiler, D. (1992) *Phonological Processes in Literacy*. York Publishers.

Brand, V. (1985) *Remedial Spelling*. Egon Publishers.

Brand, V. (1989) *Spelling Made Easy – A Multisensory Structured Spelling*. Egon Publishers.

Brereton, A. and Cann, P. (Eds) (1993) *Opening the Door – Guidance on Recognising and helping the Dyslexic Child*. London. British Dyslexia Association.

Brierley, M., Hutchinson, P., Topping, K. and Walker, C. (1989) Reciprocal peer tutored cued spelling with ten year olds. *Paired Learning*, **5**, 136–40.

British Dyslexia Association (1997). In J. Jacobson (Ed.), *The Dyslexia Handbook*, BDA.

Brooks, G., Cato, V., Fernandes, C. and Tregenza, A. (1996) *The Knowsley reading project using trained reading helpers effectively*. NFER.

Brooks, P. (1990) The effects of different teaching strategies on severe dyslexics. In G. Hales (Ed.), *Meeting Points in Dyslexia*. Reading, UK, BDA.

Brown, A., Armbruster, B. and Baker, L. (1986) The role of metacognition in reading and studying. In Oraspinu, J. (Ed.), *Reading Comprehension From Research to Practice*. Hillsdale, NJ, Lawrence Erlbaum.

Brown, G. D. and Ellis, N. C. (1994) *Handbook of Normal and Disturbed Spelling Development: Theory, Processes and Interventions*. Chichester, John Wiley.

Brown, M. (1993) Supporting learning through a whole-school approach. In Reid, G. (Ed.), *Specific Learning Difficulties (Dyslexia) Perspectives on Practice*. Edinburgh, Moray House Publications.

Brown, T. and Knight, D. F. (1990) *Patterns in Spelling*. New York, New Readers Press.

Brown, T. and Knight, D. F. (1992) *Structures in Spelling*. New York, New Readers Press.

Bruck, M. and Treiman, R. (1992) Learning to pronounce words: the limitations of analogies. *Reading Research Quarterly*, **24**(4), 375–87.

Bryant, P. E. (1990) Phonological development and reading. In Pumfrey, P. D. and Elliott, C. D. (Eds), *Children's Difficulties in Reading, Spelling and Writing*. London, Falmer Press.

Bryant, P. and Bradley, L. (1990) *Children's Reading Problems*. Oxford, Blackwell.

Buchanan, P. (1996) *Breaking Down the Barriers: Aspects of the First 25 Years of SPELD in New Zealand.* Wellington, New Zealand, SPELD.

Bullock Report, Great Britain, Department of Education and Science (1975) *A Language for Life.* Report of the Committee of Inquiry (Chairperson: Sir Alan Bullock, FBA). London, HMSO.

Burge, V. (1986) *Dyslexia Basic Numeracy.* Helen Arkell Dyslexia Centre.

Burns, R. B. (1986) *The Self-Concept in Theory, Measurement, Development and Behaviour.* London, Longman.

Burt, C. (1921) *Word Reading Test.* Revised by Vernon, P. E. (1938–67) as *Burt (Rearranged Word Reading Test).* Re-normed by Shearer, E. and Apps, R. (1975). London, Hodder & Stoughton.

Butler, K. A. (1987) *Learning and Teaching Style – In Theory and Practice.* Columbia, CT. Learners Dimension.

Buzan, T. (1984) *Use Your Memory.* London, BBC Publications.

Buzan, T. (1988) *Make the Most of Your Mind.* Pan Books.

Buzan, T. (1993) *The Mind Map Book – Radiant Thinking.* London, BBC Books.

Caine, R. N. and Caine, G. (1991) *Making Connections.* Banta.

Calfe, R. and Henry, M. K. (1985). Project Read: An inservice model for training classroom teachers in effective reading instruction. In J. Hoffman (Ed.), *The Effective Teaching of Reading: Theory and Practice,* pp. 143–60. Newark, DE, International Reading Association.

Campione, J. C. and Brown, A.L. (1989) Assisted assessment: a taxonomy of approaches and an outline of strengths and weaknesses. *Journal of Learning Disabilities,* **22**(3), 151–165.

Canfield, A. A. and Lafferty, J. C. (1970) *Learning Styles Inventory,* Detroit MI, Humanics Media (Liberty Drawer).

Capel, S. (1989) Stress and burnout in secondary school teachers: some causal factors. In Cole, M. and Walker, S. (Eds), *Teaching and Stress.* London, Open University Press.

Carbo, M. (1987) De-programming reading failure. Giving unequal learners an equal chance. *Phi Delta Kappan,* November, 196–200.

Carbo, M., Dunn, R. and Dunn, K. (1986) *Teaching Students to Read through Their Individual Learning Styles.* Englewood Cliffs, NJ, Prentice Hall.

Carlisle, J. (1993) *Reasoning and Reading – Level 1.* Cambridge, MA, Educators Publishers.

Cavey, D. W. (1993) *Dysgraphia: Why Johnny Can't Write. A Handbook for Teachers and Parents.* Austin, TX, Pro-Ed. Inc.

Chall, J. S. and Popp, H. M. (1996) *Teaching and Assessing Phonics: Why, What, When, How, A Guide for Teachers.* Cambridge, MA, Educators Publishing Service.

Chapman, J. *Understanding Learning Difficulties: A Guide for Teachers and Parents,* Massey University, New Zealand, ERDC Press.

Chasty, H. and Friel, J. (1991) *Children with Special Needs: Assessment, Law and Practice. Caught in the Act.* London. Jessica Kingsley Publishers.

Childs, S. and Childs, R. (1992) *The Childs' Spelling System – The Rules.* Better Books.

Chinn, S. (1996) *What to Do When You Can't Learn the Times Tables.* Marko Publishing.

Chinn, S. J. and Ashcroft, J. R. (1993) *Mathematics for Dyslexics – A Teaching Handbook.* London, Whurr.

Cicci, R. (1987) *Dyslexia: Especially for Parents.* Baltimore, MD, Orton Dyslexia Society.

Clark, D. B. (1988) *Dyslexia: Theory and Practice of Remedial Instruction.* Maryland, York Press.

Clay, M. (1985) *The Early Detection of Reading Difficulties: A Diagnostic Survey with Recovery Procedures.* Auckland, Heinemann Educational.

Clay, M. (1992) *Reading: the Patterning of Complex Behaviour.* London, Heinemann.

Clay, M. (1993) *An Observational Survey of Early Literacy Achievement.* Heinemann Educational.

Clifford, V. and Miles, M. (1994) Acceleread, accelewrite: *A Guide to Using Talking Computers – Helping Children to Read and Spell*. Cambridge, iansyst.

Closs, A., Lannen, S. and Reid, G. (1996) Dyslexia in further and higher education – a framework for practice. In G. Reid (Ed.), *Dimensions of Dyslexia*. Vol. 1: *Assessment, Teaching and the Curriculum*. Edinburgh, Moray House Publications.

Coles, M. (1995) *A student's guide to course work writing*. University Writing Series, University of Stirling, Stirling.

Coltheart, M., Masterson, J., Byng, S., Prior, M. and Riddoch, M. J. (1983) Surface dyslexia. *Quarterly Journal of Experimental Psychology*, **35a**, 469–95.

Conlan, J. and Henley, M. (1992) *Word Mastery*. Oxford, Oxford University Press.

Conway, N. F. and Gow, L. (1988) Mainstreaming special class students with mild handicaps through group instruction. In *Remedial and Special Education*. 5(9), 34–50.

Cooke, A. (1993) *Tackling Dyslexia: Bangor Way*. London, Whurr.

Cooper, C. (1995) Inside the WISC-III UK. *Educational Psychology in Practice*, **10**(4), 215–19.

Cooper, M., Parker, R., and Toombs, S. (1991) *Reading Assessment for Teachers (RAT-pack)*. Trowbridge, Wiltshire County Council.

Cooper, M., Toombs, S. and Parker, R. (1992) Reading assessment for teachers. The RAT pack course and materials. *Support for Learning*, **7**(2), 78–81.

Copeland, E. D. and Love, V. L. (1992) *Attention without Tension: A Teacher's Handbook on Attention Disorders*. Atlanta, GA, 3C's of Childhood Inc.

Cornelissen, P., Bradley, L., Fowler, S. and Stein, J. (1994) What children see affects how they spell. *Developmental Medicine and Child Neurology*.

Cottrell, S. (1996) Assessing the learning needs of individual students in higher education. In *Conference Proceedings. Dyslexic Students in Higher Education*. University of Huddersfield, 24 January 1996.

Cowdery, L., Montgomery, D., Morse, P. and Prince, M. (1984–88) *Teaching Reading through Spelling*. Clwyd, Frondeg Hall Technical Publishing.

Cowdery, L., McMahon, J., Morse, P. and Prince, M. (1987) *Teaching Reading Through Spelling. Diagnosis Book A*. Clwyd, Frondeg Hall Technical Publishing.

Cox, A. R. (1985) Alphabetic phonics. An organisation and expansion of Orton–Gillingham, *Annals of Dyslexia*, **35**, 187–98.

Cox, A. R. (1992) *Foundations for Literacy. Structures and Techniques for Multisensory Teaching of Basic Written English Language Skills*. Cambridge, MA, Educators Publishers

Cripps, C. (1992) *A Hand for Spelling*. Cambridge, UK, Institute of Education.

Cripps, C. and Cox, R. (1991) *Joining the ABC*. Cambridge, LDA.

Crisfield, J. (Ed.) (1996) *The Dyslexia Handbook 1996*. Reading, UK, British Dyslexia Association.

Crisfield, J. and Smythe, I. (Eds) (1993, 1994) *The Dyslexia Handbook*. Reading, UK, British Dyslexia Association.

Croft, S. and Topping, K. (1992) *Paired Science: A Resource Pack for Parents and Children*. Centre for Paired Learning, University of Dundee.

Crombie, M. (1997) *Specific Learning Difficulties (Dyslexia): A Teacher's Guide*. Northumberland, Ann Arbor Publishers.

Crombie, M. and Reid G. (1994) 5–14 Programme and specific learning difficulties. In Jordan, E. (Ed.), *A Curriculum for All? 5–14 and Special Needs*. Edinburgh, Moray House Publications.

Cudd, E. T. and Roberts, L. L. (1994) A scaffolding technique to develop sentence sense and vocabulary. *The Reading Teacher*, **47**(4), 346–349.

Cuff, C. (1989) *Study Skills*. Cambridge Educational.

Curtis, M. E. (1980) Development of components of reading skills. *Journal of Educational Psychology*, **72**(5), 656–69.

Das, J. P., Naglieri, J. A. and Kirby, J. R. (1994) *Assessment of Cognitive Processes. The PASS Theory of Intelligence*. Boston, Allyn & Bacon.

Davies, A. (1996) *Handwriting, Reading and Spelling System.* (THRASS) London, Collins Educational.

Davies, R. D. and Braun, E. M. (1997) *The Gift of Dyslexia. Why Some of the Smartest People Can't Read and How They Can Learn.* London, Souvenir Press.

De Bono, E. (1986) *CORT Thinking.* Oxford, Pergamon Press.

De Boo, M. (1992) *Action Rhymes and Games.* Scholastic Publications.

De Fries, J. C. (1991) Genetics and dyslexia: an overview. In Snowling, M. and Thomson, M. (Eds), *Dyslexia Integrating Theory and Practice.* London, Whurr.

Deford, D. E., Pinnell, G. S., Lyons, C. A. and Young, P. (1987) *Reading Recovery.* Report on the follow-up studies. Columbus Ohio Technical Report Vol. 6. Columbus Ohio State University, USA.

Dellinger, S. (1989) *Psycho-Geometrics.* Englewood Cliffs, NJ, Prentice Hall.

Dennison, P. E. and Hargrove, G. (1985) *Personalized Whole Brain Integration.* California, Educ. Kinesthetics, Glendale.

DES, (1972) *Children with Specific Reading Difficulties.* Report of the advisory committee on handicapped children (Tizard Report). London, HMSO.

DES, (1975) *A Language for Life.* Report of the Committee of Inquiry (Chair: Sir Alan Bullock). London, HMSO.

DES, (1975) *A Language for Life,* (The Bullock Report). London, HMSO.

DES, (1978) *Special Educational Needs* (The Warnock Report). London, HMSO.

Deschler, D. and Schumaker, J. B. (1987) An instructional manual for teaching students how to learn. In Graden, J. L., Zins, J. E. and Curtis, M. J. (Eds), *Alternative Educational Delivery Systems: Enhancing Instructional Aspects for all Students.* University of Kansas, Institute for Research in Learning Difficulties.

Diniz, F. A. and Reid, G. (1994) Dyslexia in Scotland. Paper presented at the twenty-first annual conference, New York Branch of the Orton Dyslexia Society. April 1994, New York, USA.

Dobie, S. (1993) Perceptual motor and neurodevelopmental dimensions in identifying and remediating developmental delay in children with specific learning difficulties. In Reid, G. (Ed.), *Specific Learning Difficulties (Dyslexia) Perspectives on Practice.* Edinburgh, Moray House Publications.

Dockrell, J. and McShane, J. (1993) *Childrens' Learning Difficulties – A Cognitive Approach.* Oxford, Blackwell.

Dodds, D. (1993) Curriculum differentiation in the secondary school. In Reid, G. (Ed.), *Specific Learning Difficulties (Dyslexia) Perspectives on Practice.* Edinburgh, Moray House Publications.

Dodds, D. (1996) Differentiation in the secondary school. In G. Reid (Ed.), *Dimensions of Dyslexia.* Vol.1 *Assessment, Teaching and the Curriculum.* Edinburgh, Moray House Publications.

Dombey, H. (1992) Reading recovery: a solution to all primary school reading problems? *Support for Learning,* **7**(3), 111–15.

Dougan, M. and Turner, G. (1993) Information technology and specific learning difficulties. In Reid, G. (Ed.), *Specific Learning Difficulties (Dyslexia) Perspectives on Practice,* Edinburgh, Moray House Publications.

Doyle, J. (1996) *Dyslexia: An Introductory Guide.* London, Whurr.

Dreary, I. (1993) Speed of information processing and verbal ability. Paper presented at the Rodin Academy for the Study of Dyslexia Conference, London.

Drummond, A., Godrey, L. and Sattin, R. (1990) Promoting parental involvement in reading. *Support for Learning,* **5**(3), 141–5.

Duane, D. D. (1991) Neurobiological issues in dyslexia. In Snowling, M. and Thomson, M. (Eds), *Dyslexia: Integrating Theory and Practice.* London, Whurr.

Duane, D. D. (1993) The meaning and utility of differential diagnoses. In 44th Annual Conference, Orton Dyslexia Society Commemorative booklet.

Duffield, J., Riddell, S. and Brown, S. (1995) *Policy, Practice and Provision for Children with Specific Learning Difficulties.* New York, Avebury Publishing.

Dunn, R. (1992) Strategies for teaching word recognition to the disabled readers. *Reading and Writing Quarterly*, **8**(2), 157–77. New York, Hemisphere.

Dunn, R. (1993). Teaching students through their individual learning styles: a practical approach learning styles training workshop. Center for the study of learning and teaching styles, St John's University, Jamaica, New York.

Dunn, R. and Dunn, K. (1992) *Teaching Elementary Students through Their Individual Learning Styles*. Boston, Allyn & Bacon.

Dunn, R. and Dunn, K. (1993) *Teaching Secondary Students through Their Individual Learning Styles*. Boston, Allyn & Bacon.

Dunn, R. and Griggs, S. A. (1989) Learning styles: quiet revolution in American secondary schools. *The Clearing House*, **63**(1), 40–2. Washington, DC: Heldref.

Dunn, R., Dunn, K. and Price, G. E. (1975, 1979, 1985, 1987, 1989) *Learning Styles Inventory*. Lawrence, KA, Price Systems, Inc.

Dyer, C. (1988) Which support?: an examination of the term. *Support for Learning*, **3**, 1, 6–11.

Dykes, B. and Thomas, C. (1989) *Spelling Made Easy*. Sydney, Hale & Iremonger.

Dyson, A. (1996) Research: the national perspective. *Paper read at Fife Dyslexia Conference*, March, Scotland.

Dyson, A. and Skidmore, D. (1996) Contradictory models: the dilemma of specific learning difficulties. In G. Reid (Ed.), *Dimensions of Dyslexia* Vol. 2: *Literacy, Language and Learning*. Edinburgh, Moray House Publications.

Dyspraxia Trust (1991) *Praxis Makes Perfect*. Hitchin, Dyspraxia Trust.

Eden, G. F., VanMeter, J. W., Rumsey, J. M., Maisog, J. M., Woods, R. P. and Zeffiro, T. A. (1996) Abnormal processing of visual motion in dyslexia revealed by functional brain imaging. *Nature*, **382**, 67–9.

Edwards, P. (1992) *Edwards Reading Test*. Heinemann Educational.

Ehri, L. (1995) The emergence of word reading in beginning reading. In P. Owen and P. Pumfrey (Eds), *Emergent and Developing Reading: Messages for Teachers*. London, Falmer Press.

Ehri, L. C. and Robbins, C. (1992) Beginners need some decoding skill to read words by analogy. *Reading Research Quarterly*, **21**(1), 13–26.

Ekwall, E. and Ekwall, C. (1989) Using metacognitive techniques for the improvement of reading comprehension. *Journal of Reading Education*, **14**(3), 6–12.

Elliot, C. D. and Tyler, S. (1986) British ability scales profiles of children with reading difficulties. *Educational and Child Psychology*. **3**(2), 80–9.

Elliott, C. D., Smith, P. and McCulloch, K. (1996) *British Ability Scales*, second edn (BAS II). NFER Nelson.

Ellis, A. (1991) *Reading, Writing and Dyslexia: A Cognitive Analysis*. Milton Keynes, Open University Press.

Ellis, N. C. (1990) Reading, phonological skills and short term memory: interactive tributaries of development. *Journal of Research in Reading*, **13**(2), 107–22.

Ellis, N. C. and Large, B. (1981) The early stage of reading: a longitudinal study. *Applied Cognitive Psychology*, **2**, 47–76.

Ellis, S. and Friel, G. (1992) *Inspirations for Writing*. Scholastic Publications.

El-Naggar, O. (1996) Specific Learning Difficulties in Mathematics – A Classroom Approach. Nasen.

Emerson, P. (1988) Parent tutored cued spelling in a primary school. *Paired Reading Bulletin*. **4**, 91–2.

Enfield, M. L. (1976) An alternative classroom approach. In *Meeting Special Needs of Children with Reading Problems*. Minneapolis, University of Minnesota. Ph.D. Dissertation.

Enfield, M. L. and Greene, V. E. (1981) There is a skeleton in every closet. *Bulletin of The Orton Society*, **31**, 189–98.

Enfield, M. L. and Greene, V. E. (1985) *Project Read: Practical Spelling Guide*. Bloomington, MN, Bloomington Public Schools.

Engelmann, J. and Bruner, E. C. (1983) *Reading Mastery I and II: Distar Reading.* Chicago Science Research Association.

Evans, A. J. (1984a) *Reading and Thinking.* Wolverhampton. Learning Materials Ltd.

Evans, A. (1984b) *Paired reading: a report on two projects.* Division of Education, University of Sheffield (unpublished paper).

Evans, A. (1989) Screening at 6+. *Dyslexia Contact*, **8**(1).

Farrer, M. (1993) Early identification – the role of the speech therapist. In Brereton A. and Cann, P. (Eds), *Opening the Door.* Reading, British Dyslexia Association.

Fawcett, A. (1989) *Automaticity – A New Framework for Dyslexic Research.* Paper presented at the First International Conference of the British Dyslexia Association, Bath 1989.

Fawcett, A. J. and Nicolson, R. I. (1995) *Dyslexia in Children, Multidisciplinary Perspectives.* Hemel Hempstead, Harvester Wheatsheaf.

Fawcett, A. J. and Nicolson, R. I. (1996) *The Dyslexia Screening Test.* London, The Psychological Corporation, Europe.

Fawcett, A. J., Nicolson, R. I. and Dean, P. (1996) Impaired performance of children with dyslexia on a range of cerebellar tasks. *Annals of Dyslexia*, Vol. XLVI. Baltimore, MD, Orton Dyslexia Society.

Feuerstein, R. (1979) *The Dynamic Assessment of Retarded Performers: The Learning Potential Assessment Device, Theory, Instruments and Techniques.* Baltimore, MD, University Park Press.

Fife Education Authority (1996) *Partnership: Parents, Professionals and Pupils.* Scotland, Fife Education Authority.

Flavell, J. H. (1979) Metacognition and cognitive monitoring. *American Psychologist*, October 906–11.

France. L., Topping, F. and Revell, K. (1993). Parent tutored cued spelling. *Support for Learning*, **8**(1), 11–15.

Frankiewicz, R. G. (1985) *An Evaluation of the Alphabetic Phonics Program Offered in the One-to-One Mode.* Houston, TX, Neuhaus Education Center.

Frederickson, N. and Reason, R. (1995) Phonological assessment of specific learning difficulties. *Educational and Child Psychology* **12**(1).

Frederickson, N. and Wilson, J. (1996) Phonological awareness training: a new approach to phonics teaching. *Dyslexia*, **2**(2), 101–20.

Frederickson, N., Frith, V. and Reason, R. (1997) *Phonological Assessment Battery.* NFER–Nelson.

Freeman, A. (1989) Coping and SEN: Challenging idealism in Cole, M. and Walker, S., *Teaching and Stress.* Milton Keynes, Open University Press.

Frith, C. and Frith, U. (1996) A biological marker for dyslexia. *Nature*, **382**, 19–20.

Frith, U. (1980) Unexpected spelling problems. In Frith, W. (ed) *Cognitive Processes in Spelling.* London, Academic Press.

Frith, U. (1985) Beneath the surface of developmental dyslexia. In K. E. Patterson, J. C. Marshall and M. Coltheart (Eds), *Surface Dyslexia.* London, Routledge & Kegan Paul.

Frith, U., (1995) Dyslexia: can we have a shared theoretical framework? *Educational and Child Psychology*, **12**(1), 6–17.

Frith, U. and Snowling, M. (1983) Reading for meaning and reading for sound in autistic and dyslexic children. *British Journal of Developmental Psychology*, **1**, 329–42.

Galaburda, A. (1988) Ordinary and extraordinary brains: nature, nurture and dyslexia. Address presented at the Annual Meeting of the Orton Dyslexia Society, Tampa, Florida, November 1988.

Galaburda A. (1993a) Cortical and sub-cortical mechanisms in dyslexia. Paper presented at 44th Annual Conference, Orton Dyslexia Society, New Orleans, LA.

Galaburda, A. (Ed.), (1993b) *Dyslexia and Development: Neurobiological Aspects of Extraordinary Brains.* Cambridge, MA, Harvard University Press.

Gallagher, A. and Frederickson, N. (1995) The phonological assessment battery (PhAB): an initial assessment of its theoretical and practical utility. *Educational and Child Psychology*, **1**, 12.

Gardner, H. (1985) *Frames of Mind.* New York, Basic Books.
Geschwind, N. and Galaburda, A. (1985) Cerebral lateralisation biological mechanisms associations and pathology: a hypothesis and a programme for research. *Archives of Neurology,* **42**, 428–59.
Gillingham, A. and Stillman, B. (1956). *Remedial Training for Children with Specific Disability in Reading, Spelling, and Penmanship.* Cambridge, MA, Educators Publishing Service.
Gilroy, D. (1995) *Applying to Higher Education for Dyslexic Students.* Bangor, University College of North Wales.
Given, B. (1993) Learning styles. Paper presented at two-day conference, Centre for Specific Learning Difficulties, June 1993, Edinburgh, Moray House.
Given, B. (1995) Five Domains of Learning. Personal correspondence.
Given, B. K. (1996) The potential of learning styles. In G. Reid (Ed.), *Dimensions of Dyslexia.* Vol. 2: *Literacy, Language and Learning.* Edinburgh, Moray House Publications.
Glaser, R., Lesgold, A. and Lejoie, S. (1987) Toward a cognitive theory for the measurement of achievement. In R. R. Ronning, J. A. Glover, J. C. Conoley and I. C. Witt (Eds), *The Influence of Cognitive Psychology on Testing.* Hillsdale, NJ, Lawrence Erlbaum.
Glynn, T., Crooks, T., Bethune, N., Ballard, K. and Smith, J. (1989) Reading recovery in context. Report for New Zealand Department of Education, Wellington, New Zealand.
Goodman, K. (1976) Reading – a psycholinguistic guessing game. In Singer, H. and Ruddell, R. B. (Eds), *Theoretical Models and Processes of Reading.* International Reading Association.
Goodman, K. (1992) I didn't found whole language. *The Reading Teacher,* **46**(3), 189–199.
Gorrie, B. and Parkinson, E. (1995) *Phonological Awareness Procedure.* Stass Publications.
Goswami, U. (1988) Children's use of analogy in learning to spell. *British Journal of Developmental Psychology.* **6**, 21–33.
Goswami U. (1992) *Analogical Reasoning in Children.* Hove, Lawrence Erlbaum.
Goswami, U. (1993) Orthographic analogies and reading development. *The Psychologist,* **6**(7), 312–16.
Goswami, U. (1994) Reading by analogy: theoretical and practical perspectives. In C. Hulme and M. Snowling (Eds), *Reading Development and Dyslexia,* London, Whurr.
Goswami, U. and Bryant, P. (1990) *Phonological Skills and Learning to Read.* Hove, Lawrence Erlbaum.
Gough, P. B. and Tunmer, W. E. (1986) Decoding, reading and reading disability, *Remedial and Special Education,* **7**, 6–10.
Grampian Region Psychological Service. (1988) *Reeling and Writhing: Children with Specific Learning Difficulties.* Grampian Education Authority, Aberdeen.
Gregorc, A. F. (1985) *Inside Styles: Beyond the Basics.* Columbia, CT, Gregorc Assoc. Inc.
Griffiths, A. and Hamilton, D. (1984) *Parent, Teacher, Child.* London, Methuen.
Hagley, F. (1987) *Suffolk Reading Scale.* NFER Nelson.
Hales, G. (1990a) *Meeting Points in Dyslexia.* London, British Dyslexia Association.
Hales, G. (1990b) Personality aspects of dyslexia. In Hales, G. (Ed.), *Meeting Points in Dyslexia. Proceedings of the First International Conference of the British Dyslexia Association.* Reading, UK, BDA.
Hales, G. (1994) *Dyslexia Matters.* London, Whurr.
Hales, G. (1995) Stress factors in the workplace. In T. R. Miles and V. Varma (Eds), *Dyslexia and Stress.* London, Whurr.
Hammill, D. D. (1990) On defining learning disabilities: an emerging consensus, UK, *Journal of Learning Disabilities* **23**(2), 74–84.
Harris, C. (1993) *Fuzzbuzz Books/Spell/Words/Letters.* Oxford, Oxford University Press.
Harrison, C. (1994) *Literature Review: Methods of Teaching Reading.* Edinburgh, SOED.

Harrison, P. and Harrison, S. (1989) *Writing for Different Purposes.* Folens.

Harrison, R. (1989) Cued spelling in adult literacy in Kirklees. *Paired Learning,* **5**, 141.

Hatcher, P. (1994) *Sound Linkage. An Integrated Programme for Overcoming Reading Difficulties.* London, Whurr.

Hatcher, P. J., Hulme, C. and Ellis, A. W. (1994) Ameliorating early reading failure by integrating the teaching of reading and phonological skills: the phonological linkage hypothesis. *Child Development,* **65**, 41–57.

Healy, J. M. (1994) *Your Child's Growing Mind.* New York, Doubleday Dell.

Healy, J. M. (1991) *Endangered Minds.* Touchstone, Simon & Schuster.

Heaton, P. (1996) Dyslexia – parents in need. London, Whurr.

Heaton, P. and Mitchell, G. (1987) *Learning to Learn – A Study Skills Course Book.* Better Books.

Heaton, P. and Winterson, P. (1986) *Dealing with Dyslexia.* Better Books.

Henderson, A. (1989) *Maths and Dyslexics.* North Wales, St. David's College.

Henry, M. K. (1993) *Words – Integrated Decoding and Spelling Instruction based on Word Origin and Word Structure.* CA, USA, Lex Press.

Henry, M. (1996) The Orton–Gillingham approach. In G. Reid (Ed.), *Dimensions of Dyslexia.* Vol. 1: *Assessment, Teaching and the Curriculum.* Edinburgh, Moray House Publications.

Henry, M. K. and Redding, N. C. (1990) *Tutor 1 – Structured, Sequential, Multisensory Lessons Based on the Orton–Gillingham Approach.* CA, USA, Lex Press.

Henry, M. K. and Redding, N. C. (1993) *Word Lists: Structured, Sequential, Multisensory.* CA, Lex Press.

Herrington, M. (1996) Examination arrangements in higher education for dyslexic students. In *Conference proceedings; dyslexic students in higher education. University of Huddersfield 24 January 1996.*

Hill, J. E. (1964) *Cognitive Style Interest Inventory.* Michigan, USA, Oakland Community College.

Hinson, M. and Smith, P. (Eds) (1993) *Phonics and Phonic Resources.* NASEN Publication.

Hinton, J. W. (1990) Stress model development and testing. In Spielberger, C. D. *Stress and Anxiety,* Vol. 14.

HMG (UK), (1981) *Education Act 1981.* London, HMSO.

Holligan, C. and Johnston, R. S. (1988) The use of phonological information by good and poor readers in memory and reading tasks. *Memory and Cognition,* **16**, 522–32.

Holt, J. (1964) *How Children Fail.* New York, Dell.

Hornsby, B. (1992) *Overcoming Dyslexia.* McDonald Optima.

Hornsby, B. (1996) *Before Alpha: Learning Games for the Under Fives.* Souvenir Press, London.

Hornsby, B. and Farmer, M. (1990 and 1993) Some effects of a dyslexia centred teaching programme. In Pumfrey, P. D. and Elliott, C. D. (Eds), *Childrens Difficulties in Reading, Spelling and Writing.* London, Falmer Press.

Hornsby B. and Miles T. R. (1980) The effects of a dyslexic-centred teaching programme. *British Journal of Educational Psychology,* **50**(3), 236–42.

Hornsby, B. and Pool, J. (1989) *Alpha to Omega: Activity Packs Stage 1, 2 and 3.* London, Heinemann Educational.

Hornsby, B. and Shear, F. (1980) *Alpha to Omega: The A–Z of Teaching Reading, Writing and Spelling.* London, Heinemann Educational.

Hulme, C. (1993) Short term memory, speech rate, phonological ability and reading. Paper presented at the Rodin Academy for the study of Dyslexia Conference. October 1993, London.

Hulme, C. and Snowling, M. (1994) *Reading Development and Dyslexia.* London, Whurr.

Hunt, M. (1996) Newcastle literacy collaborative. Paper presented at Sunderland City Challenge Reading Conference. 29 November 1996.

Hunt, R. and Franks, T. (1993) *Oxford Reading Tree Pack.* Oxford, Oxford University Press.

Hunter, J., Connolly, V., Baillie, L. and Thomson, S. (1996) *Phonological Awareness Programme for Primary One Classes.* Edinburgh, PADG, Bonnington Primary School.

Hunter-Carsch, M. (Ed.) (1989) *The Art of Reading.* Oxford, Blackwell Education.

Hynd, G. S., Marshall, R. and Gonzalez, J. (1991) Learning disabilities and presumed central nervous system dysfunction. *Learning Disability Quarterly,* **14**, 283–96.

Imich, A. J. and Kerfoots, R. (1993) Educational psychology meeting the challenge of change. Proceedings of the Annual Conference of the British Psychological Society, April 1993, Blackpool.

Irlen, H. L. (1983) Successful Treatment of Learning. Paper presented at the 91st Annual Convention of the American Psychological Association, Anaheim, CA.

Irlen, H. L. (1989) *Scotopic Sensitivity Syndrome Screening Manual,* 3rd edn. Perceptual Development Corporation.

Irlen, H. L. (1991) *Reading by the Colors: Overcoming Dyslexia and Other Reading Disabilities through the Irlen Method.* New York, Avebury Publishing.

Iversen, S. and Tunmer, W. E. (1993) Phonological skills and the reading recovery programme. *Journal of Educational Psychology,* **85**, 112–26.

Jackson, P. and Reid, G. (1997) The assessment process, unpublished paper, Centre for Specific Learning Difficulties. Moray House Institute, Edinburgh.

Jacobson, J. (1997) *The Dyslexia Handbook.* British Dyslexia Association.

Javorsky, J. (1993) *Alphabet Soup – A Recipe for Understanding and Treating Attention Deficit Hyperactivity Disorder.* Clarkston, MI, Minerva Press.

Johanson, K. V. (1992) Sensory deprivation – a possible cause of dyslexia. *Dyslexia Research Lab (BGC).* Oslo, Scandinavian University Press.

Johnston, R. S. (1992) Methods of teaching reading: the debate continues. *Support for Learning,* **7**(3), 99–102.

Johnston, R. S., Anderson, M., Perrett, D. I. and Holligan, C. (1990) Perceptual dysfunction in poor readers: evidence for visual and auditory segmentation problems in a sub-group of poor readers. *British Journal of Educational Psychology,* **60**, 212–19.

Johnston, R., Connelly, V. D. and Watson, J. (1995) Some effects of phonics teaching on early reading development. In P. Owen and P. Pumfrey (Eds), *Emergent and Developing Reading: Messages for Teachers.* London, Falmer Press.

Jones, E. R. (1989) *The Cloze Line.* Northumberland, Ann Arbor Publishers.

Jung, C. G. (1923) *Psychological Types.* London, Pantheon Books.

Kaufman, A. A. (1992) *Intelligent Testing with WISC-R.* Psychological Corp.

Keefe, J. W. (1987) *Learning Style – Theory and Practice,* Reston, VA, National Association of Secondary School Principals.

Keefe, J. W. (1991) *Learning Style: Cognitive and Thinking Skills.* Reston, VA, National Association of Secondary School Principals.

Keefe, J. W. (1993) *Learning Style: Theory: Practice: Cognitive Skills.* Reston, VA, National Association of Secondary School Principals Publications.

Keefe, J. W., Monk, J. S., Languis, M., Letteri, C. P. and Dunn, R. (1986) *Learning Style Profile.* Reston, VA, National Association of Secondary School Principals.

Kettles, G., Laws, K. and Reid, G. (1996) Specific learning difficulties: A framework for assessment, in Reid, G. (Ed.), *Dimensions of Dyslexia,* Vol. 1, *Assessment, Teaching and the Curriculum.* Edinburgh. Moray House Publications.

Kimmell, G. M. (1989) *Sound Out.* Academic Therapy Publishers.

Kirkcaldy, B. (1997) Contemporary tasks for psychological services in Scotland. *Educational Psychology in Scotland.* Spring/Summer, Issue 5, 6–16.

Kispal, A., Tate, A., Groman, T. and Whetton, C. (1989) *Test of Initial Literacy (TOIL).* NFER Nelson.

Klein, C. (1993) *Diagnosing Dyslexia – A Guide to the Assessment of Adults with Specific Learning Difficulties.* London, Adult Literacy and Basic Skills Unit.

Klein, C. (1993) *Diagnosing Dyslexia*. London, Avanti.

Kohl, M. and Tunmer, W. (1988) Phonemic segmentation skill and spelling acquisition. *Applied Psycholinguistics,* **9**, 335–56.

Kolb, D. A. (1984) *Learning Styles Inventory Technical Manual*. Boston, McBer.

Kratoville, B.L. (1989) *Word Tracking: Proverbs: High Frequency Words*. Northumberland, Ann Arbor Publishers.

Kyd, L., Sutherland, G., and McGettrick, P. (1992) A preliminary appraisal of the Irlen screening process for scotopic sensitivity syndrome and the effect of Irlen coloured overlays on reading. *British Orthothalmic Journal*, **49**, 25–30.

Kyriacou, C. (1989) The nature and prevalence of teacher stress. In Cole, M. and Walker, S., (Eds), *Teaching and Stress*. Milton Keynes, Open University Press.

Lane, K. A. (1991) *Developing Your Child for Success*. Texas, USA, JWC Louisville.

Lannen, C., Lannen, S. and Reid, G. (1997) Specific Learning Difficulties (Dyslexia): A Resource Book for Parents and Teachers. St. Annes on Sea, Red Rose Publications.

Lannen, S. and Reid, G. (1993) Psychological dimensions and the role of the educational psychologist in assessment. In Reid, G. (Ed.), *Specific Learning Difficulties (Dyslexia) Perspectives on Practice*, Edinburgh, Moray House Publications.

Lawrence, D. (1985) Improving self-esteem and reading. *Educational Research*. **27**(3), 194–200.

Lawrence, D. (1987) *Enhancing Self-Esteem in the Classroom*. London, Paul Chapman.

Lawson, J. S. and Inglis, J. (1984) The psychometric assessment of children with learning disabilities: an index derived from a principal component's analysis of the WISC-R. *Journal of Learning Disabilities*, **17**, 517–22.

Lawson, J. S., and Inglis, J. (1985) Learning disabilities and intelligence test results: a model based on a principal components analysis of the WISC-R. *British Journal of Psychology*, **76**, 35–48.

Lazear, D. (1994) *Multiple Intelligence Approaches to Assessment*, Arizona, Zephyr Press.

Lees, E. A. (1986) A Cognitive Developmental Analysis of Reading Skills in Good and Poor Readers. Paper presented at Annual Conference of Developmental Psychology Section, September 1986, British Psychological Society.

Letterland International Ltd (1997) *About Letterland '97*. Barton, Cambridge, UK, Letterland International Ltd.

Lewkowicz, N. K. (1980) Phonemic awareness training: what to teach and how to teach it. *Journal of Educational Psychology*, **72**, 686–700.

Levine, M. D. (1992) *Keeping A Head in School*. Educators Publications.

Levine, M. D. (1993) *All Kinds of Minds*. Educators Publications.

Lewis, I. and Munn, P. (1993) *So You Want to do Research*. Edinburgh. Scottish Council of Research in Education.

Liberman, I. Y. and Liberman, A. M. (1992) Whole language versus code emphasis: underlying assumptions and their implications for reading instruction. In P. B. Gough, L. C. Ehri and R. Trieman (Eds), *Reading Acquisition*. London, Lawrence Erlbaume.

Liberman, I. Y. and Shankweiler, D.P. (1985) Phonology and the problems of learning to read and write. *Remedial and Special Education*. **6**(6), 8–17.

Lidz C. S. (1991) *Practitioners Guide to Dynamic Assessment*. New York, Guilford Press.

Lindamood, C. H. and Lindamood, P. C. (1979). *The LAC Test: Lindamood Auditory Conceptualisation Test*. Allen, TX, DLM Teaching Resources.

Locke, A. and Beech, M. (1991) *Teaching Talking – Teaching Resources Handbook*. NFER Nelson.

Lovegrove, W. (1993) Visual timing and dyslexia. Paper presented at Rodin Academy for the study of Dyslexia Conference, October 1993, London.

Lovegrove, W. (1996) Dyslexia and a transient/magnocellular pathway deficit: The current situation and future directions. *Australian Journal of Psychology*, **48**.

Lunzer, E. and Gardner, K. (1984) *Learning from the Written Word*. London, Oliver & Boyd.

Macintyre, C. (1993) *Let's Find Why*. Edinburgh, Moray House Publications.

McCarthy, B. (1987) *The 4-Mat System*. Excel Incorporated.

McCleod, J. (1994) GAP Reading Comprehension Test. London, Heinemann Educational.

McCulloch, C. (1985) *The Slingerland Approach: Is it Effective in a Specific Language Disability Classroom?* MA Thesis, Seattle, Seattle Pacific University.

McKeown, S. (Ed.), (1992) *IT Support for Specific Learning Difficulties*. NCET.

McLean, B. (1993) Style counsel – Neurolinguistic programming. In *Special Children*, April, 9–11.

McLoughlin, D., Fitzgibbon, G. and Young, V. (1994) *Adult Dyslexia, Assessment, Counselling and Training*. London, Whurr.

McNicholas, J. and McEntree, J. (1991) *Games to Develop and Improve Reading Levels*. NASEN Publication.

McRoberts, R. (1984) *Writing Workshop*. Teaching Materials.

Mager, J. (1996) Local Authority Perspectives. *Paper presented at National Seminar Policy and Provision for Dyslexia*. 3 December 1996 Scottish Dyslexia Forum, Scotland.

Mailley, S. (1997) The classroom implications of visual perceptual difficulties: an exploratory study including Scotopic Sensitivity Syndrome or Irlen Syndrome. Unpublished MA dissertation, University of Leicester.

Margulies, N. (1991) *Mapping Inner Space – Learning and Teaching Mind Mapping*. Tucson, AZ, Zephyr Press.

Mathews, M. (1993) Can children be helped by applied kinesiology. Paper presented at 5th European Conference in Neuro-Developmental Delay in Children with Specific Learning Difficulties, Chester.

Mathews, M. and Thomas, E. (1993) A pilot study on the value of A. K. in helping children with learning difficulties. Paper presented at 5th European Conference in Neuro-Developmental Delay in Children with Specific Learning Difficulties, Chester.

Maxwell, P. (1997) Mnemonics – months of the year. Personal correspondence.

Meek, M. (1985) *Learning to Read*. London, Bodley Head.

Meyer, L. P. (1984) Long term academic effects of the direct instruction project. Follow through. *Elementary School Journal*, **84**, 380–94.

Miles, E. (1989) *Bangor Dyslexia Teaching System*. London, Whurr.

Miles, T. R. (1983a) *Bangor Dyslexia Test*. Cambridge, Learning Development Aids.

Miles, T. R. (1983b) *Dyslexia: The Pattern of Difficulties*. London, Collins Educational.

Miles, T. R. (1996) Do dyslexic children have IQs? *Dyslexia*, **2**(3), 175–8.

Miles, T. and Gilroy, D. (1986) *Dyslexia at College*. London, Methuen.

Miles, T. R. and Miles, E. (1991) *Dyslexia: A Hundred Years On*. Milton Keynes, Open University Press.

Miles, T. R. and Miles, E. (Eds), (1992) *Dyslexia and Mathematics*. London, Routledge.

Miles, T. R. and Varma, V. (Eds) (1995) *Dyslexia and Stress*, London, Whurr.

Miller, R. and Klein, C. (1986) *Making Sense of Spelling*. London, DCLD.

Mitchell, S. (1985) An investigation into the presence or absence of postural reflex abnormalities in children with speech problems. Unpublished Pilot Study. City of Birmingham Polytechnic.

Mommers, M. J. C. (1987) An investigation into the relationship between word recognition, reading comprehension and spelling skills in the first two years of primary school. *Journal of Research in Reading*, **2**(10), 122–43.

Monteiro, W. (1992) Neuro-linguistic processing. Paper presented at Helen Arkell Dyslexic Conference, Cambridge, April 1992.

Moore, P. J. (1988) Reciprocal teaching and reading comprehension: a review. *Journal of Research in Reading*, **11**(1), 3–14.

Morgan, R. T. T. (1976) Paired reading tuition: a preliminary report on a technique for cases of reading deficit. In *Child Care, Health and Development*, **2**, 13–28.

Moseley, D. V. (1990) Research into visual function, reading and spelling. *Dyslexia Review*.

Mosley, J. (1996) *Quality Circle Time*, Cambridge, UK, LDA.

Munn, P. and Drever E. (1990) *Using Questionnaires in Small-Scale Research. A Teachers Guide.* Edinburgh. Scottish Council for Research in Education (SCRE).

Muter, V., Hulme, C. and Snowling, M. (1997) *Phonological Abilities Test.* London, Psychological Corporation.

Myers, I. and Myers, R. (1980) *Gifts Differing*, Palo Alto, CA, Consulting Psychologists Press.

Naidoo, S. (Ed.), (1988) *Assessment and Teaching of Dyslexic Children.* London, ICAN.

Nash-Wortham, M. and Hunt, J. (1993) *Take Time.* Stourbridge, Robinswood Press.

Neale, M. (1989). *Neale Analysis.* NFER Nelson.

Neville M. H. (1975) Effectiveness of rate of aural message on reading and listening. *Educational Research*, **1**(18), 37–43.

Newby, M., Aldridge, J., Sasse, B. M., Harrison, S. and Coker, J. (1995). The dyslexics speak for themselves. In T. R. Miles and V. Varma (Eds), *Dyslexia and Stress.* London, Whurr.

Newton, M. and Thomson, M. (1982) *Aston Index.* Cambridge, LDA.

Nicolson, R. I. (1996) Development dyslexia: past, present and future. *Dyslexia*, **2**(3).

Nicolson, R. I. and Fawcett, A. J. (1990) Automaticity: a new framework for dyslexia research? *Cognition*, **35**, 159–82.

Nicolson, R. I. and Fawcett, A. J. (1993). Early diagnosis of dyslexia: an historic opportunity? Keynote address presented at BDA Early Diagnosis Conference, London, June 1993.

Nicolson, R. I. and Fawcett, A. J. (1995) Speed of processing, motor skill, automaticity and dyslexia. In A. Fawcett and R. Nicolson (Eds), *Dyslexia in Children, Multidisciplinary Perspectives.* Hemel Hempstead, UK, Harvester Wheatsheaf.

Nicolson, R. I. and Fawcett, A. J. (1996) *The Dyslexia Early Screening Test*, London, The Psychological Corporation, Europe.

Nicolson, R. I., Fawcett, A. J. and Miles, T. R. (1993) Feasibility study for the development of a computerised screening test for dyslexia in adults. *Report OL176.* Sheffield, Department of Employment.

Niklasson, M. (1993) Adding meaning to life: a matter of experience. Paper presented at the 5th European Conference of Neuro-Developmental Delay in Children with Specific Learning Difficulties, Chester.

Nisbet, J. and Shucksmith, J. (1986) *Learning Strategies.* London, Routledge.

Office of Her Majesty's Chief Inspector of Schools, New Zealand. (1993) *Reading Recovery in New Zealand.* A Report from the Office of Her Majesty's Chief Inspector of Schools. London, HMSO.

O'Hagen, F. J. and Swanson W. I. (1981) Teachers' views regarding the role of the educational psychologist in school. *Research in Education*, **29**, 29–40.

O'Hagen, F. J. and Swanson, W. I. (1983) Teachers and psychologists: a comparison of views. *Research in Education*, 36.

Orton Dyslexia Society (1991) *All Language and the Creation of Literacy.* Baltimore, MD, Orton Dyslexia Society.

Orton Dyslexia Society Research Committee (1994) G. Reid Lyon Toward a definition of dyslexia. In *Annals of Dyslexia*, **XLV**, 3–27 (1995). Baltimore, MD, Orton Dyslexia Society.

Osmond, J. (1993) *The Reality of Dyslexia.* London, Cassell.

Ostler, C. (1991) *Dyslexia – A Parents Survival Guide.* Godalming, Ammonite Books.

Ott, P. (1997) *How to Detect and Manage Dyslexia – A Reference and Resource Manual.* Oxford, Heinemann.

Oxley L. and Topping K. (1990) Peer tutored cued spelling with seven to nine year olds. *British Education Research Journal*, **16**, 63–79.

Padget, S. Y., Knight, D. F. and Sawyer, D. J. (1996) Tennessee meets the challenge of dyslexia. In *Annals of Dyslexia*, **XLVI**, 51–72. Baltimore, MD, Orton Dyslexia Society.

Palincsar, A. and Brown, A. (1984) Reciprocal Teaching of Comprehension Fostering and Comprehension Monitoring Activities. *Cognition and Instruction*, **1**(2), 117–175.

Palincsar, A. and Klenk, L. (1992) fostering literacy learning in supportive contexts. *Journal of Learning Disabilities*, **25**, 211–25.

Palmer, J., McLeod, C., Hunt, E. and Davidson, J. (1985) Information processing correlates of reading. *Journal of Memory and Language*. **24**, 59–88.

Pavlidis, G. Th. (1990a) *Perspectives on Dyslexia: Neurology, Neuropsychology and Genetics*, Vol. 1. Chichester, John Wiley.

Pavlidis G. Th. (1990b) *Perspectives on Dyslexia: Cognition, Language and Treatment*. Vol. 2. Chichester, John Wiley.

Payne, T. (1991) It's cold in the other room. *Support for Learning*, **6**(2), 61–5.

Pearson, L. E. A. and Quinn, J. (1986) *Bury Infant Check*. NFER Nelson.

Peck, A. (1993) The use of colour in visual reading difficulties. In *Centre for Specific Learning Difficulties, Moray House, Project Information No.2*. Summer 1993.

Peck, A. Wilkins, A. and Jordan, E. (1991) Visual discomfort in the classroom. *Child Language, Teaching and Therapy*. **7**(2) 326–40.

Pennington, B. F. (1990) the genetics of dyslexia. *Journal of Child Psychology and Psychiatry*, **31**, 193–201.

Pennington, B. F. (1991) *Diagnosing Learning Disorders: A Neurological Framework*. New York, Guilford Press.

Pennington, B. F. (1996) The development of dyslexia: genotype and phenotype analyses. Paper read at *47th Annual Conference*, November. Boston, MA, Orton Dyslexia Society.

Perrin, J. (1981) *Learning Style Inventory: Primary Version*. New York, St. John's University.

Perrin, J. (1983) Learning style inventory: Primary manual for administration, interpretation and teaching suggestions. Learning Styles Network, St. John's University, Center for the Study of Learning and Teaching Styles, Jamaica, NY.

Peters, M. L. (1975) *Diagnostic and Remedial Spelling Manual*. London, Macmillan Education.

Peters, M. L. (1985) *Spelling: Caught or Taught – A New Look*. London, Routledge.

Peters, M. L. and Smith, B. (1993) *Spelling in Context – Strategies for Teachers and Learners*. NFER Nelson.

Pinnell, G. S., Deford, D. and Lyons, C.A. (1988a) Reading recovery: early intervention for at risk first graders. ERS Monograph, Educational Research Service. Arlington, VA, USA.

Pinnell, G.S., Lyons, C.A., Deford, D.E. (1988b) Reading recovery. In *Sopris West Inc Educational Programmes that Work*. (14th edn). Colorado, Sopris West in cooperation with the National Dissemination Study Group.

Pinnell, G.S., Lyons, C.A., Deford, D., Bryk, A.S. and Seltzer, M. (1991) Studying the effectiveness of early intervention approaches for first grade children having difficulty in reading. *Education Report No. 16, Martha L. King Language and Literacy Centre*, Ohio State University, Columbus, OH, USA.

Pinsent, P. (Ed.) (1990) *Children with Literacy Difficulties*. Roehampton, David Fulton Publishers.

Pollock, J. (1990) *Signposts to Spelling*. London, Heinemann Education.

Portwood, M. (1994) *Developmental Dyspraxia: A Practical Manual for Parents and Professionals*. Durham, Durham County Council.

Pottage, T. (1994) *Using Computers with Dyslexics*. University of Hull, Dyslexia Computer Resource Centre.

Pratley, R. (1988) *Spelling it Out*. London, BBC Books.

Prior, M. (1996) *Understanding Specific Learning Difficulties*, Hove, Psychology Press.

Pumfrey, P. D. (1990) Integrating the testing and teaching of reading. *Support for Learning*, **5**(3), 146–152.

Pumfrey, P. D. (1996) *Specific developmental dyslexia: Basics to back.* The Fifteenth Vernon-Wall Lecture. British Psychological Society.

Pumfrey, P. D. and Reason, R. (1991) *Specific Learning Difficulties (Dyslexia) Challenges and Responses.* Windsor, NFER Nelson.

Rack, J. (1994) Dyslexia: The phonological deficit hypothesis. In R. I. Nicolson and A. J. Fawcett (Eds), *Dyslexia in Children: Multidisciplinary Perspectives,* Hemel Hempstead, Harvester Wheatsheaf.

Ramsden, M. (1992) *Putting Pen to Paper – A New Approach to Handwriting.* Devon, Southgate.

Raven, J. C. (1988) *Mill Hill Manual and Vocabulary Scale.* NFER Nelson.

Raven, J. C. (1992, 1993) *Standard Progressive Matrices.* Oxford, Oxford Psychologists Press.

Rawson, M.B. (1988) *The Many Faces of Dyslexia.* Baltimore, MD, Orton Dyslexia Society.

Ray, B. J. (1986) A cooperative teacher education and language retraining programme for dyslexics in West Texas. Paper presented at the Action in Research V Conference. Lubbock, Texas.

Reading in Partnership Project (1992) *Sunderland City Challenge, Reading in Partnership Project.* Sunderland Learning Support Service, Sunderland.

Reason, R. and Boote, R. (1986) *Learning Difficulties in Reading and Writing: A Teachers' Manual.* Windsor, NFER Nelson.

Reason, R. and Boote, R. (1994) *Helping Children with Reading and Spelling: A Special Needs Manual.* London, Routledge.

Reason, R. and Frederickson, N. (1996) Discrepancy definitions or phonological assessment. In Reid, G. (Ed.), *Dimensions of Dyslexia: Assessment, Teaching and the Curriculum,* Vol.1. Edinburgh, Moray House Publications.

Reason, R., Brown, P., Cole, M. and Gregory, M. (1988) Does the 'specific' in specific learning difficulties make a difference to the way we teach? *Support for Learning.* **3**(4), 230–6.

Reid, G. (1986) An examination of pupil stress before and after transfer from primary to secondary school. Unpublished. MEd thesis. University of Aberdeen.

Reid, G. (1987) The perceptions and attitudes of learning support teachers to specific learning difficulties and dyslexia. *Year book of the Scottish Learning Difficulties Association.*

Reid, G. (1988) Dyslexia: A case for training. *Times Educational Supplement.* 26th February.

Reid, G. (1989) The role of the educational psychologist in the identification and assessment of specific learning difficulties. *Feedback paper.* Fife Regional Council, Psychological Service, Scotland.

Reid, G. (1990) Specific learning difficulties: attitudes towards assessment and teaching. In Hales, G. (Ed.) *Meeting Points.* Reading, UK, BDA.

Reid, G. (1991a) Stress factors in teaching children with specific learning difficulties. Paper presented at the Second International Conference: Meeting the Challenge. British Dyslexia Association, April 1991, Oxford.

Reid, G. (1991b) Supporting the support teacher. Stress factors in teaching children with specific learning difficulties. *Links,* **16**(3)18–20.

Reid, G. (1992) Learning difficulties and learning styles – observational criteria. Paper presented at South East Learning Styles Conference, George Mason University, Virginia, USA.

Reid, G. (1993a) *Dyslexia: observation and metacognitive assessment.* Paper presented at 44th Annual Conference, Orton Dyslexia Society, New Orleans, LA, USA.

Reid, G. (Ed.) (1993b) *Specific Learning Difficulties (Dyslexia) Perspectives on Practice,* Edinburgh, Moray House Publications.

Reid, G. (1993c) Perspectives on reading. In Reid, G. (Ed.), *Specific Learning Difficulties (Dyslexia) Perspectives on Practice.* Edinburgh, Moray House Publications.

Reid, G. (1993d) What is reading? Unpublished study. Centre for Specific Learning Difficulties (Dyslexia). Edinburgh, Moray House Institute.

Reid, G. (1994a) Metacognitive assessment and dyslexia. Paper presented at Third International Conference of the British Dyslexia Association. April 1994. Manchester. Accepted for publication. Links II.

Reid, G. (1994b) *Specific Learning Difficulties (Dyslexia). A Handbook for Study and Practice*. Edinburgh, Moray House Publications.

Reid, G. (1996) Dimensions of Dyslexia (Vol. 1: Assessment, Teaching and the Curriculum) (Vol. 2: Literacy, Language and Learning). Edinburgh: Moray House Publications.

Reid, G. (in press) Specialist teacher training in specific learning difficulties (dyslexia): issues, considerations and future directions. In Morag Hunter-Carsch and Margaret Herrington (Eds), *Dyslexia and Effective Learning in Secondary Schools, Higher and Further Education*.

Reid, G. and Weedon, C. (1997) Insights gained from developing an instrument to profile the emerging literacy skills of six year olds. Moray House Centre for the Study of Dyslexia, Edinburgh.

Reid, G., Carson E. and Brydon P. (1989) *A Pilot Study Investigating the Merits of Segregated Provision for Primary Pupils with Severely Delayed Attainments in Reading and Spelling*. Fife Region Psychological Service, June 1989.

Reid Lyon, G. (1995) Toward a definition of dyslexia. *Annals of Dyslexia*, **XLV**. Baltimore, MD, Orton Dyslexia Society.

Retief, L. (1990) A Psychophysiological approach to panic disorder. *Doctoral Thesis*.

Richards, R. G. (1993) *Learn Playful Techniques to Accelerate Learning*. Tucson, AZ, Zephyr Press.

Richardson, A. (1985) The effects of a specific red filter on dyslexia. *British Psychological Society Abstracts*, 56.

Richardson, A. (1988) The effects of a specific red filter on dyslexia, *British Psychological Society Abstracts*, 56.

Riddell, S., Duffield, J., Brown, S. and Ogilvy, C. (1992) *Specific Learning Difficulties: Policy, Practice and Provision*. Department of Education, University of Stirling.

Riddock, B. (1996) *Living with Dyslexia*. London, Routledge.

Robertson, A. H., Henderson, A., Robertson, A., Fisher, J. and Gibson, M. (1995) *Quest Screening, Diagnostic and Support Kit*. Windsor, NFER Nelson.

Rohl, M. and Tunmer, W. (1988) Phonemic segmentation skills and spelling acquisition. *Applied Psycholinguistics*, **9**, 335–50.

Rosner, J. and Rosner, J. (1987) The Irlen treatment: a review of the literature. *Optician*, 25 September, 26–33.

Rowe, H. (1988) Metacognitive skills: promises and problems. *Australian Journal of Reading*, **11**(4), 227–37.

Rudginsky, L. T. and Haskell, E. C. (1990) *How to Spell*. Cambridge, MA, Educators Publishing Service.

Rule, J. M. (1984) *The Structure of Words*. Cambridge, MA, Educators Publishing Service.

Russell, J. (1988) *Graded Activities for Children with Motor Difficulties*. Cambridge Educational.

Russell, S. (1992) *Phonic Code Cracker*. Glasgow, Jordanhill College Publications.

Russell, S. (1993) Access to the curriculum. In Reid, G. (Ed.), *Specific Learning Difficulties (Dyslexia) Perspectives on Practice*. Edinburgh, Moray House Publications.

Scoble, J. (1988) Cued spelling in adult literacy: a case study. *Paired Reading Bulletin*, **4**, 93–6.

Scoble, J. (1989) Cued spelling and paired reading in adult basic education in Rydale. *Paired Learning*. **5**, 57–62.

Scottish Education Dept. (1978) *The Education of Pupils with Learning Difficulties in Primary and Secondary Schools in Scotland* (*Progress Report*). Edinburgh, HMSO.

Selikowitz, M. (1994) *Dyslexia and Other Learning Difficulties.* Oxford, Oxford University Press.

Selman, M. R. (1989) *Infant Teacher's Handbook.* London, Oliver and Boyd.

Selmes, I. (1987) *Improving Study Skills.* London, Hodder & Stoughton.

Seymour, P. H. K. (1986) *Cognitive Analysis of Dyslexia.* London, Routledge and Kegan Paul.

Seymour, P. H. K. (1987) Individual cognitive analysis of competent and impaired reading. *British Journal of Psychology,* **78,** 483–506.

Seymour, P. H. K. (1993) Individual variation and reaction times in dyslexia. Paper presented at Rodin Academy for the Study of Dyslexia, October 1993 Conference, London.

Seymour, P. H. K. and McGregor, C. J. (1984) Developmental dyslexia; experimental analysis of phonological, morphemic and visual impairments. *Cognitive Neuropsychology,* **1,** 43–82.

Sharon, H. (1987) *Changing Children's Minds.* London, Condor Press.

Sherman, G. F. (1993) Biological research in dyslexia: implications for differential diagnosis. Paper presented at 44th Annual Conference, Orton Dyslexia Society, New Orleans, LA, USA.

Siegal, L. S. (1989) IQ is irrelevant to the definition of learning disabilities. *Journal of Learning Disabilities,* **22,** 469–78.

Silberberg, N. and Silberberg, M.C. (1967) Hyperlexia: specific word recognition skills in young children. *Exceptional Children,* **34,** 41–2.

Sillars, S. (1992) *Spelling Rules OK!* Milton Keynes, Chalkface Project.

Singleton, C. H. (1988) The early diagnosis of developmental dyslexia. *Support for Learning.* **3**(2), 108–21.

Singleton, C. H. (Ed.) (1991) *Computers and Literacy Skills.* Hull, British Dyslexia Association Computer Resource Centre, University of Hull.

Singleton, C. H. (Ed.) (1994) *Computers and Dyslexia-Educational Applications of New Technology.* University of Hull.

Singleton, C. H. (1996a) *COPS 1 Cognitive Profiling System* Nottingham, UK, Chameleon Educational Ltd.

Singleton, C. H. (1996b) Computerised screening for dyslexia. In G. Reid (Ed.) *Dimensions of Dyslexia* Vol. 1, *Assessment, Teaching and the Curriculum.* Edinburgh. Moray House Publications.

Singleton, C H. (1996c) Dyslexia in higher education. Issues for policy and practice. In *Conference proceedings: Dyslexic Students in Higher Education.* University of Huddersfield, 24 January 1996.

Slingerland, B. H. (1971) *A Multisensory Approach to Language Arts for Specific Language Disability Children.* A Guide for Primary Teachers, Books 1–3. Cambridge, MA, Educators Publishing Service.

Slingerland, B. H. (1976) *Basics in Scope and Sequence of a Multisensory Approach to Language Arts for Specific Learning Difficulties Children.* Cambridge, MA, Educators Publishing Service.

Slingerland, B. H. (1985) *Screening Tests for Identifying Children with Specific Learning Disabilities,* Cambridge, MA, Educators Publishing Service.

Slingerland, B. H. (1993) *Specific Language Disability Children.* Cambridge, MA, Educators Publishing Service.

Smith, C. (1993) Problems with reading. *Support for Learning,* **8**(4) 139–45.

Smith, F. (1973) *Psycholinguistics and Reading.* New York, Holt, Rinehart & Winston.

Smith, F. (1985) *Reading.* Cambridge, Cambridge University Press.

Smith, F. (1988) *Understanding Reading.* A Psycholinguistic Analysis of Reading and Learning to Read (4th edn) Hillsdale, NJ, Erlbaum.

Smith, J. and Bloom, M. (1985) *Simple Phonetics for Teachers.* London, Methuen.

Snowling, M. (1987) *Dyslexia: A Cognitive Developmental Perspective.* Oxford, Blackwell.

Snowling, M. (1990a) *Dyslexia:A Cognitive Developmental Perspective.* Oxford, Blackwell.

Snowling, M. (1990b) Dyslexia in childhood: a cognitive-developmental perspective. In Pumfrey, P. D. and Elliott, C. D. (Eds), *Children's Difficulties in Reading, Spelling and Writing.* London. Falmer Press.

Snowling, M. (1991) *Children's Written Language Difficulties.* NFER Nelson.

Snowling, M. (1993a) Specific learning difficulties: A cognitive developmental perspective. Paper presented at two-day conference Centre for Specific Learning Difficulties, Moray House, Edinburgh.

Snowling, M. (1993b) What causes variation in dyslexic reading. Paper presented at the Rodin Academy for the Study of Dyslexia, October 1993 Conference. London.

Snowling, M. J. (1995) Phonological processing and developmental dyslexia. *Journal of Research in Reading,* **18**, 132–8.

Snowling, M. J. and Nation, K. A. (1997) Language, phonology and learning to read. In C. Hulme and M. J. Snowling (Eds), *Dyslexia, Biology Cognition and Intervention,* London, Whurr.

Snowling, M. and Thomson, M. (Eds), (1991) *Dyslexia – integrating theory and practice.* London, Whurr.

Springer, S. P. (1989) *Left Brain, Right Brain.* San Francisco, CA, Freeman.

Stainthorp, R. (1995) Some effects of context on reading. In P. Owen and P. Pumfrey (Eds), *Emergent and Developing Reading: Messages for Teachers.* London, Falmer Press.

Stanovich, K. E. (1980) Towards an interactive-compensatory model of individual differences in the development of reading fluency. *Reading Research Quarterly* **16**, 32–71.

Stanovich, K. E. (1986) Matthew effects in reading: some consequences of individual differences in the acquisition of literacy. *Reading Research Quarterly,* **21**, 360–407.

Stanovich, K. E. (1988) Explaining the difference between the dyslexic and the garden-variety poor readers: the phonological core model in *Journal of Learning Disabilities,* **21**(10), 590–604.

Stanovich, K. E. (1991) Discrepancy definitions of reading disability: has intelligence led us astray? *Reading Research Quarterly,* **26**(1), 7–29.

Stanovich, K. E. (1992) Speculations on the causes and consequences of individual differences in early reading acquisition. In Gouch, P. B., Ehri, L. C. and Treiman, R. (Eds), *Reading Acquisition,* pp. 65–106. Hillsdale, NJ, Erlbaum.

Stanovich, K. E. (1996) Towards a more inclusive definition of dyslexia. *Dyslexia,* **2**(3), 154–66.

Stanovich, K. E., Siegel, L. S. and Gottardo, A. (1997) Progress in the search for dyslexia subtypes. In C. Hulme and M. J. Snowling (Eds), *Dyslexia, Biology Cognition and Intervention.* London, Whurr.

Stein, J. F., (1991) Vision and language. In Snowling, M. and Thomson, M. (Eds), *Integrating Theory and Practice.* London, Whurr.

Stein, J. F. (1995) *A visual defect in dyslexics?* In R. I. Nicolson and A. J. Fawcett (Eds), *Dyslexia in Children: Multidisciplinary Perspectives.* London, Harvester Wheatsheaf.

Stein, J. F. and Fowler, M. S. (1993) Unstable binocular control in dyslexic children. *Journal of Research in Reading.* **16**(1), 30–45.

Stephenson, E. (1986) *Children with Motor/Learning Difficulties. A Guide for Parents and Teachers.* Occupational Therapy Department Royal Aberdeen Children's Hospital.

Stevens, M. (1992) *Into Print.* Edinburgh, Scottish Consultative Council on the Curriculum.

Stirling, E. G. (1990) *Which is Witch.* Checklist of Homophones. North Wales, St. David's College.

Stirling, E. G. (1991) *Help for the Dyslexic Adolescent.* Better Books.

Stoel, Van der, S. (Ed.) (1990) *Parents on Dyslexia.* Clevedon, Multilingual Matters.

Sullivan, M. (1993) A meta-analysis of experimental research studies based on the Dunn and Dunn leaking styles model. Doctoral dissertation, St. John's University, New York.

Sutherland, M. J. and Smith, C. D. (1997) The benefits and difficulties of using portable word processors with older dyslexics. *Dyslexia*, **3**(1), 15–26.

Sutton, R. (1992) *Assessment – A Framework for Teachers*. London, Routledge.

Tennessee Centre for the Study of Treatment of Dyslexia (1996). In *Tennessee Meets the Challenge of Dyslexia. The First Three Years – A Report of Accomplishments*. USA, Middle Tennessee State University.

Thomson, G. (1990) On leaving school, who tells? In Hales, G. (Ed.) Meeting points in Dyslexia. Proceedings of the First International Conference of the British Dyslexia Association, BDA, Reading.

Thomson, M. E. (1984) *Developmental Dyslexia*. London, Edward Arnold.

Thomson, M. E. (1988) *Developmental Dyslexia: Its Nature, Assessment and Remediation*. (2nd edn) London, Whurr.

Thomson, M. E. (1989) *Developmental Dyslexia* (3rd edn) London, Whurr.

Thomson, M. E. (1990) Evaluating teaching programmes for children with specific learning difficulties. In Pumfrey, P. D. and Elliot, C. D. (Eds), *Children's Difficulties in Reading, Spelling and Writing*. London, Falmer Press.

Thomson, M. and Watkins W. (1990) *Dyslexia: A Teaching Handbook*. London, Whurr.

Thomson, P. and Gilchrist, P. (1997) *Dyslexia – A Multidisciplinary Approach*. London, Chapman & Hall.

Topping, K. J. (1986) *Paired Reading Training Pack*. Dundee, University of Dundee.

Topping, K. J. (1987) Peer tutored paired reading: outcome data from ten projects. *Educational Psychology*, **7**(2), 133–45.

Topping, K. J. (1992a) *Promoting Cooperative Learning*. London, Kirklees Metropolitan Council.

Topping, K. J. (1992b) *Paired Writing Information*. London, Kirklees Metropolitan Council.

Topping, K. J. (1992c) Short and long term follow-up of parental involvement in reading projects. *British Educational Research Journal*, **18**(4) 369–79.

Topping, K. J. (1992d) *Cued Spelling Training Tape*. London, Kirklees Metropolitan Council.

Topping, K. J. (1993) Parents and peers as tutors for dyslexic children. In Reid, G. (Ed.), *Specific Learning Difficulties (Dyslexia) Perspectives on Practice*, Edinburgh, Moray House Publications.

Topping, K. J. and Lindsey, G. A. (1992) The structure and development of the paired reading technique. *Journal of Research in Reading*. **15**(2), 120–36.

Topping, K. J. and Watt, J. M. (1992) Cued spelling: a comparative study of parent and peer tutoring. Paper submitted for publication. Dundee, University of Dundee.

Topping, K. J. and Wolfendale, S. (Eds) (1985) *Parental Involvement in Childrens' Reading*. London, Croom Helm.

Traub, N. and Bloom, F. (1993) *Recipe for Reading*. Cambridge, MA, Educators Publishing Service.

Tregaskes, M. and Daines, D. (1989) Effects of metacognition on reading comprehension. *Reading Research and Instruction*, **29**(1), 52–60.

Tunmer, W. E. (1994) Phonological processing skills and reading remediation. In C. Hume and M. Snowling (Eds), *Reading Development and Dyslexia*. London, Whurr.

Tunmer, W. E. and Chapman, J. (1996) A developmental model of dyslexia. Can the construct be saved? *Dyslexia*, **2**(3), 179–89.

Tunmer, W. E., Herriman, M. L. and Nesdale, A. R. (1988) Metalinguistic abilities and beginning reading. *Reading Research Quarterly*, **23**, 134–58.

Turner, M. (1991) Finding out. *Support for Learning*, **6**(3), 99–102.

Turner M. (1993a) Testing times. *Special Children*, **65**, 12–16.

Turner M. (1993b) More testing times. *Special Children*, **66**, 12–14.

Turner, M. (1995) Children learn to read by being taught. In P. Owen and P. Pumfrey (Eds), *Emergent and Developing Reading: Messages for Teachers.* London, Falmer Press.

Turner, M. (1997) *Psychological Assessment of Dyslexia.* London, Whurr.

Tyler S. (1980) *Keele Pre-school Assessment Guide.* NFER Nelson.

Vail, P. L. (1990) *About Dyslexia – Unravelling the Myth.* Rosemount, NJ, Modern Learning Press.

Vail, P. L. (1992) *Learning Styles.* Rosemont, NJ, Modern Learning Press.

Vail, P. L. (1993) Reading comprehension: reading for reason, the reason for reading. Paper presented at the 44th Annual Conference Orton Dyslexia Society, New Orleans, LA, USA.

Vellutino F. R. and Scanlon D. M. (1986) Experimental evidence for the effects of instructional bias on word identification. *Exceptional Children,* **53**(2), 145–55.

Vernon, P. E. (1979) *Intelligence: Heredity and Environment.* San Francisco, CA, Freeman.

Vincent, D. and Claydon, J. (1982) *Diagnostic Spelling Test.* NFER Nelson.

Vincent, E. and de la Mare, M. (1987) *New Macmillan Reading Analysis.* London, Macmillan Educational.

Vitale, B. M. (1982) *Unicorns are Real (A Right-Brained Approach to Learning).* CA, Jalman Press.

Vitale, B. M. and Bullock, W. B. (1989) *Learning Inventory Manual – Tests and Remediation.* Northumberland, Ann Arbor Publishers.

Wade, B. and Moore, M. (1994) The Promise of Reading Recovery. *Educational Review Publications-Headline Series No.1.* University of Birmingham.

Walton, D. and Brooks, P. (1995) The Spoonerism Test. In N. Frederickson and R. Reason (Eds), *Phonological Assessment of Specific Learning Difficulties. Educational Child Psychology.* **12**, 50–2.

Waterfield, J. (1996) Provision for dyslexic students in higher education: A whole institution approach. In *Conference proceedings: Dyslexic Students in Higher Education.* University of Huddersfield, 24 January 1996.

Waterland, L. (1986) *Read with Me: An Apprenticeship Approach to Reading.* Stroud, Thimble Press.

Webster, A. and McConnell, C. (1987) *Children with Speech and Language Difficulties.* London, Cassell.

Wechsler, D. (1996) *The Wechsler Dimensions. The Fundamental Test between Achievement and Ability.* The Psychological Corporation.

Weedon, C., Ferguson, B., Snell, P., Smith, E. and Reid, G. (1996) *A Diagnostic Profile of Literacy Development in Early Primary.* Edinburgh, George Watson's College.

Weedon, C. and Reid, G. (1998) Some reflections upon the learning process of the able dyslexic within the normal curriculum: can they ever do themselves justice? *Education Today* (in press).

Wendon, L. (1985 and 1987) *Letterland Teaching Programme 1 and 2.* Cambridge, Letterland Ltd.

Wendon, L. (1994) *Letterland Writing Programme.* Personal correspondence.

Wendon, L. (1993) Literacy for early childhood: learning from the learners. *Early Child Development and Care,* **86**, 11–12.

West, T. G. (1991, second edition 1997) *In the Mind's Eye. Visual Thinkers, Gifted People with Learning Difficulties, Computer Images and the Ironies of Creativity.* Buffalo, NY, Prometheus Books.

White, M. (1991) *Self-esteem – Its Meaning and Value in Schools.* Cambridge, UK, Daniels Publishing.

Whittaker, E. M. (1992) Specific learning difficulty (dyslexia) and neurological research. An educational psychologist's evaluation. *Educational Psychology in Practice,* **8**(3). 139–44.

Wilkins, A. (1990) *Visual Discomfort and Reading.* Cambridge, MRC.APU.

Wilkins, A. J. (1993) *Intuitive Overlays.* I.O.O. Marketing Ltd, 56–62 Newington Causeway, London SE1 6DS.

Wilkins, A., Milroy, R., Nimmo-Smith, I., Wright, A., Tyrill, K., Holland, K. and Martin, J. (1992) Preliminary observations concerning treatment of visual discomfort and associated perceptual distortion. *Opthalmology, Physiology, Optics,* **12**, 257–63.

Wilkins, A. J., Jeanes, J. R., Pumfrey, P. D. and Laskier, M. (1996) *Rate of Reading Test R: its reliability, and its validity in the assessment of the effects of coloured overlays.* MRC Applied Psychology Unit, 15 Chaucer Road, Cambridge.

Wilkins, A. J. (1995) *Visual Stress.* Oxford, Oxford University Press.

Wilkinson, A. C. (1980) Children's understanding in reading and listening. *Journal of Educational Psychology,* **72**(4), 561–74.

Williams, L. V. (1983) *Teaching for the Two-Sided Mind.* Simon & Schuster.

Wilson, J. (1993) *Phonological Awareness Training Programme.* University College, London, Educational Psychology Publishing.

Wilson, J. and Frederickson, N. (1995) Phonological awareness training: an evaluation. *Educational and Child Psychology,* **12**(1), 68–79.

Wolf, B. J. (1985) The effect of Slingerland instruction on the reading and language of second grade children. Ph.D dissertation Seattle Pacific University, Seattle, USA.

Wolf, M. (1991) Naming speed and reading: the contribution of the cognitive neurosciences. *Reading Research Quarterly,* **26**, 123–41.

Wolf, M. (1996) *The double-deficit hypothesis for the developmental dyslexics.* Paper read at the 47th Annual Conference of the Orton Dyslexia Society, November 1996, Boston, MA.

Wolfendale, S. and Bryans, T. (1990) *Word Play.* Stafford, NARE Publications.

Wray, D. (1991) A chapter of errors: a response to Martin Turner. *Support for Learning,* **6**(4), 145–9.

Wray, D. (1994) *Literacy and Awareness,* London, Hodder & Stoughton.

Wright, A. (1992) Evaluation of the first British reading recovery programme. *British Educational Research Journal,* **18**(4), 351–68.

Wright, A. (1993) Irlen – the never ending story. Paper presented at the 5th European Conference of Neuro-developmental Delay in Children with Specific Learning Difficulties, Chester.

Wright, A. and Prance, L. J. (1992) The reading recovery programme in Surrey Education Authority. *Support for Learning,* **7**(3), 103–10.

Young, D. (1989) *Non-Reading Intelligence Tests.* London, Hodder & Stoughton.

Young, P. and Tyre, C. (1990) *Dyslexia or Illiteracy: Realising the Right to Read.* Milton Keynes, Open University Press.

Author Index

Note: Second-named and subsequent authors, normally identified by *et al*, are included in the index. Where there is only one *et al* on a page, any 'missing' authors should be found at that reference. Where there is more than one *et al*, they are distinguished by the first three letters of the first-named author. So a joint author with Cowdery (such as Montgomery) would have the page reference 104Cow.

Aaron, P. G. 4, 5, 39, 58–60, 171, 176
Adamik-Jászó, A. 25
Adams, M. J. 10, 11, 13–14, 17–18, 25,
   102–3, 170, 175
Agnew, M. 190
Aldridge, J. 114–15
Alston, J. 205
Ames, E. 202
Armbruster, B. 132
Arnold, H. 44–5, 197, 200, 202
Ashcroft, J. R. 180
Aubrey, C. 202
Augur, J. 90, 169, 176, 187
Ayres, D. B. 56, 120

Baddeley, A. 195
Baillie, L. 27, 28
Baker, L. 132
Bakker, D. J. 5, 167, 168
Ball, E. L. 46
Ballard, K. 103Gly
Ballinger, M. 130, 193
Banks, J. 7
Bar-Tal, D. 115
Barlow, S. 190
Barr, J. 33, 114, 115
Barthorpe, T. 130, 184–5
Baumer, B. A. 170
Beard, R. 176
Becker, W. C. 100
Bedford-Feull, C. 59
Beech, M. 179–80
Bell, J. 194
Bell, N. 59, 118, 119, 120, 149, 187
Bender, M. L. 120
Beretz, M. 175

Bergeron, B. 25
Berry, R. 195
Bethune, N. 103Gly
Biggar, S. 33, 114, 115
Bishop, D. V. M. 116
Blachman, B. A. 46
Black, R. S. 46
Blagg, N. 130, 193
Blair, D. 131
Blau, H. 116
Blight, J. 169
Bloom, F. 173–4
Bloom, M. 176, 188
Blyth, P. 4, 5, 119
Boder, E. 41–2, 202
Bonar, B. 53
Bono, E. de *see* De Bono, E.
Boo, M. de *see* de Boo, M.
Boote, R. 14, 113, 177, 187
Bradley, L. 15, 111–12, 116–17Cor, 123,
   176, 202
Bradshaw, J. R. 127
Brady, S. A. 176
Brand, V. 206–7
Braun, E. M. 187
Brereton, A. 201
Briggs, S. 90, 187
Brooks, G. 128–9
Brooks, P. 109
Brown, A. L. 33, 54–5, 132, 146
Brown, G. D. 207
Brown, M. 146
Brown, P. 121
Brown, S. 6–7, 163
Bruner, E. C. 100
Bryans, T. 189

Bryant, P. E. 15, 26, 111, 172, 176
Bryk, A. S. 100
Buchanan, P. 209–10
Bullock, Sir A. 12
Bullock, W. B. 197–8
Burge, V. 178
Burns, R. B. 115
Burt, C. 202
Butler, K. A. 193–4
Buzan, T. 149, 190–1, 195

Caine, R. N. & G. 195
Calfee, R. 175, 183
Campione, J. C. 33, 54–5
Canfield, A. A. 141
Cann, P. 201
Carbo, M. 121, 139
Carlisle, J. 183–4
Carsch, M. Hunter- see Hunter-Carsch, M.
Cato, V. 128–9
Cavey, D. W. 202–3
Chall, J. S. 20, 21, 22, 30, 175
Chambliss, M. 175
Chapman, J. 5, 164
Chasty, H. 169
Childs, S. & R. 207
Chinn, S. 179, 180
Cicci, R. 210
Clark, D. B. 49, 89, 95, 121, 162
Clay, M. M. 11, 14, 64–5, 68, 97, 100, 101, 102, 103, 104, 173, 176, 197, 201, 202
Claydon, J. 202, 208
Clifford, V. 186
Closs, A. 153
Coker, J. 114–15
Cole, M. 121
Coles, M. 156–7
Conlan, J. 176
Connelly, V. D. 25
Connolly, V. 27, 28
Cooke, A. 187
Cooper, C. 36
Cooper, M. 196–7
Copeland, E. D. 181–2
Cornelissen, P. 116–17
Cottrell, S. 153
Cowdery, L. 42–3, 104, 106, 187
Cox, A. R. 94, 95, 187
Cox, R. 203–4
Cripps, C. 203–4, 207
Crisfield, J. 210
Croft, S. 124
Crombie, M. 164
Crooks, T. 103Gly

Cudd, E. T. 147
Cuff, C. 192–3
Curtis, M. E. 121

Daines, D. 133
Das, J. P. 55–6
Davies, A. 187
Davies, R. D. 187
de Bono, E. 130, 146, 195
de Boo, M. 182
de Ford, D. 175
de la Mare, M. 202
de Stoel, S. Van see Van de Stoel, S.
Dean, P. 5
Deford, D. E. 100, 103, 104Pin
Dellinger, S. 137
Dennison, P. E. 120
der Vlugt, H. van see Van der Vlugt, H.
Deschler, D. 140
Dockrell, J. 166
Dodds, D. 130
Dombey, H. 103
Drever, E. 196
Duffield, J. 6–7, 163
Dunn, K. 136, 137, 139–40, 139Car, 141, 193
Dunn, R. 136, 137, 139–40, 139Car, 140–1, 193
Dykes, B. 208
Dyson, A. 5

Eaves, J. 202
Eden, G. F. 4, 5
Edwards, P. 40, 202
Ehri, L. 25–6
Ekwall, E. & C. 133
El-Naggar, O. 179
Elgar, R. Jones- see Jones-Elgar, R.
Elliott, C. D. 37, 38, 55, 169
Ellis, A. W. 21, 46, 169
Ellis, N. C. 84, 107, 207
Ellis, S. 203
Emerson, P. 124
Enfield, M. L. 98
Engelmann, J. 100
Evans, A. J. 121

Farmer, M. 84
Fawcett, A. J. 4, 5, 47, 50, 59, 161
Fenton, M. 131
Ferguson, B. 78
Fernandes, C. 128–9
Feuerstein, R. 55
Feull, C. Bedford- see Bedford-Feull, C.

Fisher, J. 202
Fitzgibbon, G. 152, 154, 210
Flavell, J. H. 132
Ford, D. de *see* de Ford, D.
Fowler, M. S. 116
Fowler, S. 116Cor
France, L. 126
Frankiewicz, R. G. 95
Franks, T. 176
Frederickson, N. M. 5, 21, 46, 107, 197
Friel, G. 203
Friel, J. 169
Frith, C. 5
Frith, U. 5, 14–15, 21, 39, 46, 93, 197

Galaburda, A. 5, 116
Gallagher, A. 46
Gardner, H. 56, 196
Gardner, K. 176
Gardner, R. 130, 193
Geiger, S. 59
Gibson, M. 131, 202
Gilchrist, P. 168–9
Gillingham, A. 183
Gilroy, D. 152–3, 169
Given, B. K. 5, 137–8
Glaser, R. 54
Glynn, T. 103
Gonzalez, J. 5
Goodman, K. 17–18, 25, 44
Gorrie, B. 47–8, 110
Goswami, U. 5, 172, 188
Gottardo, A. 116Sta
Gough, P. B. 61
Greene, V. E. 98
Gregorc, A. F. 141, 194
Gregory, M. 121
Groman, T. 199

Hagley, F. 199, 202
Hales, G. 114, 162, 169
Hargrove, G. 120
Harris, C. 176
Harrison, C. 13
Harrison, P. 205
Harrison, R. 124
Harrison, S. 114–15, 205
Haskell, E. C. 208
Hatcher, P. J. 21, 46, 47, 107, 108, 109, 178
Healy, J. M. 39, 165–6
Heaton, P. 6, 169, 194, 208–9
Henderson, A. 178, 202
Henley, M. 176
Henry, M. K. 89, 175, 182–3, 187

Herriman, M. L. 14
Herrington, M. 153
Hicks, C. 202
Hill, J. E. 141
Hinson, M. 172–3
Hornsby, B. 84, 187, 210
Hulme, C. 21, 46, 171, 176
Hunt, J. 118, 188
Hunt, M. 129
Hunt, R. 176
Hunter, J. 27, 28
Hunter-Carsch, M. 170
Huxford, L. M. 112
Hynd, G. S. 5

Inglis, J. 37
Irlen, H. L. 116, 117, 171
Iversen, S. 21

Jackson, P. 76
Jacobson, J. 161
Jarrico, S. 41–2, 202
Jászó, A. Adamik- *see* Adamik-Jászó, A.
Javorsky, J. 182
Jeanes, J. R. 117–18
Johanson, K. V. 123
Johnston, R. S. 25, 103
Jones-Elgar, R. 176, 202
Joshi, R. M. 58, 60, 171
Jung, C. G. 137

Kappers, E. J. 5Bak
Kaufman, A. A. 202
Keefe, J. W. 137, 141, 196
Kettles, G. 71
Kimmell, G. M. 187
Kirby, J. R. 55–6
Kirkcaldy, B. 6
Kispal, A. 199
Klein, C. 169, 198–9, 202, 207, 208
Klenk, L. 54
Knight, D. F. 5
Kolb, D. A. 137
Kratoville, B. L. 176, 187
Kyd, L. 117

la Mare, M. de *see* de la Mare, M.
Lafferty, J. C. 141
Languis, M. 141
Lannen, S. 153
Large, B. 107
Laskier, M. 117–18
Lawrence, D. 115, 123
Laws, K. 71

Lawson, J. S. 37
Lazear, D. 56–8
Lees, E. A. 121
Lejoie, S. 54
Lesgold, A. 54
Letteri, C. P. 141
Levine, M. D. 196
Lewis, I. 196
Liberman, A. M. 17
Liberman, I. Y. 17, 110
Licht, R. 5Bak
Lidz, C. S. 55, 200–1
Lindamood, C. H. & P. C. 49
Lindsey, G. A. 121, 123
Locke, A. 179–80
Love, V. L. 181–2
Lovegrove, W. 16–17, 116
Loveless, E. J. 116
Lowe, D. 53
Lunzer, E. 176
Lyons, C. A. 100, 103Del, 104Pin

McCarthy, B. 196
McCleod, J. 202
McConnell, C. 169
McCulloch, K. 37, 38
McEntree, J. 172, 187
McGettrick, P. 117
Macintyre, C. 196
McKeown, S. 185
McLoughlin, D. 152, 154, 210
McMahon, J. 42–3, 187
McNicholas, J. 172, 187
McShane, J. 166
Mager, J. 7
Mailley, S. 118
Maisog, J. M. 4, 5Ede
Mare, M. de la see de la Mare, M.
Margulies, N. 189
Marshall, R. 5
Masterson, J. 131
Mathews, M. 120
Meek, M. 102
Meyer, L. P. 100
Miles, E. 92, 93–4, 148, 163, 169, 185, 187
Miles, M. 186
Miles, T. R. 4, 37, 49–50, 84, 114, 148, 161,
    163, 169, 185, 195, 202
Miller, R. R. 169, 207, 208
Milne, A. 131
Mitchell, G. 194
Mitchell, S. 120
Mommers, M. J. C. 23
Monk, J. S. 141

Montgomery, D. 104Cow, 106Cow, 187
Moore, M. 176
Morgan, R. T. T. 120
Morse, P. 42–3, 104Cow, 106Cow, 187
Morton, A. 131
Moseley, D. V. 117
Mosley, J. 116, 130, 195
Moyse, S. 59
Munn, P. 196

Naggar, O. El- see El-Naggar, O.
Naglieri, J. A. 55–6
Naidoo, S. 169
Nash-Wortham, M. 118, 181, 188
Nation, K. A. 116
Neale, M. 40–1, 202
Nesdale, A. R. 14
Neville, M. H. 120
Newby, M. 114–15
Newton, M. 202
Nicolson, R. I. 4, 5, 47, 50, 161
Nisbet, J. 146, 147, 148, 196

Osmond, J. 210
Ostler, C. 209
Ott, P. 163
Oxley, L. 125–6

Padget, S. Y. 5
Palincsar, A. 54, 146
Palmer, 59
Parker, R. 196–7
Parkinson, E. 47–8, 110
Pascal, L. 190
Pavlidis, G. Th. 116, 166–8
Pearson, L. E. A. 199
Pennington, B. F. 5
Perrin, J. 141
Peters, M. L. 205–6
Petty, M. 130, 193
Pinnell, G. S. 100, 103Def, 104
Pinsent, P. 169
Pollock, J. 196, 208
Pool, J. 187
Popp, H. M. 20, 21, 22, 30
Portwood, M. 204–5
Pottage, T. 186
Prance, L. J. 103
Pratley, R. 208
Price, G. E. 141
Prince, M. 42–3, 104Cow, 106Cow, 187
Prior, M. 168
Pumfrey, P. D. 1, 4, 5–6, 40, 68, 117–18,
    159, 169

Quinn, J. 199

Rack, J. 93, 107
Ramsden, M. 203, 205
Raven, J. C. 55, 202
Rawson, M. B. 161–2
Ray, B. J. 95
Reason, R. 5, 14, 21, 40, 46, 113, 121, 159, 177, 187, 197
Redding, N. C. 183, 187
Reid, G. 4, 6, 10, 63, 71, 75–6, 78, 79, 132, 141, 153, 159–60
Reid Lyon, G. 3–4
Retief, L. 120
Revell, K. 126
Richards, R. G. 191
Richardson, A. 117
Richardson, S. 175
Riddell, S. 6–7, 163
Riddock, B. 208
Roberts, L. L. 147
Robertson, A. 202
Robertson, A. H. 202
Rohl, M. 111
Rosner, J. 117
Rowe, H. 133
Rudginsky, L. T. 208
Rumsey, J. M. 4, 5Ede
Russell, J. P. 118, 187, 204
Russell, S. 109, 111, 187

Sasse, B. M. 114–15
Sawyer, D. J. 5
Scanlon, D. M. 121
Schumaker, J. B. 140
Scoble, J. 124–5
Selikowitz, M. 164, 210
Selman, M. R. 187
Selmes, I. 196
Seltzer, M. 100
Seymour, P. H. K. 208
Shankweiler, D. P. 110, 176
Sharron, H. 169, 196
Shucksmith, J. 146, 147, 148, 196
Siegal, L. S. 36–7, 39, 60, 116Sta
Sillars, S. 208
Singleton, C. H. 5, 50–1, 151, 158, 185, 188
Skidmore, D. 5
Skidmore, S. 190
Slingerland, B. H. 43–4, 188, 202
Smith, B. 206
Smith, C. 26
Smith, C. D. 153
Smith, E. 78

Smith, F. 11, 25
Smith, J. 103Gly, 176, 188
Smith, P. 37, 38, 172–3, 205
Smythe, I. 210
Snell, P. 78
Snowling, M. J. 5, 15, 116, 123, 160, 169, 171, 175, 176
Springer, S. P. 196
Stainthorp, R. 26
Stanovitch, K. E. 3, 5, 10, 17, 18, 39, 45–6, 93, 107, 116
Stein, J. F. 93, 116, 116Cor
Stevens, M. 176
Stillman, B. 183
Stirling, E. G. 176, 196
Stoel, S. Van der see Van der Stoel, S.
Sullivan, M. 141
Sutherland, G. 117
Sutherland, M. J. 153
Sutton, R. 198, 202

Tal, D. Bar- see Bar-Tal, D.
Tangel, D. M. 46
Tate, A. 199
Taylor, J. 205
Thomas, C. 208
Thompson, M. 202
Thomson, M. E. 37, 160, 169, 188
Thomson, P. 168–9
Thomson, S. 27, 28
Toombs, S. 196–7
Topping, F. 126
Topping, K. J. 103, 121, 122, 123, 124, 125–6, 126, 176, 188, 205, 208
Traub, N. 173–4
Tregaskes, M. 133
Tregenza, A. 128–9
Triay, I. 131
Tunmer, W. E. 5, 14, 17, 21, 61, 111
Turner, M. 24, 25, 26, 59, 196
Tyler, S. 200, 202
Tyre, C. 169, 176

Vail, P. L. 166, 190
Van der Stoel, S. 169, 209
Van der Vlugt, H. 168
VanMeter, J. W. 4, 5Ede
Varma, V. 114, 195
Vellutino, F. R. 121
Vincent, D. 202, 208
Vincent, E. 202
Visser, J. 130, 184–5
Vitale, B. M. 192, 197–8
Vlugt, H. van der see Van der Vlugt, H.

Wade, B. 176
Waller, E. 196
Walton, D. 109
Waterfield, J. 151
Waterland, L. 176
Watkins, W. 188
Watson, J. 25
Watt, J. M. 124
Webster, A. 169
Weedon, C. 4, 78, 79
Welchman, M. 169
Wendon, L. 85, 188
West, T. G. 5, 130, 192
Whetton, C. 199
White, M. 116, 130
Wilkins, A. J. 4, 5, 116, 117–18, 188
Wilkinson, A. C. 120

Williams, G. 130, 193
Williams, J. 175
Williams, L. V. 196
Wilson, J. 5, 21, 107, 177–8
Winterson, P. 169
Wolf, M. 4–5, 47
Wolfendale, S. 103, 176, 189
Woods, R. P. 4, 5Ede
Wortham, M. Nash- *see* Nash-Wortham, M.
Wray, D. 24–5, 133, 134
Wright, A. 100, 102, 103, 104, 117

Young, D. 201
Young, P. 103Del, 169, 176
Young, V. 152, 154, 210

Zeffiro, T. 4, 5Ede

Subject Index

ability scales 37–9
About dyslexia: unravelling the myth (Vail) 166
abstract visual logic, assessment of 79
Acceleread, accelewrite: a guide to using talking computers... (Clifford & Miles) 186
accuracy, of reading 30
achievement scales 37
ACID profile, of dyslexia 37
Action rhymes and games (de Boo) 182
Adult dyslexia: assessment, counselling, training (McLoughlin *et al*) 210
adults
  resources for 208–10
  screening tests for 50
  see also dyslexic adults
affective dimensions, of learning styles 137
All language and the creation of literacy 175
Alpha to Omega 88–9
alphabet
  teaching 90–1, 96–7, 105
  see also letters
Alphabet soup (Javorsky) 182
Alphabetic Phonics programme 94–6
alphabetic stage, of reading development 15, 18
Analogical reasoning in children (Goswami) 188
Annals of dyslexia 162
application forms, for further and higher education 151–2
areas of influence, and learning styles 137–8
Arithmetic, Coding, Information and Digit Span tests 37
The art of reading (Hunter-Carsch) 170
Assessment: a framework for teachers (Sutton) 198
assessment
  of adults 210

aims 31–2
baseline schemes 50–1
by class teachers 68, 102
by specialist teachers 68
checklists for 52–3
components approach 58–61
criteria 77
and curriculum 81–2
curriculum-based 56–8
diagnostic 35–49, 50, 51–2, 64–5, 102
dynamic tests 55, 200–1
framework 71–7, 78
metacognitive 53–61
multiple intelligence approaches 56–8
normative 32, 54
observational 61–5, 102
outcomes 33–4
and parents 68
PASS model 55–6
pre-reading 43, 70
process 67–80
purpose 32–3
resources 159–60, 196–202
for secondary schools 77, 197–8
standardised 35–41
static tests 54–5
strategies 33, 34–65, 68, 70, 77
and systematic observation 64–5, 102
and teaching 32, 33, 68, 81–2
see also diagnosis; screening; specific subjects with the subheading *assessment*
Assessment, teaching and the curriculum (Reid) 159–60
Assisted Assessment 54–5
assisted learning strategies 83, 120–6, 128–9
Aston Index 39–40
Aston Portfolio 113–14
Aston Portfolio Assessment Checklist 40
attention, assessment of 61, 76
attention deficit disorders 181–2, 201

Attention without tension (Copeland & Love) 181–2
auditory factors, in reading skills development 11–12, 93, 123
auditory skills, assessment of *see* listening comprehension; phonological assessment
automaticity *see* over-learning

background knowledge, and comprehension 145
balanced reading programmes 26
Ballinger, M.: *Somerset thinking skills* 146, 193
Bangor Dyslexia Teaching System 92–4
Bangor Dyslexia Test 49–50
baseline assessment schemes 50–1
Beginning to read: the new phonics in context (Adams) 170
bibliographies, for essays 156–7
binocular instability 116–17
Blagg, N.: *Somerset thinking skills* 146, 193
Boder Test of Reading and Spelling Patterns 41–2
books
    familiarity with, assessment 64–5
    favourites 132–3
    see also reading
boredom, problems with 93, 105
bottom-up reading process model 15–16, 17–19, 25
    see also top-down reading process model; whole-language teaching
brain *see* headings beginning with *neuro*
Brain Gym programme 120
Breaking down the barriers: aspects of the first 25 years of SPELD in New Zealand (Buchanan) 209–10
British Ability Scales 37–9
British Dyslexia Association
    Computer booklets 186
    Third International Conference 171
Bullock Report 12
Bury infant check (Pearson & Quinn) 199

checklists, for diagnosis 52–3
child development 165–6
children
    perceptions of reading 10–11
    self-perception *see* self-image
    see also dyslexic children
Children's learning difficulties: a cognitive approach (Dockrell & McShane) 166
circle time 130, 195

class teachers
    assessment by 68, 102
    and dyslexia 5, 6
    thinking aloud 140
classroom environment *see* learning context
Cognition, language and treatment (Pavlidis) 167–8
cognitive ability scales 37–8
cognitive approaches, to dyslexia 166
cognitive dimensions, of learning styles 137
cognitive profile, of dyslexia 37
Cognitive Profiling System 50–1
cognitive skills *see* thinking skills
colour filters, for reading 117–18, 171
communication
    between professionals 6–7, 69, 131
    between schools 132
communication skills, teaching 142–6
community involvement, in literacy 128, 129
components approach, to assessment 58–61
comprehension 58, 59, 60–1
    assessment 38, 62
    and background knowledge 145
    see also listening comprehension; reading comprehension
computerised screening programmes 50–1
computers
    for dyslexic students 153
    in education 185–6
Computers and dyslexia: educational applications of new technology (Singleton) 185
concentration *see* attention
concept driven reading process *see* top-down reading process
confidence
    assessment of 76
    developing 145–6
    see also motivation; self-image
consultation, between professionals 69, 70, 131
context, and study skills 143, 144–5
contextual clues
    and reading 17–18, 19, 23–4, 27–30, 121
    see also top-down reading process; whole-language teaching
COPS 50–1, 191
core variable model, of phonological competence 21, 46
counselling

of dyslexic adults 210
of dyslexic children 114–16
creative writing
    development 99–100
    teaching 165
creativity, and dyslexia 192
cued spelling 124–6
curriculum
    and assessment 56–8, 81–2
    assessment of 32
    and IQ 32
    and learning styles 134–41
    and metacognition 134–5
    and provision for dyslexia 69, 127, 134
    and self-esteem 115
    and whole school models 130
    see also National Curriculum

data driven reading process see bottom-up
    reading process
decision making see thinking skills
decoding 59–61, 97, 120–1
    and etymology 182–3
    strategies, and assessment 65
Developmental dyspraxia (Portwood)
    204–5
Diagnosing dyslexia: a guide to the
    assessment of adults... (Klein) 198–9
diagnosis 3–4, 6, 163, 167, 198–9, 201
    checklists for 52–3
    and listening comprehension 4, 60–1
    medical model 68
    see also assessment; screening
diagnostic assessment 35–49, 50, 51–2,
    64–5, 102
Diagnostic reading record (Arnold) 45, 200
differences, assessment of 34–5, 75–6
differentiation 130, 184–5
Differentiation: your responsibility
    (Barthorpe & Visser) 184–5
difficulties, assessment of 34, 71–3
Dimensions of dyslexia, vols 1–2 (Reid)
    159–60
Direct Instruction System of Teaching
    Arithmetic and Reading 24, 100, 115
discrepancies
    in dyslexia 3–4
        assessment of 34, 58, 74–5
        and resource allocation 6
DISTAR programme 24, 100, 115
distractability see attention
Doing your research project (Bell) 194
dynamic tests, in assessment 55, 200–1
dyseidetic dyslexia 42

Dysgraphia: why Johnny can't write
    (Cavey) 202–3
dysgraphia see writing skills
dyslexia
    ACID profile 37
    assessment see assessment
    characteristics 2, 4–5, 37, 60, 79–80
    and class teachers 5, 6
    cognitive approaches 166
    and creativity 192
    and curricular provision 69, 127, 134
    definitions 1–3
    diagnosis see diagnosis
    directories 161
    discrepancies see discrepancies
    early intervention 6
    eye movements in 167
    general texts on 159–69
    and genetics 163
    and IQ see IQ
    journals 161, 162
    and neurological abnormalities 5, 166
    and neurological research 163
    provision for 5–7
    and psychology 168, 196
    research 168
    resources on 159–210
    and stress 195
    types 41–2
    and visual processing 5, 93
    Working Party on (HEFC) 158
    see also comprehension; decoding;
        hyperlexic readers; literacy;
        numeracy; reading; writing skills
Dyslexia: a hundred years on (Miles &
    Miles) 163
Dyslexia: integrating theory and practice
    (Snowling & Thomson) 160
Dyslexia: an international journal of
    research and practice 161
Dyslexia: a multidisciplinary approach
    (Thomson & Gilchrist) 168–9
Dyslexia: parents in need (Heaton) 208–9
Dyslexia: a parents' survival guide (Ostler)
    209
Dyslexia: theory and practice of remedial
    instruction (Clark) 162
Dyslexia basic numeracy (Burge) 178
Dyslexia in children: multidisciplinary
    perspectives (Fawcett & Nicolson) 161
Dyslexia Early Screening Test 50
Dyslexia handbook (Jacobson) 161
Dyslexia and mathematics (Miles & Miles)
    185

Dyslexia matters (Hales) 162
Dyslexia and other learning difficulties: the facts (Selikowitz) 164
Dyslexia Screening Test 50
Dyslexia and stress (Miles & Varma) 195
dyslexic adults
 biographies 192
 diagnosis 198–9
 supporting 210
dyslexic children
 assessment *see* assessment
 comprehension *see* comprehension
 counselling 114–16
 diagnosis *see* diagnosis
 and examinations 131–2
 teaching *see* specialist teaching; teaching
dyslexic students
 computers for 153, 185–6
 and further and higher education 151–8
dysphonetic dyslexia 41–2
dyspraxia *see* motor skills

Early Years Battery, of ability scales 37
education *see* teaching
education authorities, and dyslexia provision 5–7
educational kinesiology 120
educational priorities, and the Warnock Report 127
Edwards Reading Test 40
effects *see* outcomes
emotional needs, of dyslexic children 114–16, 195
Endangered minds (Healy) 165–6
environment, and reading skills development 13–14
essays, techniques 154–7
etymology, as a teaching technique 182–3
examinations, and dyslexic children 131–2
eye dominance 116–17
eye movements, in dyslexia 167

failure, sense of 34, 115–16, 126
filters, coloured, for reading 117–18, 171
funding *see* resources, allocation
further education, and dyslexic students 151–8

Games to improve reading levels (McNicholas & McEntree) 172
Gardner, R.: *Somerset thinking skills* 146, 193
genetics, and dyslexia 163
gestalt hemisphere, weakening 118

Get better grades (Agnew *et al*) 190
The gift of dyslexia (Davies & Braun) 187
Graded activities for children with motor difficulties (Russell) 204
grammatical context, in reading 27–9, 44
graphemes *see* letters

habits, in learning styles 137–8
handwriting *see* writing skills
Head Start programme 24
Helping children with reading and spelling (Reason & Boote) 113, 177
hemispheric specialisation 118, 167, 191, 192
Hickey Multisensory Language Course 90–2
higher education, and dyslexic students 151–8
Higher Education Funding Council, Working Party on dyslexia 158
home environment, and reading skills development 13–14
How to detect and manage dyslexia (Ott) 163
How to teach your dyslexic child to read (Baumer) 170
hyperactivity 181–2, 201
hyperlexia 39
hyperlexic readers, characteristics 59–60

identification *see* diagnosis
In the mind's eye (West) 192
individual learning styles *see* learning styles
individualised programmes 82, 83, 84–105
individuality, in reading 19
initiative, assessment of 63
Inspirations for writing (Ellis & Friel) 203
intelligence quotient *see* IQ
interaction with others, assessment of 62, 76
interactive compensatory model, of the reading process 18–19, 26
interactivity, of reading 23–4
interviews, for further and higher education 152–3
IQ
 and the curriculum 32
 and reading skills 3–4, 39
 tests 201
 validity 36–7, 60
Irlen overlays (lenses) 117–18, 171
IT *see* computers

IT support for specific learning difficulties (McKeown) 185

Joining the ABC (Cripps & Cox) 203–4

Keele pre-school assessment guide (Tyler) 200
kinesiology 120
knowledge framework *see* background knowledge; schemata
Knowsley Reading Project 128–9, 132–3

LAC Test 49
language experience model, of teaching 23
language factors, in reading skills development 11–12
A language for life (Bullock Report) 12
language skills
    assessment 37, 38, 62, 180
    and movement 188
    and the reading process 18–19, 104
    teaching 23, 179–80, 189
    see also literacy; reading; writing skills
laptops *see* computers
Learn playful techniques to accelerate learning (Richards) 191
learning
    organisation of 61–2, 76
    responsibility for 139
    transferability 56, 100, 103, 127, 146–7
    see also assisted learning strategies
learning context
    assessment of 63
    and teaching strategies 81, 139, 140
learning difficulties
    assessment, procedures 6, 34–9
    see also dyslexia; hyperactivity; hyperlexia
learning habits 137–8
Learning inventory manual: tests and remediation (Vitale & Bullock) 197–8
Learning Potential Assessment Device 55
learning process *see* metacognition
learning skills
    resources 188–94
    see also study skills; thinking skills
learning styles
    assessment 63, 76, 141
    and the curriculum 134–41
    resources 190, 193–4
    and teaching strategies 82, 121, 138–9, 140–1
Learning styles (Vail) 190
Learning Styles Inventory 141

learning support, whole-school models 131
Learning and teaching style: in theory and practice (Butler) 193–4
Learning to learn (Heaton & Mitchell) 194
LEAs, and dyslexia provision 5–7
lenses, tinted, for reading 117–18, 171
Letterland 85–8
letters
    phonic equivalences 14, 15, 71–2, 107
    shapes, and reading 13, 14
    see also alphabet
liaison, between professionals 69, 70, 131
lifestyle, and child development 165–6
light sensitivity 117, 171
Lindamood Auditory Conceptualisation Test 49
linguistics *see* language skills
listening comprehension
    assessment 74, 78
    and diagnosis 4, 60–1
    and reading skills 39, 59, 60, 61, 80
Listening, language and learning (Reid) 160
literacy
    acquisition, factors 10
    assessment 37–8, 78–80, 199, 201
    community involvement 128, 129
    teaching
        by parents 103, 121–2, 124, 128, 168
        Neurological Impress Method 123, 167–8
        resources 160, 162
        in secondary schools 93–4, 131–2
        strategies 175
        whole-school models 127–9
    see also reading; spelling; writing skills
Living with dyslexia (Riddock) 208
local education authorities *see* education authorities
logographic stage, of reading development 14–15, 18
look and say model, of teaching reading 21–2, 167
LPAD tests 55

The many faces of dyslexia (Rawson) 161–2
Mapping inner space (Margulies) 189
mapping skills, teaching 148
mathematics *see* numeracy
Mathematics for dyslexics (Chinn & Ashcroft) 180
Maths and dyslexics (Henderson) 178

meaning *see* semantic context
medical model, of diagnosis 68
memory, assessment 38, 79
memory skills, teaching 148–9
metacognition
    and the curriculum 134–5
    in reading skills development 132–4,
        140–1
metacognitive assessment 53–61
metacognitive strategies, teaching 133–4
The mind map book: radiant thinking
    (Buzan) 190–1
mind mapping 133, 148, 149, 189, 190–1
miscue analysis 44–5, 197
mnemonics 93, 148, 149, 191
motivation
    assessment of 63, 76
    development 145–6
    see also self-image
motor skills
    assessment of 76
    teaching
        resources 204–5
        strategies 118–20, 188
multiple intelligence approaches, to
    assessment 56–8
multiplication *see* numeracy
multisensory teaching techniques 84,
    89–97, 139, 148–9
    resources 183
    for spelling 112, 206
muscles, and reflexes 120

naming *see* memory
National Curriculum attainment,
    assessment of 75, 198, 200
Neale Analysis of Reading Ability 40–1,
    74
*Neuro-psychological correlates and
    treatment, vols 1–2* (Bakker & Van der
    Vlugt) 168
neurological abnormalities, and dyslexia 5,
    166
neurological development 165–6
    see also hemispheric specialisation
Neurological Impress Method, of literacy
    teaching 123, 167–8
neurological research 163
neurological systems, for processing
    information 56
neurological usage, and reading 118, 167,
    191, 192
Neurology, neuro-psychology and genetics
    (Pavlidis) 166–7

New Macmillan Reading Analysis 74
New Zealand Federation of Specific
    Learning Disabilities Associations
    209–10
Newcastle Literacy Collaborative 129
Non-reading intelligence tests 201
non-word reading tests 73
norm-referenced tests 35–41
normative assessment 32, 54
note-taking, for essays 155
numeracy
    assessment 37, 38
    teaching 178–9, 180, 185

observational assessment 61–5, 75–6, 102,
    201
*An observational survey of early literacy
    achievement* (Clay) 201
Office of Her Majesty's Chief Inspectors
    of Schools, *Reading recovery in New
    Zealand* 174–5
onset and rhyme games 27, 177–8
*Opening the door: guidance on recognising
    and helping the dyslexic child* (Brereton
    & Cann) 201
oral errors, significance 46
organisation
    of communication *see* communication
        skills
    of learning, assessment of attitudes
        61–2, 76
    of thoughts
        teaching 142–5
        see also thinking skills
orientation skills, teaching 148
orthographic stage, of reading
    development 15
Orton–Gillingham programme 89–90, 94,
    96, 104, 183
outcomes, of assessment 33–4
over-learning 84, 148–9
    and boredom 93, 105

paired reading 120–4
parental pressure, and resource allocation
    6
parents
    and assessment 68
    and cued spelling 125
    liaison with schools 33, 68, 70
    and literacy development 103, 121–2,
        124, 128, 168
    resources for 208–9
Parents on dyslexia (Van der Stoel) 209

PASS model of assessment 55–6
peer tutoring 83, 125–6, 129
personality types, and learning styles 137–8
Perspectives on dyslexia, vols 1–2 (Pavlidis) 166–8
Petty, M.: *Somerset thinking skills* 146, 193
PHAB *see* Phonological Assessment Battery
phonemes 22, 89, 107
Phonic Code Cracker 109–10, 111
phonic equivalences, of letters 14, 15, 71–2, 107
phonic models
    of teaching 19–21, 25–6, 46, 88–92, 103
        programmes 94–6, 99, 104–5, 107–12
        resources 167–8, 170, 172–4, 177–8, 181
Phonic rhyme time (Nash-Wortham) 181
phonics, and spelling 15
Phonics and phonic resources (Hinson & Smith) 172–3
Phonological Assessment Battery 46–7, 71, 197
Phonological assessment of specific learning difficulties (Frederickson & Reason) 197
phonological awareness
    assessment 21, 41–2, 45–9, 71–3, 78–9, 197
    strategies 27, 28, 47–8, 107–12, 177–8
Phonological Awareness Procedures 47–8, 109, 110
Phonological Awareness Programme for Primary One classes 27, 28
Phonological awareness training (Wilson) 177–8
phonological competence, core variable model 21, 46
phonological processing, and reading skills 39
Phonological skills and learning to read (Goswami & Bryant) 172
photosensitivity 117, 171
physiological dimensions, of learning styles 137
pictograms 85, 86, 87
Planning, Attention, Simultaneous and Successive processes *see* PASS
Policy, practice and provision for children with specific learning difficulties (Duffield *et al*) 163
postural reflexes 119–20

Practitioner's guide to dynamic assessment (Lidz) 200–1
Praxis makes perfect 204
pre-reading 23–4
    assessment 43, 70, 199, 200
primary schools, liaison with secondary schools 132
primitive reflexes, inhibition 119–20
print
    familiarity with, assessment 64–5
    and the reading process 18
    visual awareness of *see* visual factors
    see also reading
problem solving
    strategy development 56
    see also thinking skills
professional development *see* training
professionals
    communication between 6–7, 67, 69, 131
    see also class teachers; teachers
Project Read 97–100, 183
psycholinguistic guessing games 17, 44
Psychological assessment of dyslexia (Turner) 196
psychology, and dyslexia 168, 196
Putting pen to paper: a new approach to handwriting (Ramsden) 203

Quality circle time in the primary classroom (Mosley) 195
Quest Screening, Diagnostic and Support Kit 51–2, 112–13

Rat pack (Cooper *et al*) 196–7
Rate of Reading Test 117–18
reading 19
    accuracy 30
    assessment 62–3, 102
        components approach 58
        miscue analysis 44–5, 197
        resources 40–6, 50, 51–2, 102, 196–7, 199, 200
        strategies 71–4, 78
        see also phonological awareness, assessment
    and brain usage 118, 167, 191, 192
    and contextual clues *see* contextual clues
    for essays 155
    individuality in 19
    and interactivity 23–4
    and letter shapes 13, 14
    perceptions of, by children 10–11
    semantic context 27, 29, 44

reading (*cont.*)
  syntactic context 27–9, 44
  and word recognition skills 17
  see also alphabet; books; decoding;
    language skills; letters; literacy; pre-
    reading; print; spelling; writing
*Reading assessment for teachers (RAT
  pack)* (Cooper *et al*) 196–7
Reading by colours (Irlen) 171
reading comprehension
  assessment 74, 78
  and decoding 121
  development, resources 97, 99, 183–4
  and diagnosis 4
Reading development and dyslexia (Hulme
  and Snowling) 171
Reading in Partnership Project 128
*Reading problems: consultation and
  remediation* (Aaron & Joshi) 171
reading processes
  interactive compensatory model 18–19,
    26
  and language 18–19, 104
  models 9, 15–19, 25, 26, 44, 93
  and print 18
  self-monitoring 133
  visual factors 11–12, 13–14, 15, 16–17
reading records, diagnostic 45, 200
Reading recovery in New Zealand 174–5
Reading Recovery Programme 14, 64, 97,
  100–2
  evaluation 102–4, 174–5
reading skills
  indicators 133
    see also reading, assessment
  and IQ 3–4, 39
  and listening comprehension 39, 59, 60,
    61, 80
  and phonological processing 39
reading skills development 9–10, 11–15, 18
  assisted learning strategies 83, 120–4,
    128–9
  factors 10, 11–12, 13, 24, 93, 123
    see also visual factors
  and home environment 13–14
  individualised programmes 82, 83,
    84–105
  and metacognition 132–4, 140–1
  resources 170–6, 177–8, 181, 182–3, 197
  strategies 19–30
  support strategies 82, 83, 105–10, 111,
    112–14
reading standards, decline 24–5
reading tests *see* reading, assessment

reasoning, assessment 38
Reasoning and reading: level 1 (Carlisle)
  183–4
Recipe for reading (Traub & Bloom)
  173–4
Reciprocal Teaching 54, 146–7
references, for essays 156–7
reflex inhibition 119–20
relaxation, assessment of 63, 76
reliability, of standardised tests 36
Remedial spelling (Brand) 207
repetition *see* over-learning
research techniques, for students 154–5,
  194
resources
  for adults 208–10
  allocation 5–6, 7
  for assessment 159–60, 196–202
  on dyslexia 159–210
  for parents 208–9
  for teaching *see* teaching, resources;
    specific subjects with the subheading
    teaching
responsibility, for learning 139
rhyme 181, 182
  games 27, 177–8
  and spelling 111–12
right hemisphere, weakening 118
Running Records 102

scaffolding 146–7
schemata development, teaching 143–5,
  149
School Age Battery, of ability scales 37
school provision *see* whole-school models
schools
  liaison between 132
  liaison with parents 33, 68, 70
  procedures for identifying learning
    difficulties 6
scotopic sensitivity syndrome 117, 171
screening tests 39–40, 49–53, 78–80, 96,
  112–13
  for adults 50
  pre-reading 43, 70
  see also assessment; diagnosis
secondary schools
  assessment of dyslexia 77, 197–8
  liaison with primary schools 132
  literacy teaching 93–4, 131–2
self-image 34, 114–16, 126, 132, 166, 195
  assessment of 63, 76
  see also confidence; motivation
semantic context, and reading 27, 29, 44

sensitivity, to light 117, 171
sentence construction, teaching 147
sequencing
    assessment of 62
    teaching 143
sequential teaching strategies 84, 92–4,
    167
simultaneous processing, assessment of 56
Slingerland Assessment 43–4
Slingerland Programme 96–7, 98
social interaction, assessment of 62, 76
Somerset thinking skills course (Blagg *et
    al*) 146, 193
sound linkage assessment 47
Sound Linkage programme (Hatcher) 47,
    107–9, 178
Special educational needs (DES) *see*
    Warnock Report
specialist teaching
    for dyslexic children 67, 127
    see also professionals
specific learning difficulties *see* dyslexia
*Specific learning difficulties (dyslexia):
    challenges and responses* (Pumfrey &
    Reason) 159
*Specific learning difficulties (dyslexia): a
    teacher's guide* (Crombie) 164
*Specific learning difficulties in mathematics:
    a classroom approach* (El-Naggar) 179
SPELD (New Zealand Federation of
    Specific Learning Disabilities
    Associations) 209–10
Spelling: caught or taught: a new look
    205–6
spelling
    assessment 37, 38, 41–2, 50, 71, 78
    and etymology 182–3
    and phonics 15
    and phonological awareness 110–12
    and rhyme 111–12
    teaching 91–2, 104–5, 111–12, 113, 124–6
        resources 177, 182–3, 191, 203–4,
        205–8
*Spelling in context: strategies for teachers
    and learners* (Peters & Smith) 206
*Spelling made easy: multi-sensory
    structured spelling* (Brand) 206–7
spoonerisms, in teaching reading 109
staff, training 6, 68–9, 103
standardised assessment 35–41
standards, of reading 24–5
static tests, in assessment 54–5
strategic classroom environments 140
stress, and dyslexia 195

structured teaching strategies 84, 89–94,
    104–5, 167
study skills 154–7
    teaching 141–50
        resources 190, 192–3, 194
    see also learning skills; thinking skills
Study skills (Cuff) 192–3
subjects, for essays, selection 154
success factors, in further and higher
    education 153
successive processing 56, 136
Suffolk reading scale (Hagley) 199
support strategies 82, 83, 105–20
    in further and higher education 153
sustained visual sub-systems 16–17
syntactic context, in reading 27–9, 44
systematic observation, for assessment
    64–5, 102

Take time (Nash-Wortham & Hunt) 188
talking *see* language skills
teachers
    training 6, 68–9, 103
    see also class teachers
teaching
    and assessment 32, 33, 68, 81–2
    and computers 185–6
    and learning styles 82
    phonic models *see* phonic models, of
        teaching
    resources 159–60, 164, 177–88
    in secondary schools 93–4, 131–2
    specialist 67, 127
    strategies 81–126, 93, 163, 165
        assisted learning 83, 120–6, 128–9
        evaluation 24–6
        individualised 82, 83, 84–105
        and the learning context 81, 139, 140
        and learning styles 82, 121, 138–9
        multisensory *see* multisensory
            teaching techniques
        sequential 84, 92–4, 167
        structured 84, 89–94, 104–5, 167
        support strategies 82, 83, 105–14, 150
    see also specific subjects
*Teaching elementary students through their
    individual learning styles* (Dunn &
    Dunn) 193
Teaching Reading Through Spelling 42–3,
    104–5, 106
*Teaching talking: teaching resources
    handbook* (Locke & Beech) 179–80
tension *see* relaxation
Test of initial literacy (Kispal *et al*) 199

tests
  ranking of difficulty 79–80
  see also assessment; examinations; IQ,
    tests
text see books; print; reading
theoretical causal model, of phonological
  competence 21, 46
thinking skills
  teaching 146, 189, 190–1
    programmes 130, 193
  see also learning skills; organisation, of
    thoughts; study skills
tinted lenses, for reading 117–18, 171
top-down reading process model 15, 16,
  17, 18, 25, 93
  and the balanced approach 26
  and miscue analysis 44
  see also bottom-up reading process
    model; contextual clues; whole-
    language teaching
topics, for essays, selection 154
training, for staff 6, 68–9, 103
transferability, of learning 56, 100, 103,
  127, 146–7
transfers, between schools 132
transient visual sub-systems 16–17
Tutor 1: structured, sequential, multisensory lessons based on the Orton–
  Gillingham approach (Henry &
  Redding) 183
tutors, in further and higher education
  157

Understanding learning difficulties
  (Chapman) 164
Understanding specific learning difficulties
  (Prior) 168
Unicorns are real: a right-brained approach
  to learning (Vitale) 192
Unscrambling spelling (Klein & Miller)
  207
Using computers with dyslexics (Pottage)
  186

validity
  of IQ tests 36–7, 60
  of standardised tests 36
verbal memory, assessment 79
verbal skills, assessment 37, 38
visual factors
  in the reading process 11–12, 13–14, 15,
    16–17, 93

  in reading skills development 116–18
visual logic, assessment of 79
visual memory, assessment of 79
visual processing, and dyslexia 5
visual skills
  assessment 38, 62
  teaching 118, 119, 148, 191
Visualizing and verbalizing for language
  comprehension and thinking (Bell) 118,
  119
vocabulary development 99
  see also word recognition skills

Warnock Report
  and differentiation 184
  and educational priorities 127
Wechsler Individual Achievement Test 37
Wechsler Intelligence Scale 36–7, 56
What to do when you can't learn the times
  tables (Chinn) 179
whole-language teaching 24–6, 175
  see also contextual clues; top-down
    reading process
whole-school models
  and curriculum 130
  of dyslexia provision 67, 69–70, 78, 80,
    83
  of learning support 131
  of literacy teaching 127–9
  principles 129–30
Williams, G.: Somerset thinking skills 146,
  193
word imaging 118, 119
Word play (Wolfendale & Bryans) 189
word processing 185
word reading tests 71, 72–3
word recognition skills
  and reading 17–18, 61
  see also vocabulary development
word slides (reading activity) 27
Words: integrated decoding and spelling
  instruction based on word origin and
  word structure (Henry) 182–3
Working Party on dyslexia (HEFC) 158
writing skills
  assessment 50, 64, 74, 199
  for essays 155–6
  teaching 15, 96
    resources 202–4, 206
  see also creative writing; literacy

Your child's growing mind (Healy) 165

Index compiled by Sylvia Potter

Related titles of interest...

DYSLEXIA

An International Journal of Research and Practice

THE JOURNAL OF THE BRITISH DYSLEXIA ASSOCIATION
A forum for professionals and academics with interests in the skills and
difficulties of those with specific dyslexia.

Contact the Journals Administration Office for subscription details:
Fax: +44 1243 843 232 e-mail: cs-journals@wiley.co.uk

Understanding and Teaching Children with Autism

Rita Jordan and **Stuart D. Powell**

The book specifically addresses the needs of children, but much of it will remain
relevant to those working with adults who will appreciate the book's exploration
of the roles played by emotion and cognition in the autistic condition and the way
in which these affect teaching and learning.

0471-95888-3 188pp 1995   Hardback
0471-95714-3 188pp 1995   Paperback

Teaching Children with Autism to Mindread

A Practical Guide

Patricia Howlin, Simon Baron-Cohen, Julie Hadwin and **John Swettenham**

This is the first practical book on applying theory of mind to children with autism.
Theory of mind - the theoretical basis to the ability to infer other's mental states
and the ability to use this information to interpret what they say, make sense of
their behaviour and predict what they will do next - is used effectively in the
treatment of social and communicative difficulties in autistic children.

0471-97623-7   336pp   January 1998

Controlling Your Class

A Teacher's Guide to Managing Classroom Behaviour

Bill McPhillimy

Aimed at teachers and student teachers of both primary and secondary pupils, this
book provides a short, readable set of ideas and guidelines that a busy student or
teacher can relate to his or her own experience, and put into practice.

0471-96568-5   162pp   1996 Paperback

Visit the Wiley Home Page http:\\www.wiley.co.uk